A Multicultural Dictionary of Literary Terms

A Multicultural Dictionary of Literary Terms

by
Gary Carey *and*
Mary Ellen Snodgrass

McFarland & Company, Inc., Publishers
Jefferson, North Carolina, and London

The present work is a reprint of the illustrated case bound edition of A Multicultural Dictionary of Literary Terms, *first published in 1999 by McFarland.*

Illustrations by Raymond M. Barrett, Jr.

LIBRARY OF CONGRESS CATALOGUING-IN-PUBLICATION DATA

Carey, Gary.
    A multicultural dictionary of literary terms / by Gary Carey
and Mary Ellen Snodgrass.
        p.   cm.
    Includes bibliographical references and index.

    ISBN-13: 978-0-7864-2950-9
    ISBN-10: 0-7864-2950-X
    (softcover : 50# alkaline paper) ∞

    1. Literature—Dictionaries.   I. Snodgrass, Mary Ellen.
II. Title.
PN41.C28   2006
803—dc21   98-35221

British Library cataloguing data are available

Cover art by Gary Carey

Manufactured in the United States of America

McFarland & Company, Inc., Publishers
   Box 611, Jefferson, North Carolina 28640
      www.mcfarlandpub.com

Acknowledgments

Lynne Reid Bolick
Wanda Rozzelle
  Reference Librarians
  Catawba County Library
  Newton, North Carolina

Avis Gachet
  Wonderland Books
  Granite Falls, North Carolina

Frances Hilton
  Chapter One Books
  Hickory, North Carolina

Arnie Jacobson
  Consultant
  Omaha, Nebraska

Corki Miller
  Deputy Director
  Elbert Ivey Memorial Library
  Hickory, North Carolina

Louisa S. Nye
  Author, Consultant
  Norfolk, Virginia

James L. Roberts
  Professor Emeritus
  University of Nebraska

Mark Schumacher
  Reference Librarian
  Jackson Library, UNC-G
  Greensboro, North Carolina

Greg W. Tubach
  Editor, Author
  Lincoln, Nebraska

Table of Contents

Preface

The plan of *The Multicultural Dictionary of Literary Terms* is to present terms essential to a thorough, comprehensive study of world literature, including print literature as well as stage drama. Entries name devices, modes, literary periods, writers, titles, and characters as a means of defining and exemplifying the full span of classic literature worldwide. To fill this tall order, we have combed high school and college texts in current use for direction and models to guide our choice of the most significant additions to the reader's vocabulary. Entries listed alphabetically provide alternate spellings and pronunciations of difficult terms, textual definition and commentary, citations, dates of publication where possible, and cross-references. The text features three illustrations—the Freytag diagram of a literary plot, the plan of the Greek stage, and a model Venn diagram. As an adjunct to self-directed reading, study, analysis, literary research, library reference, and lesson planning, this volume appends these self-explanatory study aids:

- complete chronological listings under the headings of the Booker McConnell Prize, Poet Laureate Consultants in Poetry to the Library of Congress, Nobel Prize for Literature, and Pulitzer Prize for Drama, Fiction, and Poetry;

- a time line of world literature, naming in chronological order works dating from Egyptian hymns composed in 1350 B.C. to works from current times and demonstrating the global scope of literary classics;

- a bibliography of print and electronic sources that range from literary handbooks and overviews to in-depth studies of world drama, modern usage, and genre analysis, such as Hugh Holman and William Harmon's *A Handbook to Literature* and Laurie Henry's *The Fiction Dictionary*, and timely print and Internet articles from literary research and current journals, including *Bilingual Review, Americas,* and *Studies in Latin American Popular Culture*;

- a comprehensive index to the text, which guides the reader to terms within the dictionary entries. These terms represent literary genres, subgenres, styles, devices, characters, performers, motifs, neologisms, standard phrases, and periods; e.g., drama and liturgy, shaggy dog story, lyricism and romanticism, understatement, Anancy, Punch and Judy, cantor, coming-of-age, E-zines, *carpe diem,* and Victorianism.

Significant to this volume are introductions to foreign terms derived from world cultures, for example, *mechane, corrido, koshare, surah, kyogen, trouvère, mesholim, nasib, ghazal, ta'ziyah, senryu, deus ex machina, katauta,* and *tekerleme.* At the heart of the work is the intent to lessen the newness of multiculturalism and to introduce and explain unfamiliar forms of literary expression.

For maximum inclusion, we have drawn styles, titles, and models from the whole cloth of literature—scripture, young adult novels, children's stories, hymns, oratory, current fiction, classic history, fables, and traditional works ranging from Alaskan and African epic, Hawaiian myth, Arab-American ode, Asian talk-story, minstrel and puppet shows, Argentine saga, Chinese aphorism, Caribbean call-and-response, medieval French beast fable, Japanese stage production, Australian national anthem, Bosnian journal, Zuñi ritual, Gullah dialect, advertising, and the media. A casual reading of this *Handbook* compels the reader, writer, teacher, librarian, researcher, or editor to explore a wider range of texts and to contemplate the creativity of the men and women who capture all aspects of human behavior in the world's literature.

Introduction

Since the advent of multiculturalism in schools, higher education, book stores, libraries, and the media in the 1980s, consumers have been perplexed by the newness of styles and modes of expression and by a daunting unfamiliarity with prize-winning titles and authors. Inclusion has taken students and teachers from the white-centered, male-dominant coursework of past generations into a broader, more even-handed selection of works by male and female authors worldwide. To the standard syllabus selections of novel, short story, poem, epic, and essay, publishers have added a challenging list of forms including the Japanese renga, sub–Saharan beast lore, Sioux vision quest, Cantonese folk tale, Australian saga, Mexican corrido, and Arabic surah. The result is an expanded awareness of literary possibilities enhanced by these world classics:

- Akhenaten's "Hymn to the Sun"
- Confucius's *Analects*
- *Ramayana*
- Lao-tzu's *Tao Te Ching*
- Ossian's *Fingal*
- T'ao Ch'ien's shih poetry and Li Po's lyric verse
- Tu Fu's anti-war verse
- Murasaki Shikibu's *Genji*
- The Sufist Rumi's *Mathnawi* and *Divani Shamsi Tabriz*
- *Sundiata*
- *Carmina Burana*
- Hafiz's *Divan*
- Seami Motokiyo's *Atsumori*
- Luis Vaz de Camoëns's *The Luciad*
- Chikamatsu Monzaemon's kabuki drama
- Aphra Behn's *The Rover* and *Oroonoko*
- Mary Wollstonecraft's *A Vindication of the Rights of Woman*
- Lady Hong of Hyegyong Palace's *A Record of Sorrowful Days*
- *Walum Olum*
- Harriet Ann Brent Jacobs's *Incidents in the Life of a Slave Girl, Written by Herself*
- Frederick Douglass's "What the Black Man Wants"
- Asadullah Khan Ghalib's ghazals
- Chief Joseph's "I Will Fight No More Forever"
- Sarah Winnemucca's *Life Among the Piutes, Their Wrongs and Claims*
- King David Kalakaua's *The Legends and Myths of Hawaii*

The study of the twentieth century henceforth cannot stop at William Faulkner, Ernest Hemingway, Ezra Pound, and T. S. Eliot. The list of female authors must grow beyond Willa Cather, Eudora Welty, Virginia Woolf, and Katherine Anne Porter. A full overview of all elements of society calls for a span of points of view that numbers among the old classics these authors and works of fiction and nonfiction:

- Kate Chopin's *Bayou Folk*
- Mary Hunter Austin's *The Land of Little Rain*
- Juan Ramón Jiménez's *Elegías lamentables*
- Charlotte Perkins Gilman's *Herland*
- Rabindranath Tagore's *The Hungry Stones*
- Yevgeny Zamyatin's *We*
- Lu Hsun's *Call to Arms*
- Johan Bojer's *The Emigrants*
- Hsiao Hung's *Market Street*
- Mari Sandoz's *Crazy Horse: The Strange Man of the Oglalas*
- Czeslaw Milosz's "Song of a Citizen"
- Nikos Kazantzakis's *Zorba, the Greek*
- Marjory Stoneman Douglass's *The Everglades: River of Grass*
- Américo Paredes's "El Corrido de Gregorio Cortez"
- Mariano Azuela's *The Underdogs*
- Isak Dinesen's "Babette's Feast"
- Friedrich Dürrenmatt's *The Visit*
- V. S. Naipaul's *The Mystic Masseur*
- Sandra Cisneros's *The House on Mango Street*
- James Vance Marshall's *Walkabout*
- Octavio Paz's *Cuento de los Jardines*
- Adrienne Rich's *Charleston in the 1860s: Derived from the Diaries of Mary Boykin Chesnut*
- Beth Henley's *Crimes of the Heart*
- Harvey Fierstein's *Torch Song Trilogy*
- Isabel Allende's *House of the Spirits*
- Marsha Norman's *'night Mother*
- Paul Monette's *Borrowed Time*
- May Swenson's "How Everything Happens"
- *The Songs of Henry Lawson*
- Derek Walcott's *Omeros*
- Kazuo Ishiguro's *Remains of the Day*
- Lois Lowry's *The Giver*
- Sonia Sanchez's *Does Your House Have Lions?*

The task of the well-read pleasure reader and theater-goer is no different from that of the student, librarian, teacher, researcher, and editor—to sample an array of national literatures, genres, and authors and to comprehend each work's addition to the body of world literature. To make this job as simple and enjoyable as possible, we have compiled a volume of terms and genres, along with a variety of models from familiar classics by

Homer, Molière, and William Shakespeare to the most recent additions to the canon of world writing—the songs of Mary Hunter Austin; fiction of Laura Esquivel, Kazuo Ishiguro, and Michael Ondaatje; poetry of Sonia Sanchez and Octavio Paz; tales of Paul Keens-Douglas, J. J. Reneaux, and Ken Corsbie; saga of Sylvia Lopez-Medina; stories of Leslie Marmon Silko; children's fiction of Lois Lowry; and autobiographies of Nelson Mandela, Mark Mathabane, and Rigoberto Menchu.

Rather than rehash the time-honored models of simile, epic, verse, rhythm, and personification, we have chosen from an expanded field. Our choices avoid the dominance of British authors over American, white over nonwhite, male over female, Judeo-Christian over other world faiths, and straight over gay. Our choices tempt the thoughtful reader to study the rhyme schemes of Emma Lazarus along with those of Alexander Pope and to savor sagas by Colleen McCullough and Isabel Allende as well as by James Fenimore Cooper. Our title suggestions include the *Sundiata* alongside the *Iliad* and *Odyssey*, and kabuki drama as well as staple Restoration plays and Broadway hits. With this volume in hand, the savvy reader can pronounce and fathom unfamiliar terms, add new names to the must-have list, and plot a course to a greater appreciation of what it means to be well read.

The Dictionary

abridgment   a simplified, shortened, or condensed version that pares a work down to its basic elements to save space, to remove confusing or tedious segments, or to enhance appeal for unsophisticated readers, for instance, abbreviated editions of lengthy novels such as Herman Melville's *Moby-Dick* (1851) and Victor Hugo's *Les Misérables* (1862). Unlike paraphrasing, abridgment shortens while maintaining original wording. A censorious form of abridgment, bowdlerization, removes potentially offensive passages; for example, indecency, swearing, and blasphemy. The term derives from the name of Thomas Bowdler, an English doctor and editor who published *The Family Shakespeare* (1818), a compendium of William Shakespeare's plays from which Bowdler removed passages that he thought might shock or demoralize young readers.

abstract   a critical term characterizing themes, diction, and topics that avoid people, animals, and names of tangible objects by focusing on non-concrete terms that express ideas, categories, or concepts; for instance, the subject of marriage in Carson McCullers's *A Member of the Wedding* (1946), the theme of loss in James Agee's *A Death in the Family* (1956), the concept of tribalism in Chinua Achebe's *Things Fall Apart* (1959), and the lively paradoxes of Polish-Palestinian poet Shin Shalom's "The Dance of the Torches" (1968). Another meaning of abstract is a summary or précis of a speech, book, or document, as in a news account of a presidential State of the Union address, a simplification of a philosophy, or a plot outline on a book jacket. *See also* précis.

absurdism   the attempt to account for unreal, irrational, disordered, or incoherent events and to cope with nothingness, anxiety, isolation, or the malaise that afflicts humanity after the collapse of tradition and values. The philosophy of absurdism impinges on modern novels—notably, Franz Kafka's "The Metamorphosis" (1915), Albert Camus's *The Myth of Sisyphus* (1942), Ralph Ellison's *Invisible Man* (1947), Samuel Beckett's *Waiting for Godot* (1952), Joseph Heller's *Catch-22* (1961), Kurt Vonnegut's *Slaughterhouse-Five* (1966), and Margaret Atwood's *The Handmaid's Tale* (1985). In absurdism, there are no givens, no justice, as depicted in the droll interrogation in Heinrich Böll's "My Melancholy Face":

> "Last employment?"
> "Prisoner ..."
> "Former offense?"
> "Happy face."

In Albert Camus's *The Stranger* (1946), doubts about God, patriotism, sanity, and self supplant previous philosophies that assured human worth, direction, purpose, and reward. The refusal of the protagonist Meursault to conform to society's expectations costs him credibility in a court trial where he fights a murder charge. In his one angry outburst, he declares that his inability to weep for his mother is the sole reason for the court's convicting him of premeditated murder. A famous absurdist stage play, Friedrich Dürrenmatt's *The Visit* (1956), depicts a greedy town that condones the public execution of an innocent man, whose corpse is disclosed tidily covered by a checkered tablecloth. Other hallmarks of the theater of the absurd include plays by Jean Genet, Vaclav Havel, Ann Jellicoe, Eugène Ionesco, Edward Albee, Bertolt Brecht, Jean Anouilh, Marsha Norman, Hugh Leonard, David Mamet, and Harold Pinter.

See also existentialism.

acrostic   a riddle, occasional poem, essay, love letter, advertisement, or newspaper column arranged so that a sequence of letters, syllables, or words spells out a hidden message, as in the first letters of the religious emblem "Jesus Christ, Son of God, Savior," which in Greek spells *ichthus*, or fish, a Christian symbol. Acrostics are mental gymnastics; touches of such wit can found in the Bible, the alphabetized stanzas in Geoffrey Chaucer's poem "ABC" (ca. 1369), Ben Jonson's play *The Alchemist* (1610), and love verse by Edgar Allan Poe. In *Through the Looking Glass* (1871), author Lewis Carroll salutes his young friend Alice by composing a poem that spells out her full name in the first letters of each line.

act-tune   music composed and performed between the acts of a play, a standard feature of Elizabethan dramas. Most of the writers of this genre were anonymous, with the exception of Henry Purcell, the most versatile and celebrated composer of his era. Music as a component of theater has a long tradition, dating back as far as performances for Egypt's god king, Turkish puppet productions, Hindu tamborinists, and the Chinese theater music that accompanied such between-the-acts performances as jugglers, acrobats, and mimes.

adage   a tradional saying; often a short, sometimes trite proverb that uses a metaphor to express a common belief—for example, "a stitch in time saves nine" and "a rolling stone gathers no moss" from Benjamin Franklin's *Poor Richard's Almanack* (1733–1758). Ambrose Bierce produced a collection of biting adages in *The Devil's Dictionary* (1906). *See also* aphorism, epigram.

alexandrine   a twelve-syllable line of prose or a line of iambic hexameter verse, often a variation of a monotonous series of lines in iambic pentameter. Common to elevated drama of twelfth-century French literature, it was a standard stanza conclusion in Edmund Spenser's *The Faerie Queene* (1596) and appears in William Shakespeare's plays—for example, in the confrontation with the former king's ghost in *Hamlet* (ca. 1599–1600), Hamlet inserts a twelve-syllable line among ten-syllable lines when he asks:

> … What may this mean,
> that thou, dead corse, again, in complete
>   steel,
> Revisit'st thus the glimpses of the moon,
> Making night hideous; and we fools of
>   nature
> So horridly to shake our disposition
> With thoughts beyond the reaches of
>   our souls?
> Say, why is this? wherefore? What
>   should we do?
>
> (I, iv, 55-61)

The alexandrine is also common in verse by Sir Philip Sidney, Alexander Pope,

John Dryden, John Keats, Robert Browning, and Robert Bridges.

See also meter, Spenserian stanza.

alienation effect   a theatrical concept that drama must appeal to reason and not to emotion. The proponent, Bertolt Brecht, adopted this idea from the Chinese style of acting. By rejecting the traditional Greek intent to entertain and rid the viewer of harmful emotions, Brecht distanced spectator from actor by engaging the audience's mind and critical faculties over feelings. Brechtian drama such as his *Drums in the Night* (1922) became known as Epic Theater, an antibourgeois focus on ethical human behavior and unbiased judgment of actions, particularly those of the working class.

allegory   a literary work or form of visual imagery that functions on two or more levels of meaning by comparing objects to symbols beyond the scope of the work—for instance, Washington Irving's short story "The Devil and Tom Walker" (1824), Kate Chopin's story "Emancipation: A Life Fable" (1869), Derek Walcott's folk play *Ti-Jean and His Brothers* (1972), and Mark Twain's "The Man Who Corrupted Hadleyburg" (1898), a bitter allegory on hypocrisy and greed. Through direct or implied comparison, allegory results in either moralizing or satire and is common to mystery plays, aphorism, fable, exemplum, parable, and religious epic, as found in the *Second Shepherds' Play*, Confucian and Sufi homilies, Daoist and Buddhist verse, Japanese haiku, native American beast fables, the parables of Christ, and Dante's epic poem *The Divine Comedy* (1321).

A monumental allegory, John Bunyan's *The Pilgrim's Progress* (1678) compares the obstacles on a journeyman's literal path to the symbolic hindrances and temptations faced by a Christian who tries to live a pure and blameless life in anticipation of reward in an afterlife. Benjamin Franklin employs allegory in one of the didactic adages from *Poor Richard's Almanack* (1733–1758): "He that riseth late must trot all day, and shall scarce overtake his business at night; while Laziness travels so slowly that Poverty soon overtakes him."

Other important allegories include Plato's cave myth in *The Republic* (Fourth century B.C.), the biblical *Song of Solomon* (ca. sixth century B.C.), the medieval morality play *Everyman* (late fifteenth century), Edmund Spenser's *The Faerie Queene* (1596), Jonathan Swift's *Gulliver's Travels* (1726), Samuel Taylor Coleridge's *The Rime of the Ancient Mariner* (1798), Nathaniel Hawthorne's "Young Goodman Brown" (1846) and *The Scarlet Letter* (1850), Herman Melville's *Moby-Dick* (1851) and *Billy Budd* (1951), Samuel Butler's *Erewhon* (1872), Karel Capek's *R.U.R.* (1921), James Thurber's *Fables for Our Times* (1940), George Orwell's *Animal Farm* (1945), Albert Camus's *The Plague* (1948), Thomas Pynchon's *V* (1963), Edward Albee's *Tiny Alice* (1964), Richard Adams's *Watership Down* (1972), and Maya Angelou's "On the Pulse of the Morning" (1993).

See also fable, parable.

alliteration   the repetition of consonant sounds, even those spelled differently; for example, the *z* sound in busy, scissors, xylophone, zone, and frizz, or the *zh* sound in mirage, pleasure, derision, vizier, and azure. As a method of linking words for effect, alliteration is also called head rhyme or initial rhyme, the connective element of Old English and Old Norse verse, as in *Beowulf* (ca. 600) and the *Edda* (ca. 1150–1250). As demonstrated in *Beowulf*, strong pairings of consonants solidified the lusty trochaic meter, as in the repeated *g* and *d* in line one and the *w* and *d* in line two of this couplet:

> God mid Gaetum Grendles daeda
> [God amid the Geats Grendel's deeds]
> Wlanc Wedera leod word aefter spraec.
> [The proud Weder lord words after spoke.]

Examples of alliterated titles from American literature include Francis Scott Key's patriotic poem "The Star-Spangled Banner" (1814), A. B. Guthrie's historical fiction *The Way West* (1949), and Sonia Sanchez's verse collections *Homegirls and Handgrenades* (1984) and *Under a Soprano Sky* (1987). Additional examples include the *k* sounds in Mary Stewart's *The Crystal Cave* (1970), *th* sounds of S. E. Hinton's *That Was Then, This Is Now* (1971), initial *w*'s in Maxine Hong Kingston's *The Woman Warrior* (1975), repeated *r*'s in Mildred Taylor's *Roll of Thunder Hear My Cry* (1976), and sibilance in Joaquin Miller's *Song of the Sierras* (1871) and Maya Angelou's *Now Sheba Sings the Song* (1987).

Alliteration has a rhythmic and musical effect in children's literature such as Dr. Seuss stories and riddles and tongue-twisters—for instance, "She sells seashells down by the seashore." Repeated consonant sounds also predominate in rap, doggerel, and advertising jingles, as in the product name "Denham's Dandy Dental Detergent" in Ray Bradbury's *Fahrenheit 451* (1953) and similar media slogans in Don DeLillo's *White Noise* (1991). A unique segment of alliteration is sibilance, the hissing repetition of the *s* or *sh* sound, a unifying factor in the opening line of the prologue to Geoffrey Chaucer's *The Canterbury Tales* (1385): "Whan that Aprill with his shoures soote...."

allusion   a brief or indirect reference to something or someone known to most people—for example, the land of cotton for the American South, stars and stripes for the American flag, Turkey Day for Thanksgiving, and the jolly fat man in the red suit and white whiskers for Santa Claus. A memorable example from American oratory comes from Martin Luther King, Jr.'s "I Have a Dream" speech, which patterns a sentence after the Gettysburg Address: "Fivescore years ago, a great American, in whose symbolic shadow we stand, signed the Emancipation Proclamation," a reference to Abraham Lincoln's memorial statue in Washington, D.C.

Titles often draw on earlier works of fiction and art or events from history, like the biblical site mentioned in the title of John Steinbeck's *East of Eden* (1952), the reference to Horace's *Ars Poetica* in the title of Palestinian poet Maxim Ghilan's "Ars Po" (1968), the name of an imprisoned female figure in Greek mythology in the title of Michael Crichton's *The Andromeda Strain* (1969), and a line from *Macbeth* in the title of Robert Frost's poem "Out, Out—."

In Edmond Rostand's *Cyrano de Bergerac* (1897), references to Ulysses and Penelope from Homer's *Odyssey* precede the concluding image of Roxane as a pensive widow sitting in the convent garden embroidering her tapestry, just as Homer's Penelope sews a winding cloth for her father-in-law, Laertes, to keep suitors from forcing her into marriage.

Southern novelist Flannery O'Connor made a left-handed compliment in reply to critics who compared her stories to those of master Southern writer William Faulkner: "Nobody wants his mule and wagon stalled on the same track the Dixie Limited is roaring down."

Allusions may be categorized by the source of their meaning, for example, the biblical and mythological allusions mentioned above as well as these:

• literary allusion, the focus of Lee Ann Roripaugh's "Good-Bye to Never-Never Land" (1989), which refers to J. M. Barrie's *Peter Pan* in the title and to L. Frank Baum's *The Wizard of Oz* in the line, "the gates of Oz and the Emerald City/ have been closed."

• personal allusion to events, situations, and family and acquaintances from the author's life, for example, Louisa May Alcott's description of a weak father in *Little Women* (1869) and John Steinbeck's references to his companion, biologist Ed Ricketts, in *Cannery Row* (1945).

• topical allusions to current events, a major purpose of the political satire in Washington Irving's *A History of New York* (1809) and Margaret Atwood's *The Handmaid's Tale* (1986).

• structural allusion, as with the Homeric journey motif in Derek Walcott's *Omeros* (1990) and Charles Frasier's *Cold Mountain* (1997).

• imitative allusion or parody, the style of John Gardner's *Grendel* (1971), a witty retelling of *Beowulf* from the monster's point of view.

ambiguity   a deliberate fusion of meanings in a single image or phrase to promote meaning, nuance, or ambiance, as found in connotation, pun, and paradox, all of which are subtleties of language open to multiple interpretations. For example, "the darkest evening of the year," a familiar phrase from Robert Frost's "Stopping by Woods on a Snowy Evening" (1923), suggests both the winter solstice and a bleak emotional depression.

An extended ambiguity colors the dual image of the dead hero in A. E. Housman's "To an Athlete Dying Young" (1896), in which the hero is carried "shoulder-high," both in the procession at the time of his victory and when borne by pall bearers to his grave. To the poet, both

public adulation and life itself are too short.

A useful literary device, ambiguity heightens significance, particularly poetry, as found in Gerard Manley Hopkins's "Inversnaid" (1889), Amy Lowell's "Patterns," and Randall Jarrell's "The Death of the Ball Turret Gunner" (1955).

Ambiguity can result from the intentional implications of homophones, as in the overlay of meanings for berth/birth in "Berth's Garage," a setting in John Updike's poem "Ex-Basketball Player," and the implications of sole/soul in the description "a gentleman from sole to crown" and reflections of the heart or core in the title of E. A. Robinson's "Richard Cory" (1910). Likewise compelling is Kaye Gibbons's novel *Ellen Foster* (1987), in which the title character adopts a new surname after she joins a foster family.

anachronism   a detail or sentiment that is inconsistent with the historical milieu of a work, as in William Shakespeare's reference to a clock and to men with hats pulled down in *Julius Caesar* (ca. 1599), which is set in a time when male characters dressed in Roman togas. Mark Twain heightens the satire in *A Connecticut Yankee in King Arthur's Court* (1886) by forcing the protagonist back 1200 years, when he teaches citizens of King Arthur's Camelot to play baseball and ride bicycles. Rather than reflecting a careless error, the use of anachronism may establish a sense of universality, time fusion, or timelessness, a frequent theme or motif in utopian and science fiction based on time travel, particularly H. G. Wells's *The Time Machine* (1895), Virginia Woolf's *Orlando* (1928), Ray Bradbury's *The Martian Chronicles* (1950), Arthur C. Clarke's *Childhood's End* (1953), and John Fowles's satiric side notes in *The French Lieutenant's Woman* (1969).

analogy a literary parallel or comparison between like situations, objects, or ideas, often overtly expressed as a simile or implied as a conceit, image, or metaphor, as in references to death as a form of sleep in William Shakespeare's *Hamlet* (ca. 1599–1600), Emily Dickinson's comparison of a book to a frigate in "There Is No Frigate Like a Book" (ca. 1873), Isak Dinesen's feminine description of a heavenly body in "the African new moon lying on her back" from *Out of Africa* (1937), and Octavio Paz's analogy of time and mortality in his statement "We are condemned to kill time: Thus we die bit by bit" from *Cuento de los Jardines* (1968).

More extensive analogies dominate an entire work, as in Robert Louis Stevenson's vision of toys on a bedspread as soldiers on a battlefield in "The Land of Counterpane" (1885), Walt Whitman's making a sea captain an analogue to President Abraham Lincoln in "O Captain, My Captain" (1855), and May Swenson's controlling architectural image in "body my house" from the poem "Question" (1954).

See also conceit, image, metaphor, simile.

anapest a metrical foot or unit that contains three syllables, two unstressed syllables followed by a stressed syllable (‿‿´), the controlling rhythm of a tribute to De Soto in Stephen Vincent and Rosemary Benét's *The Book of Americans* (1933), which proclaims:

> He discovered the great Mississippi,
> He faced perils and hardships untold,
> And his soldiers ate bacon, if I'm not
>   mistaken,
> But nobody found any gold.

Less stately and noble than the iamb, the anapest often alternates with the iamb and produces a variable and suitably mobile measure, as found in George Leybourne's popular song "The Man on the Flying Trapeze" (1860), which begins,

> Oh, he flies through the air with the
>   greatest of ease
> This daring young man on the flying
>   trapeze.

Joel Chandler Harris applied the same genial flow for a dialect revival hymn:

> Oh, what shill we do w'en de great day
>   comes,
> Wid de blowin' er de trunpits en de ban-
>   gin' er de drums?
> How many po' sinners'll be kotched out
>   late
> En fine no latch ter de goldin gate.
>   (1880)

In verse from the romantic and Victorian eras, anapests govern Sir Walter Scott's "Lochinvar" (1808), Lord Byron's "The Destruction of Sennacherib" (1815), Percy Bysshe Shelley's "The Cloud" (1820), Clement Moore's "A Visit from St. Nicholas" (1823), Robert Browning's "How They Brought the Good News from Ghent to Aix" (1845), and Algernon Swinburne's "A Forsaken Garden" (1878). Anapestic rhythm adapts to the needs of both the frontier melodramas of Robert Service's "The Shooting of Dan McGrew" (1907) and "The Cremation of Sam McGee" (1907) and John Masefield's pensive "Sea Fever" (1902), which exults, "I must go down to the seas again, to the lonely sea and the sky."

anecdote a brief, uncomplicated, but often penetrating narrative that reflects an incident, attitude, or detail relevant to a person's life and behavior or to an event—for example, the story of Washington cutting down the cherry tree in Mason Lock Weems's *The Life of Washington, with Curious Anecdotes* (1800), isolated conversations with friends in Marjorie Kinnan Rawlings's autobiography *Cross Creek* (1942), the inclusion of chance meetings or humorous misadventures in Laura Ingalls Wilder's reflective travelogue *West from Home: Letters, San Francisco, 1915* (1974), and the description of a native American courtship ritual in Antoine LeClaire's *The Autobiography of Black Hawk* (1833):

> He goes to the lodge when all are asleep, (or pretend to be), lights his matches, which have been provided for the purpose, and soon finds where his intended sleeps. He then awakens her, and holds the light to his face that she may know him—after which he places the light close to her. If she blows it out, the ceremony is ended, and he appears in the lodge next morning, as one of the family. If she does not blow out the light, but leaves it to burn out, he retires from the lodge.

The anecdote varies in style and purpose, as with the war story, a gossipy item or hurtful dig at a famous person, a curious circumstance, or an amusing sidenote told for the purpose of establishing some unique quality or trait.

The anecdote is a staple in second-century B.C. Taoist lore of Chuang Tzu, Lieh Tzu, and Lui An, the sayings of Saadi, the Sufi poet of Persia, and the Japanese writings collected in Sei Shonagon's *The Pillow Book* (ca. 1050) and Yoshida Kenko's *Essays in Idleness* (ca. 1350).

In American literature, anecdotes dot the text of Mark Twain's *Roughing It* (1872) and *Life on the Mississippi* (1883), small-town events enliven Olive Anne Burns's *Cold Sassy Tree* (1984), and family anecdotes enrich Sarah Delany and Elizabeth Delany's *Having Our Say* (1993), in which laughter from one side of a duplex apartment convinces a guest in the adjacent apartment that the building is haunted.

antagonist the prime character, being, or force that opposes or causes conflict for the main character or protagonist in a drama or narrative. In the biblical story of Samson and Delilah, the antago-

nist Delilah persuades the protagonist Samson to disclose the secret of his strength, then betrays him to his enemies. The antagonist may appear in a number of guises:

- a villain, notably William Shakespeare's Iago in *Othello* (ca. 1603–1604)
- a rival, such as Ashley Wilkes in Margaret Mitchell's *Gone with the Wind* (1936)
- a generalized enemy, as with the French army in Erich Maria Remarque's *All Quiet on the Western Front* (1929) and the North Vietnamese army in Walter Dean Myers's *Fallen Angels* (1968)
- a personal enemy or opponent, as with the grandmother in Richard Wright's *Black Boy* (1945)
- a culture or way of life, as depicted in Dorothy Johnson's story "A Man Called Horse" (1949) and racism in August Wilson's *Fences* (1986)
- a force of nature, as found in Jack London's survival story "To Build a Fire" (1900).

anticlimax a concluding afterthought or the introduction of a lesser point after the main point or issue has been presented, as in J. M. Barrie's prediction that Peter Pan will survive "so long as children are gay and innocent and heartless." Anticlimax is usually an abrupt lapse or rapid transition from a lofty, noble, or serious element to something mundane, insignificant, or even ridiculous—for example, in Alexander Pope's *The Rape of the Lock*, the heroine's worry that she will

> … stain her honour, or her new brocade;
> Forget her prayers, or miss a masquerade,
> Or lose her heart, or necklace, at a ball.

An example from Winston Churchill derives from a witty put-down, "They told me how Mr. Gladstone read Homer for fun, which I thought served him right." Satirist Dorothy Parker summons anticlimax to create cynicism in her adage, "The two most beautiful words in the English language are 'check enclosed.'" The unforeseen lapse in suspense or a decline in dramatic intensity from serious to trivial makes anticlimax the key factor in bathos. *See also* bathos.

anti-hero, anti-heroine   a protagonist or central figure who is devoid of the usual heroic qualities of an admirable person or leader, particularly skill, grace, honesty, courage, and truth; a non-hero who does not embody admirable traits or who blunders into heroism by chance. An anti-hero is found in Joseph Conrad's *Lord Jim* (1900), Thomas Berger's *Little Big Man* (1965), Marsha Norman's *'night, Mother* (1982), and Barbara Kingsolver's *The Bean Trees* (1988).

Meursault, the focus of Albert Camus's *The Stranger* (1946), risks a death sentence by refusing to scheme or lie or present himself as other than what he is. His refusal to mourn his mother with tears and his explanation of how the sun on the sea precipitated the shooting demonstrate an inability to dissemble on the witness stand, even if his statements doom him to decapitation for premeditated murder.

An anti-hero from American literature, James Thurber's Walter Mitty, from *My World and Welcome to It* (1942), models the comic aspect of the non-traditional central figure. The character Mitty has added to the English language a colorful term for a curiously inadequate person with good intentions who lacks the strength, drive, or opportunity to complete a heroic act.

Unlike Mitty's wimpish figure of the browbeaten husband, serious depictions of the anti-hero often question the nature of the quest, as with Miguel de Cervantes's

Don Quixote (1615), or ridicule a class, substratum, or generation of people, as with the inept title characters in Gustave Flaubert's *Madame Bovary* (1857) and T. S. Eliot's "The Love Song of J. Alfred Prufrock" (1917), Ernest Hemingway's failed soldier in *A Farewell to Arms* (1929), Willy Loman in Arthur Miller's *Death of a Salesman* (1949), Yossarian in Joseph Heller's *Catch-22* (1961), mismatched roommates in Neil Simon's *The Odd Couple* (1965), the hapless, retarded hero of Daniel Keyes's *Flowers for Algernon* (1967), and the jilted women in Terry McMillan's *Waiting to Exhale* (1992) and Margaret Atwood's *The Robber Bride* (1993).

anti-masque   a short interlude performed during the masque in a mood antithetical to the mood of the masque itself. British dramatist Ben Jonson (1573–1637) was particularly fond of using the anti-masque to sharpen his satire. Jonson's masques were so elaborate that they finally challenged the artistic invention of Inigo Jones (1573–1652), Britain's famed scenic designer.

antithesis   a balanced statement of contrasts that juxtaposes opposing points of view in parallel words, phrases, clauses, images, or themes—for example, a line from May Sarton's poem "My Sisters, O My Sisters" (1974), "She was born a good grandmother, not a good lover," and the implied paradox of Muriel Rukeyser's intriguing opening statement in *Letter to the Front* (1944): "To be a Jew in the twentieth century/Is to be offered a gift." The simplest of antitheses derives from paralleling nouns, as in the truism "Ignorance is bliss" and Catherine II of Russia's command, "Reign or die." Martin Luther King, Jr., creates terse antithesis by stating opposites on either side of a linking verb: "Injustice anywhere is a threat to justice everywhere."

A more demanding form of antithesis occurs in the pairing of the two clauses of a compound sentence: Jane Austen's declaration, "Business, you know, may bring money, but friendship hardly ever does," and Queen Anne's observation, "I have changed my ministers, but I have not changed my measures." Parallel sentences often demonstrate the pairing of contrasting ideas. An example from Ayn Rand occurs in a statement in *The Fountainhead* (1943): "Civilization is the progress toward a society of privacy. The savage's whole existence is public."

Antithesis is a common rhetorical device in maxims illustrating appropriate behavior, as in "A wrathful man stirreth up strife: but he that is slow to anger appeaseth strife" (Proverbs 15:18), and "Faithful are the wounds of a friend; but the kisses of an enemy are deceitful" (Proverbs 27:5-6). Similarly, actions and ideas can present polar opposites, but with more emphasis on thought and less on parallel grammatical structures—for instance, Edith Wharton's description of the title character of *Ethan Frome* (1911): "Every one in Starkfield knew him and gave him a greeting tempered to his own grave mien; but his taciturnity was respected and it was only on rare occasions that one of the older men of the place detained him for a word."

Another purpose of antithesis is to form the second element of a dialectic, a controlled disputation that examines each element in a reasoned search for the truth. Aldous Huxley's *Brave New World* (1932) focuses on the tit-for-tat exchange in a discussion of religion: Mustapha Mond contends, "People believe in God because they've been conditioned to believe in God," to which the Savage replies, "But all the same ... it is natural to believe in God when you're alone—quite alone, in the night, thinking about death."

anti-utopia   a failed attempt to create a perfect world; a dystopia. An influential anti-utopian pamphlet, Thomas Malthus's *An Essay on the Principle of Population As It Affects the Future of Society* (1798), demonstrates the use of anti-utopianism in nonfiction by warning outright that unbridled growth will eventually compromise the earth's ability to feed and shelter the population. Many fictional literary examples display the imaginary creation of hell on earth:

• the collapse of an ideal natural world in Samuel Johnson's *Rasselas* (1759)

• threats of violence in H. G. Wells's *The Island of Dr. Moreau* (1896) and *The War of the Worlds* (1898) and Margaret Atwood's *The Handmaid's Tale* (1985)

• disillusionment with the mechanics of utopia in L. Frank Baum's *The Wonderful Wizard of Oz* (1900) and Yevgeny Zamyatin's *We* (1921)

• the decline in belief systems in John G. Neihardt's *Black Elk Speaks* (1932)

• the loss of personal rights in Ralph Ellison's *Invisible Man* (1947), George Orwell's *1984* (1949), and Marge Piercy's *Woman on the Edge of Time* (1976).

aphorism   a concise, often witty truism or principle stated in a brief phrase or sentence to serve as an insightful observation, moral precept, or form of instruction—for example, Ambrose Bierce's biting adages in *The Devil's Dictionary* (1906). In describing the use of fear as a disciplinary measure in *One Day in the Life of Ivan Denisovich* (1963), novelist Alexander Solzhenitsyn condenses his remarks to a single instance: "Beat a dog once and you only have to show him the whip," a meaningful image that depicts the level of fear that cows human prisoners while it compares them to whipped dogs. In Hermann Hesse's novel *Siddhartha* (1951), the title character proves he is literate by writing two illustrative maxims in parallel grammatical form: "Writing is good, thinking is better. Cleverness is good, patience is better."

apocalyptic literature [uh•pah•kuh•LIHP•tihk]   writing that features a holocaust, the end of the world, divine intervention in sinful or evil acts, the secrets of the future, or the ultimate judgment on humankind, as in the biblical story of the eradication of the sinful cities of Sodom and Gomorrah in Genesis 19:1–29, the dire predicament of the spider dangling over the abyss in Jonathan Edwards's sermon "Sinners in the Hands of an Angry God" (1741), and the presence of death in an Algerian city besieged by a deadly contagion in Albert Camus's novel *The Plague* (1947).

Other intense apocalyptic works include the biblical Book of Revelation, William Blake's verse cycle "America: A Prophecy" (1793), Edgar Allan Poe's stories "The Fall of the House of Usher" (1839) and "The Masque of the Red Death" (1842), T. S. Eliot's "The Wasteland" (1922) and "The Hollow Men" (1925), William Butler Yeats's poem "The Second Coming" (1933), Nathanael West's *The Day of the Locust* (1939), Ray Bradbury's dystopic *Fahrenheit 451* (1953), Doris Lessing's *The Four-Gated City* (1969), H. Lindsey's *The Late Great Planet Earth* (1970), and Gabriel García Márquez's *One Hundred Years of Solitude* (1970).

apologia [ap•uh•LOH•jyuh]   a literary defense of a person or situation, also an explanation or detailed accounting of an event, institution, dogma, or philosophy—for example, Varina Davis's *Jefferson Davis, Ex-President of the Confederate States of America, A Memoir* (1890), which clears up myths and misconceptions about her husband's role as president of the short-lived Confederate States of America.

apostrophe   an emotion-charged call, command, or statement addressed directly to an absent or dead person, abstract quality, object, or hypothetical being, as in Edna St. Vincent Millay's cry, "O world, I cannot hold thee close enough!" (1917), and Thomas Wolfe's lyric call in *Look Homeward, Angel* (1929):

> O sea! (he thought) I am the hill-born, the prison-pent, the ghost, the stranger, and I walk here at your side. O sea, I am lonely like you, I am strange and far like you, I am sorrowful like you; my brain, my heart, my life, like yours, have touched strange shores.

Apostrophe is a standard rhetorical device, dignifying the Egyptian hymn to Aten (ca. 1360 B.C.), the hymn to the night in the *Rig Veda* (ca. 1000 B.C.), the Tewa "Song of the Sky Loom," Phillis Wheatley's "To His Excellency, George Washington" (1776), Percy Bysshe Shelley's "Ode to the West Wind" (1820), Hilda Doolittle's "Oread" (1914) and "Tribute to the Angels" (1945), and Derek Walcott's "Sunday Lemons" (1971).

One of America's most poignant apostrophes occurs in Frederick Douglass's *Narrative of the Life of Frederick Douglass* (1845), when, at the depths of despair, the Maryland slave calls to a ship,

> O that I were free! O, that I were on one of your gallant decks, and under your protecting wing! Alas! betwixt me and you, the turbid waters roll. Go on, go on. O that I could also go! Could I but swim! If I could fly. O, why was I born a man, of whom to make a brute!

Less serious are Anton Chekhov's use of facetious apostrophe in *The Cherry Orchard* (1904) and Mark Twain's melodramatic quip in *Europe and Elsewhere* (1923), "O kind missionary, O compas-

sionate missionary, leave China! Come home and convert these Christians!"
See also invocation.

approximate rhyme words that come close to rhyme without copying the exact sound pattern, as in clear/there, mood/blood, and itches/leeches in a passage ridiculing astral healing according to phases of the moon from Samuel Butler's *Hudibras* (1662):

> Her secrets understood so clear,
> That some believed he had been there,
> Knew when she was in fittest mood,
> For cutting corns or letting blood.
> When for anointing scabs and itches,
> Or to the bum applying leeches;
> When sows and bitches may be spayed,
> And in what sign best cider's made.

Note that the final couplet rounds out the verse in true rhyme, spayed/made.

Also called off-rhyme, pararhyme, or slant, oblique, near, or imperfect rhyme, the pairing of similar sounds may indicate a shift in English pronunciation over time, as in the Elizabethan use of join (jine) to rhyme with pine.

Approximate rhyme is also a factor in translations—for example, Abraham Birman's English version of Yehudah Karni's "Evening in Jerusalem" (1968), which chooses soul/gone/fall/dun and fetters/night/batters/tight for the second and third stanzas.

The poet may intend to stray from too much perfection for effect, as in Sterling Brown's "Slim in Hell" (1932), which pairs unlikely strings of words: said Slim/at him, it's a fac'/devil's track, cabarets/Memphis days, devilish broad/Lawd, Lawd, Lawd, and was firing/presspirin'.
See also rhyme.

apron the part of the stage that protrudes in front of the proscenium arch, sometimes extending over the pit. Tradi-

tionally, Shakespearean soliloquies such as the "to be or not to be" speech in *Hamlet* (ca. 1599–1600) are delivered by actors standing apart from the rest of the cast on the apron, where the audience can see the actors' visual expression and where oral projection is most clear. An exaggerated apron, known as a thrust stage, protrudes into the audience. Musical theater productions often require a thrust stage for solos and duets, for example, Jerry Herman's *Hello, Dolly!* (1963).

archaism [ar•KAY•izm] obsolete or out-of-date language, phrasing, spelling, or idiom that belongs to ancient times—for example, amongst, methinks, haply, withal, perchance, alarum, fain, holp, yclept, vouchsafe, or forsooth, all found in William Shakespeare's poetry and dramas, or "Ye Olde Shoppe" for settings in colonial America. Ancient language also establishes the traditions of the past—for example, a reading of the King James version of Ruth 1:16 for a wedding, or Psalm 23 at a funeral.

Authors may deliberately choose antique language to set a mood, to create sonorous lines, or to adapt writing to an earlier era; for example, using *quoth* and *smote* to parody or to give a biblical flavor, a device common to the English romantic and Victorian poets, particularly John Keats and Alfred Lord Tennyson.

In the twentieth century, Heywood Broun reprises archaic terms for "The Fifty-First Dragon" (1941), a fable about a knight's development of courage. John Gardner establishes a tie with the past by calling for "a new set of nonce-rules" in *Grendel* (1971). The electronic bard in Stanislaw Lem's "The First Sally (A) OR Trurl's Electronic Bard" (1974) blends technobabble with Elizabethan phrases and *thee* and *thy*. Florence King creates satire from comparisons of current feminism to the medieval era in *The Florence King Reader* (1995).

archetype [AR•kuh•type] a recurrent theme, character, setting, or motif from early epic literature to present heroes and adventures stories in fiction, film, television, and video games; for example, the game Dungeons and Dragons, life cycles in Richard Adams's beast epic *Watership Down* (1972), and Mary Stewart's popular Merlin series, which opens *The Crystal Cave* with "I am an old man now, but then I was already past my prime when Arthur was crowned King" (1970).

Twentieth-century science fiction, elemental myth, and quest novels—J. R. R. Tolkien's *The Hobbit* (1937) and the Lord of the Rings trilogy (1956), Mary Renault's mythic recreations in *The King Must Die* (1958) and *The Last of the Wine* (1975), Ursula Le Guin's Earthsea trilogy (1972), Marion Zimmer Bradley's *Mists of Avalon* (1983), and Anne McCaffrey's late twentieth century fantasy dragon adventures—reprise chivalric lore and create figures similar to knights, dragon slayers, princesses, and voyagers of old who championed elemental right while battling evil in an era predating codified law.

Essential to the study of archetypes are standard critical writings—Sir James G. Frazer's *The Golden Bough* (1915), Carl Jung's *Modern Man in Search of a Soul* (1920), Joseph Campbell's analysis of mythology, notably his study of primordial leaders in *The Hero with a Thousand Faces* (1949), and Northrop Frye's *Anatomy of Criticism* (1957).

aside private commentary spoken *sotto voce* or in an undertone, discreet emotional outbursts, or whispers that the speaker limits to another character or characters in a play or to the audience—for example, Mark Antony's smug comment "Now let it work" after his manipulative funeral speech over the body of the title character in William Shakespeare's *Julius Caesar* (ca. 1599). Common to the Renaissance, the use of asides was redirected from serious drama to melodrama and comedy in the nineteenth century.

In the twentieth century, Thornton Wilder updated the stage convention in *Our Town* (1938), a framework drama that requires communication between the audience and the stage manager and discussion among spirits in the cemetery that the living characters cannot hear. In 1945, Tennessee Williams created for *The Glass Menagerie* the character/narrator Tom Wingfield, who is both active onstage and separated from the action by retreats to an outer framework during which he comments on events and character motivation. A familiar aside concludes the play: "Blow out your candles, Laura—and so goodbye...."

assonance repetition of a vowel sound, as in ache/eight/way, soul/moan/wrote, and cool/soup/rule—for example, the short *a* sound in Edgar Allan Poe's title *Al Aaraaf, Tamerlane, and Minor Poems* (1829). Less obvious than consonance, assonance or vocalic rhyme is a subtle form of sound linkage, usually euphonious and predominantly occurring in accented syllables, as found in these titles:

- long *a* in Jules Verne's adventure novel *Around the World in Eighty Days* (1870) and Randall Jarrell's poem "Lady Bates" (1955)
- long *e* in Jessamyn West's *Except for Me and Thee* (1949) and Marlo Thomas's collection *Free to Be ... You and Me* (1974)
- long *i* in Maya Angelou's *I Know Why the Caged Bird Sings* (1970) and Margaret Craven's *I Heard the Owl Call My Name* (1973)

• long *o* in Rose Wilder Lane's *On the Way Home* (1962) and Eldridge Cleaver's *Soul on Ice* (1968)

• long *u* in Edgar Allan Poe's "Ulalume" (1847), Moss Hart and George S. Kaufman's *You Can't Take It with You* (1936), and Marjorie Kellogg's *Tell Me That You Love Me, Junie Moon* (1972).

See also consonance, rhyme.

atmosphere   the prevailing aura or ambience triggered by a work's mood and tone and by incidental text clues that predispose the audience to a particular mindset or expectation of outcome, as in the foreboding of Edgar Allan Poe's verse romance, "Eldorado" (1849), poverty in Montreal in Gabrielle Roy's *The Tin Flute* (1945), and the grim ghetto of Alice Childress's play *A Hero Ain't Nothin' but a Sandwich* (1973), in which a street evangelist disrupts the peace with a cry of "Freeeeeeeedom now! Freeeeeeeeeeeeeeeedom now!" Other examples cover the spectrum of emotional response:

• ominous, brooding supernatural presence that introduces William Shakespeare's *Macbeth* (ca. 1603-06) and governs gothic lore and the fiction of Joseph Conrad and Stephen King

• dreamy acquiescence in Sidney Lanier's nature poem "The Marshes of Glynn" (1878) and Christina Rossetti's lyric "Song" (1848)

• tension that mounts to crisis in Shirley Jackson's story "The Lottery" (1948), Harper Lee's novel *To Kill a Mockingbird* (1960), Carlos Fuentes's *Old Gringo* (1961), and Wilson Rawls's *Where the Red Fern Grows* (1985)

• family camaraderie in Beth Henley's play *Crimes of the Heart* (1979)

• zany air of unpredictability that guides the character attitudes and action of Moss Hart and George S. Kaufman's *You Can't Take It with You* (1936)

• repressed mirth and genial nonchalance of Mary Chase's *Harvey* (1944).

audition   an assembling of actors, trying out for specific roles in a drama, comedy, or musical. Usually auditions are held on the stage where the play will be performed, the director sitting in what has come to be known as "the director's row," somewhere about two to nine rows back from the front of the stage, depending on the size and configuration of the theater.

autobiography   a long reflective narrative or memoir written by a person about his or her own life and accomplishments—traditionally either in chronological order or augmented by flashbacks. American models of this form of writing include Frederick Douglass's *Narrative of the Life of Frederick Douglass* (1845), Harriet Ann Brent Jacobs's *Incidents in the Life of a Slave Girl, Written by Herself* (1861), Benjamin Franklin's *Autobiography* (1867), Sarah Winnemucca's *Life Among the Piutes, Their Wrongs and Claims* (1883), Charles Eastman's *Indian Boyhood* (1902), Andy Adams's *The Log of a Cowboy* (1903), Thomas Henry Tibbles's *Buckskin and Blanket Days* (1904), *The Life and Adventures of Nat Love, Better Known in the Cattle Country as Deadwood Dick* (1907), Luther Standing Bear's *My Indian Boyhood* (1931), Maria Chona's *Papago Woman* (1936), Zora Neale Hurston's *Dust Tracks on a Road* (1942), Ella Deloria's *Waterlily* (1944), Santha Rama Rau's *Home to India* (1945), Anne Frank's *Diary of a Young Girl* (1952), Jason Betzinez's *I Fought with Geronimo* (1959), Maya Angelou's *The Heart of a Woman* (1981), and Zlata Filipovic's *Zlata's Diary* (1994).

A significant contribution to nonwhite autobiography of the late twentieth century is Mark Mathabane's *Kaffir Boy* (1986), which expresses personal and family reactions to fear, discontent, frustration, and deprivation. From a first-person point of view, the author discloses the dangers of the poverty, crime, rebellion, and rioting he experiences while growing up in South Africa.

An autobiography may be dictated to a ghost writer or stenographer, particularly when the work is to be published in another language, as is the case with Antoine LeClaire's *The Autobiography of Black Hawk* (1833), S. M. Barrett's *Geronimo's Story of His Life* (1906), John G. Neihardt's *Black Elk Speaks* (1932), Frank B. Linderman's *Pretty Shield, Medicine Woman of the Crows* (1932), Joseph Epes Brown's *The Sacred Pipe* (1953), Charles S. Brant's *Autobiography of a Kiowa Apache Man* (1969), and Richard Erdoes's *Lame Deer: Seeker of Visions* (1972). Alex Haley published *The Autobiography of Malcolm X* (1965) at the direction of the subject, who was killed before the book's completion.

Fiction may reflect autobiographical elements, as in Saki's repressive family and the dreary landscape of the vengeful short story "Sredni Vashtar" (1911), growing up in New Zealand in Katherine Mansfield's story collection *The Garden Party* (1922), memories of a North Carolina childhood in Thomas Wolfe's *Look Homeward, Angel* (1929), Gertrude Stein's *The Autobiography of Alice B. Toklas* (1933), Mary Hunter Austin's *Earth Horizon* (1933), Pat Conroy's exposé of Southern educational shortcomings for blacks in *The Water Is Wide* (1972), and the fictional recreation of the Argentine Revolution in Isabel Allende's *House of the Spirits* (1982).

avant-garde [A•vahnt•GAHRD] startling, shocking, or titillating new forms of art, painting, writing, or theater that break new ground or employ techniques that may attack or supplant established styles and forms, as is the case with anti-realism, surrealism, and absurdism. Tennessee Williams's *The Glass Menagerie* (1944), his so-called memory play, presents unconventional scenes that focus on impressionist acting techniques. Lighting is dreamy and operatic to filter around the characters and often holds cameo-like scenes apart from the rest of the stage. Williams again changed the look of American avant-garde theater with new, high standards in *A Streetcar Named Desire* (1947), a drama that was as rough and realistic as *The Glass Menagerie* was tender and touching.

B

backdrop a large curtain or canvas, extending across the back of a stage, on which are painted or projected trees, mountains, buildings, crowd scenes, and other elements of the play's setting, for example, marble-like columns for a revival of a Greek tragedy. A boom—a long pole, supportive arm, or brace—extends a microphone, camera, or lights in front of the backdrop. Additional props such as a noose or swing may be lowered or raised before the backdrop from the catwalk, a narrow walkway or bridge that extends across the top of the theater.

For a stage version of Roger Miller's *Big River: The Adventures of Huckleberry Finn* (1985), a backdrop may unfurl the Mississippi River, which seems to flow onstage and disappear in the distance. The backdrop creates a sense of depth and isolation from society as characters Huck and Jim float on their raft. At night, lighting effects cause the Mississippi to vanish and the sky to fill with twinkling stars. When the play closes production, stagehands strike the set by removing the backdrop and packing up flat scenery, all of which are stripped of paint for another production.

balanced sentence   a sentence, like a balance-beam scale, composed of equal elements on each side of a conjunction, conjunction and comma, or semicolon, which creates caesura or pause as an emphasis on the proportional comment on either side. Poet Carl Sandburg uses a conjunction to divide two parts of a prediction: "Sometime they'll give a war and nobody will come." Balanced sentences may corroborate an idea, as in Gwendolyn Brooks's line, "My mother is jelly-hearted and she has a brain of jelly" in the poem "Jessie Mitchell's Mother" (1960). Lines from the introduction to Toni Morrison's *The Bluest Eye* (1970) demonstrate the use of a semi-colon as the connector at the pause: "Cholly Breedlove is dead; our innocence too. The seeds shriveled and died; her baby too." Balance may also convey contrast or antithesis in themes and subjects, as in the introduction to Sojourner Truth's speech "Keeping the Thing Going While Things Are Stirring" (1867): "My friends, I am rejoiced that you are glad, but I don't know how you will feel when I get through."

ballad   a dramatic, straightforward story-poem intended to be read aloud, recited by a storyteller or balladeer, or sung with musical accompaniment and audience participation, as found in Elizabeth Madox Roberts's *The Great Meadow* (1930), an historical novel containing a vigorous, lethal Kentucky hunting song, "Bangum Went to a Wild Boar's Den," composed in chivalric tradition:

> Bangum drew his trusty knife,
> Cut 'im down, cut 'im down.
> And he stabbed that wild boar outen his life,
> Cut 'im down, cut 'im down.

The folk ballad flourished from the Middle Ages through the Renaissance, for example "Twa Corbies," "Mother, Get Up and Bar the Door," "Lord Randal," "The Demon Lover," "Robin Hood and Allen a Dale," and "Barbara Allen," the most familiar of English folk ballads. Derived from preliterate periods of composition, the ballad demonstrates standard oral qualities:

- abrupt retelling of chronological events
- simple dialect or colloquial narration or vivid conversation
- interruption at regular intervals by a repeated line or refrain, often altered in increments to reflect shifts in the narration
- stereotyping in stock descriptions, e.g., flaxen-haired, bold lover, and blood-red wine
- impersonal recitation of grim details, e.g. arrest and hanging, sudden death by poisoning.

Traditional ballads have no identifiable author and exist in numerous versions over time, as in the variations of the Chinese *Book of Songs*, which dates to the sixth century B.C., and nineteenth-century Mexican corridos. These story-poems tell of winsome young girls, soldiers, sailors, and farm folk involved in stories of unrequited love, longing, sensational revenge plots, imprisonment, execution or tragic loss, rebellion against tyranny, prophecy, and supernatural incidents. Parodied versions follow the general outline, but carry melodrama and tragedy to ridiculous lengths.

The folk ballad follows a standard meter and groups events into four-line stanzas of alternating iambic tetrameter/iambic trimeter rhyming abcb. Edward Paramore's parody of Robert Service's *The Ballad of Yukon Jake* (1921) illustrates an artful copy of the traditional ballad stanza:

> But, miles away, in Keokuk, Ia.,
> Did a ruined maiden fight
> To remove the smirch from the Baptist Church

By bringing the heathen light...
So, two weeks later, she took a freighter,
For the gold-cursed land near the Pole,
But Heaven ain't made for a lass that's
     betrayed—
She was wrecked on Shark Tooth Shoal!

After the advent of printing, the English ballad appeared on broadsides, a folio sheet printed with a reworded ballad or narrative of current events, such as miracles, public executions, political scandal, catastrophes, or adulation of popular and legendary figures, for example, Robin Hood, Rob Roy, Nell Gwyn, Tom Dooley, the Boston Strangler, Frankie and Johnny, Stagolee, Big John, Jesse James, Bonnie and Clyde, and Casey Jones. Street distributors recited stirring or titillating verses while strolling among potential customers and selling copies for a few cents each.

Australian tradition from New South Wales names the transported convict Francis "Frank the Poet" McNamara, native to Tipperary, as creator of impertinent colonial verse ballads such as the protest song "For the Company Underground" and the anti-authoritarian "A Convict's Tour in Hell" (1885), which begins:

You prisoners of New South Wales
Who frequent watchhouses and gaols,
A story to you I will tell:
'Tis a convict's tour to hell.

These ballads draw on the "Kelly" tradition of Irish ballads, which typically open with "Oh Paddy, dear, did you hear the news that's going round?/On the head of bold Ned Kelly they have placed a thousand pound." Early twentieth-century Australian rhymer Henry Lawson published a number of folk recitatives, including "Ballad of the Drover," "Freedom on the Wallaby," "Andy's Gone with Cattle," and a bawdy ditty, "The Bastard from the Bush," published in an anthology, *The Songs of Henry Lawson* (1989).

The literary or art ballad imitates the style and conventions of anonymous traditional narratives such as Po Chu-Yi's "Song of Everlasting Regret" (ca. 845 A.D.), Samuel Taylor Coleridge's *The Rime of the Ancient Mariner* (1798), John Keats's "La Belle Dame Sans Merci" (1820), Heinrich Heine's "The Lorelei" (1827), Henry Wadsworth Longfellow's *Ballads and Other Poems* (1841), Philip Pendleton Cooke's *Froissart Ballads, and Other Poems* (1847), Dante Gabriel Rossetti's "Sister Helen" (1854), Harriet A. Glazebrook's "Lips That Touch Liquor Shall Never Touch Mine" (1878), Rudyard Kipling's "Danny Deever" (1890) and *Barrack Room Ballads* (1890), W. S. Gilbert's *Bab Ballads* (1869), Oscar Wilde's *The Ballad of Reading Gaol* (1898), Sir Walter Scott's *The Lay of the Last Minstrel* (1805) and *Minstrelsy of the Scottish Border* (1803), and Alfred Noyes's *The Highwayman* (1913).

The North American frontier produced its own ballad tradition, which focuses on mining, livestock, banditry, and summary justice. Most popular for public performance were Robert Service's *The Shooting of Dan McGrew* (1903) and *The Cremation of Sam McGee* (1905), which made the poet's reputation. Frequently anthologized are an anonymous anti-Mormon ballad, "The Mountain Meadows Massacre," Joaquin Miller's *Joaquin et al.* (1869), Nora Perry's "The Love-Knot" (ca. 1875), Bret Harte's California ballads, Marie Ravenal de La Coste's "Somebody's Darling" (1881), Francis Miles Finch's "The Blue and the Gray" (1909), and Américo Paredes's "El Corrido de Gregorio Cortéz," collected in the 1950s. Two major collections of frontier balladry come from the Lomax family: John Lomax's *Cowboy Songs and Other Frontier Ballads* (1910) and John and Alan Lomax's *American Ballads and Folk Songs* (1934). *See also* corrido.

ballade [bal•LAHD] a demanding Old French verse form in iambic or anapestic tetrameter, often dedicated to a patron in an artful show of poetic skill. Made popular in the 1500s, the poem consists of three eight-line stanzas rhyming ababbcbc. It concludes with a four-line envoi or refrain rhyming bcbc and summarizing the previous action, the style of vagabond poet François Villon's "Ballade of Dead Ladies" in *Le Grand Testament* (ca. 1462), which ends with his famous question, "Mais où sont les neiges d'antan!" [But where are the snows of yesteryear!].

The intricacies of the ballade are central to a grudge match between Cyrano and Valvert in Act I of Edmond Rostand's *Cyrano de Bergerac* (1898). Cyrano pauses before initiating the duel and selects rhymes for his lengthy poem, which includes three eight-line stanzas and a four-line refrain, "Then, as I end the refrain, thrust home!"

In "Ballade of Dead Gentlemen," C. S. Lewis adapts the artificiality of the ballade to parody Villon. Lewis's envoi warns, "Princesses all, beneath your sway/In this grave world they bowed the knee;/Libertine airs in Elysium say," and concludes in French with a rhetorical question, "Mais où sont messieurs les maris?" [But where are the gentlemen their husbands?].

barnstormer a member of a dedicated, but low-paid theatrical company that tours small towns to perform light comedy and local-color drama. Barnstormers carry their own scenery and props. They arrive in town often late in the afternoon, set up a show in a few hours, and are ready to perform minutes later. After the show, the pace becomes hectic and exhausting as actors double as drays to load scenery and props on a bus or caravan of buses and vans and drive toward the next performance.

bathos [BAY•thohs] overstatement, excessive pathos, or anticlimax that emphasizes loss, sentiment, or tragic circumstances to the point of creating humor or melodrama, applied by critics to Beth Henley's play *The Miss Firecracker Contest* (1983). Alexander Pope delineates the parameters of bathos in an essay, *On Bathos, or, Of the Art of Sinking in Poetry* (1728), a witty send-up of Longinus's *On the Sublime*.

Unintentional humor can result from a poet's overreach of emotion, for example, in Percy Bysshe Shelley's "Ode to the West Wind" (1819), which complains, "I fall upon the thorns of life! I bleed!" and the unfortunate internal rhyme in Gerard Manley Hopkins's "The Windhover" (1918), which declares, "My heart in hiding/Stirred for a bird."

Examples from American verse include Mark Twain's humorously dismal "Ode to Stephen Dowling Bots, Dec.d" (from *Huckleberry Finn*, 1884) and Edwin Arlington Robinson's melodramatic "Mr. Flood's Party" (1920), which pictures a town drunk on a bender under what appears to be a double moon. The mellow tippler shakily places his jug on the ground and repines that "most things break," a sentimental reference to relationships fractured by his alcoholic misbehavior.

In Isabel Allende's historical novel *Of Love and Shadows* (1987), the protagonist, journalist Irene Beltran, attends a community pig roast. The overfed beast, oblivious to imminent death, is dragged in on short, wobbly legs. The animal is blinded by the light and stiff with terror. In Allende's overdrawn comparison, the butcher becomes an officiating Aztec priest, who sacrifices the howling pig with a stroke of the knife. The scene foreshadows the capture and murder of Evangelina, an innocent child whose remains her killer tosses into a pile of victims in a remote area where they won't be found.

beast fable an amoral animal tale or allegorical satire that places the beast characters in a farmyard, jungle, or forest setting in a comic or seriocomic action to reveal folly, pride, and other character flaws, as found in the trickery of the pig hero Kamapua'a, a deity and shape-shifter featured in an anonymous epic in the Hawaiian-language newspaper *Ka Leo o ka Lahui* (1891). A classic English example is Geoffrey Chaucer's "The Nun's Priest's Tale" (1385), the mock epic story of Chaunticleer the rooster and his flight from a fox.

Originated by Aesop in the sixth century B.C., the beast fable contains short conversational episodes that depict small animals in power struggles with large predators or human beings. Each Aesop fable concludes in a simplistic moral or adage, for example, "To change place is not to change nature," "Some would rather have a bad reputation than no attention at all," or "Danger comes from where we least expect." The use of animals to expose or lampoon human foibles is a typical ruse of the underclass or slaves, who created wry stories to mask criticism or contempt for their masters and overlords.

The beast fable is common to African, European, Asian and Middle Eastern, and native American and Southern lore, as found in Anansi the Spider stories from West Africa and the Caribbean, India's *Panchatantra* (ca. 200 B.C.), Marie de France's *Fables* (ca. 1175), and Jean de La Fontaine's Reynard the Fox stories (1694), as well as native American Coyote trickster tales and Uncle Remus stories (ca. 1880s).

Twentieth-century developments in beast fable include Rudyard Kipling's *Just-So Stories* and "Rikki Tikki Tavi" (1912), the tale of a wily mongoose who bests a cobra, Richard Adams's *Watership Down* (1972), and Virginia Hamilton's *The People Could Fly* (1985).

bedroom farce a comedy focused on or set in a bedroom, often with the bed itself as stage center and numerous doors through which characters appear and disappear at a mad pace. Such comedies abound with *double entendre* and themes of amorous escapades, disguise and deception, infidelity, and illegitimate births. The conventions of sexual farce have their western roots in the bawdy Greek comedies of Aristophanes and satyr plays, European *fabliaux*, and seventeenth-century romps such as William Wycherley's *The Country Wife*. Bedroom farce, such as Joe Orton's *What the Butler Saw* (1969), Alan Ayckbourn's *Bedroom Farce* (1979), and Michael Frayn's *Noises Off* (1983), remains in vogue.

belles lettres [behl•LEHTR] a French term referring to fine writing or artistic efforts, including poetry, drama, essay, vignette, memoir, criticism, and fiction, as in the Arabic verse of Badi al-Zaman, the late tenth-century court poet and author of *Maqamat*, and the literary epistles of his contemporary, Abu Bakr al-Khwarizmi, producer of *Maqama*, a compendium of rhymed anecdotes.

In *The Adventures of Huckleberry Finn* (1884), Mark Twain mocks the artificial strivings of Emmeline Grangerford, who paints pictures captioned "Shall I Never See Thee More Alas" and "I Shall Never Hear Thy Sweet Chirrup More Alas," and who fills a scrapbook with original verse tributes derived from "obituaries and accidents and cases of patient suffering." After reading her ode to a boy who fell down a well and drowned, Huck marvels, "If Emmeline Grangerford could make poetry like that before she was fourteen, there ain't no telling what she could 'a' done by and by."

Twentieth-century American belletrists include William Faulkner, whose esthetic verse "L'Après-Midi d'un Faune" (1919) imitates European style and subject matter. He later discarded the style in favor of experimental fiction about Mississippi settings and subjects.

Often used pejoratively, the term tends to dismiss or denigrate overly elegant, ornate, or clumsy verse and prose by the amusing dilettante or inept poetaster who aims too obviously toward the sublime, for example, imitators of Joseph Addison and aesthetes from Southern plantations, notably, Mississippian Irwin Russell, who ignored the realities of slave life in his holiday piece, *Christmas-Night in the Quarters* (1878), which honors the first banjo.

A female essayist often labeled a belletrist is Anne Morrow Lindbergh, author of *Gift from the Sea* (1955).

Bernadon   a stock comic figure, usually male, who developed from the Viennese theatrical tradition. He usually enters and exits the stage with much heaving and panting and runs out again only to encounter fearful creatures of the night, usually imaginary. Southern minstrel shows usually contained skits in which a black male was obsessed about demons and ghosts that he believed lurked outside. In the South during the 1940s, black characters were usually assigned these roles, a bit of folk stagecraft sure to get a laugh. Early cinema transformed Bernadon into a screen version.

bildungsroman   [BIHL•duhnz•roh•mahn]   literally a "formation novel," which describes the coming-of-age of an untried or naive youth, for example, Charlotte Brontë's *Jane Eyre* (1847), Charles Dickens's *David Copperfield* (1850) and *Great Expectations* (1861), Thomas Mann's *Buddenbrooks* (1901), James Joyce's *Portrait*

of the Artist As a Young Man (1916), Thomas Wolfe's *Look Homeward, Angel* (1929), Marjorie Kinnan Rawlings's *The Yearling* (1938), Betty Smith's *A Tree Grows in Brooklyn* (1943), Fred Gipson's *Old Yeller* (1956), Wilson Rawls's *Where the Red Fern Grows* (1961), Hal Borland's *When the Legends Die* (1963), Theodora Kroeber's *Ishi* (1964), Maya Angelou's *I Know Why the Caged Bird Sings* (1970), Jean Craighead George's *Julie of the Wolves* (1972), Rudolfo Anaya's *Bless Me, Ultima* (1973), Maxine Hong Kingston's *The Woman Warrior* (1975), Pat Conroy's *The Great Santini* (1976), Elizabeth Speare's *The Sign of the Beaver* (1983), and Amy Tan's *The Joy Luck Club* (1989). In his survival novel *The River* (1991), young adult fiction writer Gary Paulsen parallels the challenge of passage down a river with the trials of growing up. By the time the protagonist recovers from a rigorous canoe trip to a trading post, he is more mature and more self-assured of his capabilities than he was before he ventured into the Canadian northwest.

biography   a life story or history that stresses habits, lifestyle, dignity, morality, or motivations of a particular person, for example, Mari Sandoz's study of her father for *Old Jules* (1935) and Fawn Brodie's biography of Thomas Jefferson (1974). Biographies span literature, providing in-depth study of the aims, motivation, and achievement of significant world figures: the deeds of the Buddha in *Buddha-carita* (second century A.D.), Plutarch's *Parallel Lives* (A.D. 115), Suetonius's *Lives of the Caesars* (ca. A.D. 121), John Filson's *The Adventures of Col. Daniel Boon* [sic], *Containing a Narrative of the Wars of Kentucke* (1784), James Boswell's *Life of Johnson* (1791), *The Narrative of William Wells Brown; a Fugitive Slave* (1851), Elizabeth Gaskell's *Life of Charlotte Brontë* (1857), Thomas D. Bonner's

The Life of James Pierson Beckwourth, Mountaineer, Scout, Pioneer and Chief of the Crow Nation (1856), E. M. Forster's *Life of Charles Dickens* (1874), Lytton Strachey's *Queen Victoria* (1921), Carl Sandburg's *Abraham Lincoln* (1939), Mari Sandoz's *Crazy Horse: The Strange Man of the Oglalas* (1942), Marchette Chute's *Shakespeare of London* (1950), Bailey C. Hanes's *Bill Pickett, Bulldogger* (1977), and Ruthann Lum McCunn's *Thousand Pieces of Gold* (1981), the life of Lalu Nathoy, a Chinese captive enslaved and forced into prostitution in an Idaho mining camp, and Judith Thurman's *Isak Dinesen: The Life of a Storyteller* (1982).

A branch of fiction that imitates biography is the biographical novel, which builds with dialogue and interpolated events the life of a famous person, for instance, Irving Stone's *Lust for Life* (1934), the fictional life story of Vincent Van Gogh, Mary Renault's *The Persian Boy* (1972), a retelling of the life of Alexander the Great, Louise Erdrich's *Love Medicine* (1984), about her Ojibway ancestors, and Toni Morrison's *Beloved* (1987), the completion of the true story of an escaped slave.

See also autobiography.

black humor a morbid, bitter, or grotesque form of comedy that emphasizes suffering, macabre jokes, or comic patter about sickness, deformity, accident, mishap, death, or any grave or grievous situation; for example, Mercutio's dark jests in his death scene in William Shakespeare's *Romeo and Juliet* (ca. 1593-1595) and the seriocomic description of a father's death in Reynolds Price's *A Long and Happy Life* (1962):

> swept away by the Holy Ghost, bag and baggage, in a pillar of fire instead of drunk and taken at dusk by a pickup truck he never saw but walked straight into as if it was a place to rest.

Black humor thrives in the novel, stage, film, and television version of Richard Hooker's *MASH* (1968) and the novel and screen versions of Joseph Heller's *Catch-22* (1961) and Kurt Vonnegut's *Slaughterhouse-Five* (1966) as well as dystopic novels—Kurt Vonnegut's *Cat's Cradle* (1963), Marge Piercy's *Woman on the Edge of Time* (1976), and Margaret Atwood's *The Handmaid's Tale* (1985)—and drama, particularly Samuel Beckett's *Waiting for Godot* (1952), James Goldman's historical drama *The Lion in Winter* (1968), Harvey Fierstein's *Torch Song Trilogy* (1979), Beth Henley's witty family comedy, *Crimes of the Heart* (1979), and Marsha Norman's suicide play, *'night Mother* (1982).

Black humor often situates wit or comedy at an inappropriate or awkward moment; for example, in William Blinn's screenplay *Brian's Song* (1972), the term "put you to sleep" is a wry play on words suggesting euthanasia or mercy killing at a turning point of the life of Brian Piccolo, the first white major league football player to room with a black teammate. A grotesque version of black humor concludes Larry Larson, Levi Lee, and Rebecca Wackler's *Tent Meeting* (1987), a stage comedy that parodies tent revivals by lampooning Reverend Ed, an itinerant evangelist who sires Arlene, a grossly deformed infant, by his daughter Becky. The comedy ends as Ed attempts to drown the swaddled infant in a baptismal font, not realizing that Becky has substituted an eggplant in Arlene's baby blanket.

blackout a stage technique in which all lights onstage are extinguished or obscured. The effect is immediate and often occurs during suspenseful scenes. Occasionally, blackouts are reversed, for example, a scene in darkness in which a player discusses blindness as the lights slowly come up. Often, blackouts occur suddenly and dramatically at the end of serious tragedy, followed by a quick curtain.

blank verse   an unrhymed arrangement of short and long beats into a five-measured line of metrical feet (´/´/´/ ´/´/), which can be varied and adapted according to need with caesura, enjambment, dialect, and incidental metrical changes, particularly spondee, anapest, and trochee. After its introduction by Henry Howard, the Earl of Surrey, in the sixteenth century, Renaissance playwrights Christopher Marlowe and William Shakespeare found the form flexible and reflective of the natural rhythms of English. The strict line was often varied for effect, as in *Othello* (ca. 1603-1604), in which Shakespeare blends prose, rhymed song, and blank verse passages to vary the texture of speeches, reflection, and everyday exchanges.

More faithful to the meter are Marlowe's *Dr. Faustus* (1593), John Milton's epic *Paradise Lost* (1667), William Wordsworth's "Lines Composed a Few Miles above Tintern Abbey" (1798), Elizabeth Barrett Browning's *Aurora Leigh* (1857), and Alfred, Lord Tennyson's "Ulysses" (1842) and *Idylls of the King* (1885).

Still a favored form of metrical expression in the twentieth century, blank verse permeates Stephen Vincent Benét's *John Brown's Body* (1928) and is Robert Hayden's choice for *Middle Passage* (1962), which applies unrhymed iambic pentameter to a stream-of-consciousness journal passage:

> 8 bells. I cannot sleep, for I am sick
> with fear, but writing eases fear a little
> since still my eyes can see these words
>   take shape
> upon the page & so I write, as one
> would turn to exorcism.

boards   the actual flooring of a stage or music hall. The term derives from the phrase "treading the boards," a synonym for the acting profession or a differentiation between acting onstage as opposed to acting on a set before a television or film camera. First performances of a play are often said to be "on the boards."

book   the script or text of a musical. Typically, one partner writes the book, the other composes the music. In the case of Richard Rodgers and Oscar Hammerstein, Hammerstein wrote the sharply critical lyrics for *The King and I* and Rodgers set them to music.

boy company   Elizabethan acting troupes that assigned female roles to boys whose voices had not deepened. Usually eight to twelve per company, the boys performed religious drama and Latin plays and, by the seventeenth century, competed with adult companies for audiences. Favorites of Queen Elizabeth I, these popular young performers often trained as choirboys; for example, the boys of Chapel Royal, whom Richard Edward directed, and the "children of Paul," a troupe of St. Paul's Cathedral's choir school, coached by Sebastian Westcott and Richard Farrant. Farrant merged the children of Windsor and Chapel Royal at Blackfriars Theatre, where they were directed by William Hunnis after Farrant's death. Under King James I, Henry Evans and Edward Kirkham formed the Children of the King's Revels, favorites of the queen.

English Renaissance dramatists Ben Jonson, George Chapman, Thomas Marston, Thomas Dekker, Thomas Middleton, John Webster, Nathan Field, and John Lyly met the demand for materials suited to the boy companies. The Children of the King's Revels fell from favor with the production of *Eastward Ho!* (1605), a controversial work by Jonson, Chapman, and Thomas Marston that offended King James with hints of sedition.

Boy actors such as Charles Hart and Edward Kynaston earned their parts for looks, grace, and voice and were tutored and boarded free for their services. The heyday of children's troupes ended with the eighteenth century, when young players were absorbed into adult troupes.

breeches part (also pants role)   a stage role intended for a man, but played by a teenage girl or slender, small-framed woman, who often revealed the shape of her legs in tight knee breeches and hose. As extra audience appeal, directors often cast women as young pages in Italian and French opera. Breeches parts were deliberately comic, as that of Cherubino in Wolfgang Amadeus Mozart's *The Marriage of Figaro* (1786), memorable for quick changes, disguises, and mistaken identities.

In the nineteenth century, Madame Elizabeth Vestris played Giovanni in Covent Garden. Her contemporary, Louisa Lane, established a reputation for breeches roles by playing Romeo, Mark Antony, and other male characters from Shakespeare.

broadside (also broadsheet)   a sheet of paper printed on one side and occasionally illustrated with a woodcut; for example, "Botany Bay" and other popular warning verses from Great Britain that were distributed throughout colonial Australia, the Irish street song "There's Whiskey in the Jar," and the southern humor and tall tales attributed to Davy Crockett.

A sixteenth-century forerunner of the modern newspaper, the English broadside contained announcements, sensational news stories and scandals, courtroom melodrama, political harangue,

scurrilous verse set to popular melodies, elegies, epitaphs, and love ballads, and was sold on London streets for a nominal price by independent agents called chapmen. Replicated in the eighteenth and nineteenth centuries in American cities, these "penny dreadfuls" included political protest, as in Penelope Barker's female protesters and their *Daughters of Liberty in Edenton* (1774), a colonial protest of the tea tax in Edenton, North Carolina.

The broadside remained in vogue until linotype revolutionalized mass news publication. Favorites were posted on the walls of bars and inns. The Mexican version, the corrido, tended to glamorize newsworthy bandits and rebels along the Rio Grande border. *See also* ballad, corrido.

bugaku [boo•GAH•koo]   literally "music dance," a traditional court performance for the Japanese imperial family and guests. Often based on Chinese and Korean texts, bugaku pairs Chinese and Korean sources, known as "dances of the left" and "dances of the right." Dating back over 1200 years, bugaku, such as the popular duo of "Ryo-O" and "Nasori," is performed by richly costumed and masked figures to the lively music of three percussion and two wind instruments.

burlesque [bur•LEHSK]   absurd exaggeration of actions, manners, or costumes to ridicule people, religious rituals, government, and social situations, as the bumptious play "Pyramus and Thisbe" in William Shakespeare's *A Midsummer Night's Dream* (ca. 1593-1595) and Francis Beaumont's *The Night of the Burning Pestle* (ca. 1607), a spoof of knight errantry.

Subsequent examples of derisive stage entertainment, essay, and verse include Samuel Butler's *Hudibras* (1662), John Dryden's *The Hind and the Panther* (1687), John Gay's *The Beggar's Opera* (1728),

Henry Fielding's *Tom Thumb* (1730), Alexander Pope's *The Dunciad* (1743), Richard Sheridan's *The Critic* (1779), Washington Irving's *A History of New York, from the Beginning of the World to the End of the Dutch Dynasty* (1809), John Brougham's *Po-Ca-Hon-Tas, or the Gentle Savage* (1855), Lewis Carroll's "You Are Old, Father William" (1865), critic H. L. Mencken's *A Book of Burlesques* (1916), and Ernest Hemingway's *The Torrents of Spring* (1926), a burlesque on the style of novelist Sherwood Anderson.

A traditional form of religious burlesque prevails among Zuñi mudheads, who dress in clay masks topped by lumps and ridicule priests by performing comic rituals, prancing about, and eating soil. Similarly, the Pueblo clown society or *koshare*, a troupe of mummers paralleling the antics of Cherokee boogers, cavort, act foolishly, and ape officials at sober fertility rites. Coated in black body paint striped in white to mimic a skeleton, the clowns counter serious tribal rituals by tripping each other, swiping food from participants, mimicking holy men, cross-dressing, and mocking ritual acts. The antics of the *koshare* enliven a chapter of Barbara Kingsolver's *Animal Dreams* (1990), in which the Anglo protagonist observes droll celebrants at a native festival pantomiming a mock Western shoot-out.

Stage burlesque became popular in the United States in the early 1900s, incorporating song, dance, skits, and variety acts. In the 1920s, burlesque merged with striptease, notably performed by Gypsy Rose Lee. With the introduction of prohibition, burlesque houses dwindled.

busker   a young amateur magician or mime who entertains in subways or sidewalks where lines of people wait to buy tickets or enter restaurants. Busking troupes include jugglers, contortionists, guitarists, and other instrumentalists.

C

cabaret [ka•buh•RAY]   a theatrical performance in a small setting. Traditionally, cabaret is bitingly satiric and drenched in politics. The art form reached its apex in pre–World War II Berlin, where Bertolt Brecht's works were favorites. His collaborator, Kurt Weill, was married to Lotte Lenya, an actress who starred in Weill's *Threepenny Opera* (1928). She made the cabaret part of Jenny, a prostitute, her signature role. Currently, cabaret refers to a small posh club featuring a lone, smoky-voiced chanteuse and pianist. Increasingly, men perform cabaret, often accompanying themselves on piano.

cacophony [kuh•KAH•foh•nee]   a pattern or grouping of harsh, grating, jangling, or discordant sounds—usually consonants—to create or heighten such negative effects as annoyance, inarticulation, tension, disharmony, or conflict, as in Louis L'Amour's tough-sounding title *Conagher* (1964), a cowboy romance offset by wrangling, accusations, and fighting.

A cacophonous line may stress dental letters [d, t], guttural sounds [g, gr], sibilance [s, sh, z, zh], or combinations of hard sounds [ch, ck, j, qu, tch, x]. An example laden with g and t sounds is the Cornish prayer, "From ghoulies and ghosties and long-leggety beasties and things that go bump in the night, good Lord deliver us!"

Cacophony is a subtle sound clue to the author's purpose. It can contribute to humor, as in the tongue-twister "How much wood would a woodchuck chuck if a woodchuck could chuck wood?" In serious and dramatic literature, cacophony is often an element of mood or tone, as displayed in the looming greed and vitriolic family squabbling of Tennessee Williams's *Cat on a Hot Tin Roof* (1955) and dramatic confrontations between Indians and white settlers in Conrad Richter's young adult novel, *The Light in the Forest* (1953). In Richter's final scene, Cuyloga, the Lenni Lenape father, emphasizes g, k, t, s, and sh when he orders his son in stolid, predominantly one-syllable words: "Now go like an Indian, True Son, ... Give me no more shame."

cadence   a unified, rhythmic phrase or sound pattern, which may vary for effect from mellifluous oneness to a brittle staccato. Emily Dickinson, a master of cadence, creates a smooth mobility with

> Because I could not stop for Death—
> He kindly stopped for me—
> The Carriage held but just Ourselves—
> And Immortality. (1890)

The poem illustrates, with its placement of words into genteel reportage, the civility of death, a polite, unhurried carriage driver who bears the speaker inexorably "toward Eternity."

In contrast, American poet e. e. cummings illustrates the cadences and exuberance of children at play in "Chanson Innocent, I" (1923), with a wide-space layout:

> the queer
> old balloonman whistles
> whistles far and wee
> and bettyandisbel come dancing
> from hop-scotch and jump-rope.

In a more serious vein, Randall Jarrell's frenzied subject in "Woman at the Washington Zoo" (1960) emits breathy gasps as she pleads, "You know what I was, /You see what I am: change me, change me!"

Poetry written in blank verse breaks up the flow of too many end-stopped lines

with the sensitive placement of caesura, or pause, and enjambment, which carries a cadence from one line into the succeeding line. An effective patterning of thoughts occurs in William Wordsworth's "She Dwelt Among the Untrodden Ways" (1800), which concludes, "But she is in her grave, and, oh,/The difference to me!" The grouping of phrases on either side of the emotional pause demonstrates the separation between speaker and subject.

caesura   a natural pause, interruption, or break in a line of verse to acknowledge the normal flow of thought and syntax or to emphasize thought or emotion, as in Robert Burns's declaration of love in "A Red, Red Rose" (1796), in which he arrives at a reassuring stopping point with his promise, "And I will come again, my luve,/Though it were ten thousand mile." More thoughtful in a moment of contemplation is a line from A. E. Housman's "Loveliest of Trees" (1896), in which the speaker acknowledges, "Now, of my threescore years and ten,/Twenty will not come again."

Caesura contributes to the pacing of humor, especially satire, as demonstrated by Truvy's sincere compassion in a bit of gossip confided piecemeal to customers of her beauty salon in Robert Harling's play *Steel Magnolias* (1988):

> Ruth Robeline ... now there's a story. She's a twisted, troubled soul ... Husband killed in World War II. Her son was killed in Vietnam. I have to tell you, when it comes to suffering, she's right up there with Elizabeth Taylor.

call and response   live interaction with a storyteller, speaker, or minister, a trait of Southern gospel revivalism; for example, the group prayer scene in DuBose Heyward's folk novel *Porgy* (1925). Call and response takes the form of chant in the native American performance poems of Joy Harjo, Peter Blue Cloud, and Simon Ortiz and in the jazzy, vocal texts performed by black poets Amiri Baraka and Jayne Cortez. Storyteller Linda Goss draws on audience response to her stories with a simple, rhythmic give and take:

> caller: Gather 'round, my people
> response: *Well, well.*
> caller: Gonna tell you a story.
> response: *Well, well.*
> caller: Listen now, my children.
> response: *Well, well.*
> all: *Well, well, well, well.*

calypso   light-hearted, expressive, and mildly satiric songs, poems, and stories of the Caribbean folk tradition. Calypso performers recite or sing with an infectious, danceable rhythm that encourages audience participation, clapping, and foot tapping, as with Barbadian poet Mighty Gabby's "Jack" (1982) and the nostalgic calypso memories in the songs and poems of Guyanese poet Dave Martins.

camp   a stylized form of satire that employs exaggerated mannerisms, anachronism, and self-mocking gimmicks to counter society's flawed ideas about women, homosexuals, Jews, immigrants, and other marginalized groups. Camp effectively protests exclusion, cliquishness, and prejudice by overplaying theatrical artifice for the sake of humor in classics ranging from Virginia Woolf's surreal novel *Orlando* (1928), Mart Crowley's wryly mocking screenplay *The Boys in the Band* (1970), the thriller cult film *The Attack of the Killer Tomatoes* (1978), and Harvey's Fierstein's bittersweet play *Torch Song Trilogy* (1979) to Anne Fine's young adult satire *Alias Madame Doubtfire* (1988), the nucleus of the film *Mrs. Doubtfire*. A standard of arch comedy, camp exists in Greek phallic skits, English morris dance, native American *koshare* clowning, and the

exaggerated mugging of Japanese kabuki theater. Equally at home onstage, in film and television sitcom, and at a Mardi Gras masquerade ball, camp relies on trading social and sex roles.

A significant charade in Charlotte Brontë's *Jane Eyre* (1847) involves the cross-dressing of Edward Rochester, who plays a gypsy fortune-teller, Mother Bunches, as a means of learning more about his guests and discovering the heroine's opinion of him. When Jane discovers the ruse, the camp scene dissolves, returning the novel to traditional relationships.

canon   a body of writing that is traditionally accepted as undoubted, authentic, or authorized, for example, the 66 books of the Protestant Bible, which omits a body of suspect writings collectively known as the Apocrypha, or "hidden books."

Canon can also refer to the traditional titles of great or classic works that are valued by a culture or regularly appear on approved reading lists and syllabi for university study and literary analysis. This formal grouping of works was formerly dominated by white male authors until the civil rights and women's movements opened the standard list to include more works by women and non-white authors as well as literature that espouses minority philosophies, particularly anti-colonialism, anti-patriarchy, Marxism, New Age, gay points of view, and millennialism.

canto   a major section or numbered subdivision of a long poem, such as a mock epic; a unified thematic whole in a complex work; for instance, Dante's *Divine Comedy* (ca. 1321), Lord Byron's *Don Juan* (1824), Henry Wadsworth Longfellow's *The Song of Hiawatha* (1855), George Eliot's sonnet sequence *Brother and Sister* (1869), A. E. Housman's *A*

Shropshire Lad (1896), Edna St. Vincent Millay's *Sonnets from an Ungrafted Tree* (1923), Ezra Pound's *Cantos* (1969), and Adrienne Rich's *Twenty-One Love Poems* (1978).

canzone [kan•TSOH•nay]   a melodic air or love song, the Italian equivalent of the French *chanson*. *See* chanson.

caricature   an outlandish exaggeration of appearance and behavior to create absurd portraits of literary figures; for example, Dame Pertelote, the satiric image of a wife in Geoffrey Chaucer's "The Nun's Priest's Tale" (1385), the wily servant in William Shakespeare's *A Comedy of Errors* (ca. 1580s-1594), the title character in Aphra Behn's *The Rover* (1677), the lovely Cunegonde in Voltaire's *Candide* (1759), a government official in W. S. Gilbert and Arthur Sullivan's *The Mikado* (1885), Sitting Bull in Herbert and Dorothy Fields's *Annie Get Your Gun* (1940), the alien in Gore Vidal's *A Visit to a Small Planet* (1955), and General George Armstrong Custer in Thomas Berger's *Little Big Man* (1965).

Caricature is a central element in Greek satyr plays, Roman comedy, *commedia dell'arte*, camp theater, Caribbean Carnival masque, and world trickster lore. Notable figures in literature stand out with overplayed idiosyncrasies: the pinchpenny Jew Shylock in William Shakespeare's *The Merchant of Venice* (ca. 1596-1598), the spoiled princeling Pao-yu in Tsao Hsueh-chin's classic Chinese novel *The Dream of the Red Chamber* (ca. 1791), snobs and gossips in Jane Austen's *Emma* (1816), Charles Dickens's inflated plutocrat Mr. Bounderby in *Hard Times* (1854), and the churlish Snopes clan in William Faulkner's *The Hamlet* (1940), *The Town* (1957), and *The Mansion* (1960).

Modern comedy relies on overdrawn characters for Joseph Heller's war protest, *Catch-22* (1961), Burt Shevelove, Larry Gelbart, and Stephen Sondheim's slapstick comedy, *A Funny Thing Happened on the Way to the Forum* (1963), Richard Hooker's satiric *MASH* (1968), the boastful marshal Rooster Cogburn in Charles Portis's Western adventure tale *True Grit* (1968), Terry McMillan's semi-autobiographical novel *Mama* (1987), and Anne Fine's young adult novel *Alias Madame Doubtfire* (1988). A tragicomic monster mother commandeers daughters and cows servants in Laura Esquivel's romantic fable *Like Water for Chocolate* (1992), an imaginative folk tale about love recipes in which the spinster daughter turns out a wedding cake that causes the mother and her guests to weep for past loves.

catastrophe   the conclusion, final resolution, or dénouement of a conflict in which a tragic hero suffers punishment, defamation, social or economic ruin, or death as a result of character flaws. Examples include the blinding and self-exile of the title character in Sophocles's *Oedipus Rex* (409 B.C.), the death of the ruling family of Denmark and demise of their dynasty in William Shakespeare's *Hamlet* (ca. 1599-1600), the collapse of a marriage in Henrik Ibsen's *A Doll's House* (1879), institutionalization of a deranged woman in Tennessee Williams's *A Streetcar Named Desire* (1947), the ruin and demise of a decent man and his neighbors in Arthur Wilson's *The Crucible* (1953), and the death of a failed father and husband in August Miller's *Fences* (1986). At the end of the falling action in *Death of a Salesman* (1949), playwright Arthur Miller augments the widow's mourning of her husband, Willy Loman, by implying that he is barely respected by his sons and is forgotten by people he once considered his friends and valued business associates.

catharsis   the draining or purgation of pity and fear as a result of identification with the plight and suffering of a tragic hero. Derived from Aristotle's *Poetics* (fourth century B.C.), the term applies to modern drama; for instance, the audience's purification and therapeutic release of emotion from compassionate response to the loneliness of Miss Alma, the repressed old maid of Tennessee Williams's emotional drama *Summer and Smoke* (1948), or tension at the alienation and yearning of the elderly protagonist in Horton Foote's play *The Trip to Bountiful* (1953).

chanson [shahn•SAHN] an original love song or plaint composed of dazzling, clever lyrics expressing the male speaker's devotion to his lady in accordance with the requirements of courtly love. A vehicle for the medieval troubadours of Provence, each *chanson* contained five or six interlinking stanzas and a summary *envoi* or chorus, usually half as long as the stanza.

character an individual, animal, or fantastic creature that performs actions that make up a fictional plot; for example, the human focus of "Words Under the Words" (1995) by Arab-American poet Naomi Shihab Nye, which describes a grandmother's hand that soothed a sick grandchild and made bread with a "round pat-pat and the slow baking."

Each fictional character expresses moral qualities through dialogue and action, for instance, the villainous Regina Giddens in Lillian Hellman's play *The Little Foxes* (1939), the endearing old lady in Clyde Edgerton's *Walking Across Egypt* (1987), and the companions who run the cafe in Fannie Flagg's *Fried Green Tomatoes at the Whistle Stop Cafe* (1987).

Characters may take shape from the author's description as a result of participation in events, or from the description of other characters, as in Will Tweedy's reflection on his step-grandmother, Miss Love Simpson Blakeslee, in Olive Ann Burns's *Cold Sassy Tree* (1984).

Identifiable character types flesh out the cast of fiction:

• narrator or speaker, whose point of view dominates the text; for example, Nick Carraway in F. Scott Fitzgerald's social novel *The Great Gatsby* (1925)

• protagonist, the central character, the one about whom the plot turns, such as Shakespeare's title characters—Hamlet, Juliet, Macbeth, Julius Caesar, Richard II, and Henry IV

• antagonist, the villain or aggressor, a major participant in the action who torments, manipulates, or threatens the protagonist; for instance, the manipulative mother in Laura Esquivel's whimsical fable *Like Water for Chocolate* (1992)

• round character, a realistic being who possesses a complex or multifaceted array of traits—a description of Inman, the returning veteran in Charles Frazier's historical novel *Cold Mountain* (1997)

• stock character, a figure who recurs in literature, such as Satan, Everyman, Punch and Judy, and Toby, the country bumpkin of early twentieth-century melodrama who bests the city slicker and wins the girl

• flat character or stereotype, a one-dimensional person who performs a single function or represents a quality—for example, patriotism, duty, or parental love —but reveals no depth of involvement, intent, or emotional growth, as displayed by the furmity seller in Thomas Hardy's novel *The Mayor of Casterbridge* (1886)

• static character, a stable figure, usually of secondary importance, who remains unchanged by the action—a description of Mr. Addams, the father of the protagonist in Carson McCullers's play *The Member of the Wedding* (1946)

• dynamic character, a participant in the action who alters in attitude and behavior as a consequence of the action. Protagonists are dynamic characters, as is obvious in the creation of the lusty immigrant Antonia Shimerda Cuzak in Willa Cather's *My Antonia* (1926)

• supernumeraries, onstage participants who have no lines to speak. These are usually members of crowd scenes, supplicants, servants, or spear-carriers.

See also antagonist, foil, protagonist, trickster.

characterization the author's revelation and development of believable human qualities, words, thoughts, influence, and actions in fictional beings; for instance, the African slave known as Bras Coupé, the protagonist of the kernel story in George Washington Cable's *The Grandissimes* (1880), and Julia, a friend of the speaker in Lillian Hellman's autobiographical *Pentimento: A Book of Portraits* (1973). *See also* chorus, code hero.

character name a method of displaying or revealing character traits, attributes, or attitudes through the choice of symbolic names, which may contain a descriptive term; for example, the amoral Mr. Gray in Robert Cormier's thriller novel *I Am the Cheese* (1977) and Colonel Bull Meecham, the ogre-father in Pat Conroy's *The Great Santini* (1976). In *Les Misérables* (1862), Victor Hugo produces starkly emblematic characters, such as Leblanc (The White) and Lenoire (The Black), Cosette (Little Thing), Madame Magloire (My Glory), Fantine (Little Fallen Leaf), Sister Simplice (Simply), Toussaint (All-Saint), and Bishop Bienvenu (Welcome), a description of the priest's openhanded Christianity. A humorous alias is Ultimus (The Last) Fauchelevent, Valjean's name while he

serves the convent as assistant gardener and younger brother of Fauchelevent.

In *Invisible Man* (1947), novelist Ralph Ellison selects symbolic names for characters, such as Sybil, the lustful temptress whose name suggests the seer in Virgil's *Aeneid* (19 B.C.) who leads Aeneas to the Underworld, a hellish supernatural setting that Ellison mirrors in the Harlem riot. Other names that ring true to image are Trueblood, Bledsoe, Ras, Barrelhouse, Rinehart, and Clifton, the pivotal character at a social precipice who cannot escape martyrdom. Ironically, the narrator has two names—his own and his Brotherhood alias—but reveals neither one.

chiaroscuro [kee•uh•roh•SKOO•roh] a deliberate contrast of light and dark to highlight movement or intensify a particular figure or setting; for instance, alternating patterns of moonlight and darkness in the orchard courtship scene in William Shakespeare's *Romeo and Juliet* (ca. 1593-1595). The contrast reflects the uncertainty of a love match between Romeo and Juliet, two young, naive members of warring families. Likewise, the uncertainty of Juliet's marital status worsens the dilemma she faces as she conceals her secret marriage to a family enemy while trying to forestall a forced betrothal to a man of her father's choosing. *See also* motif.

choka [CHOH•kah] a Japanese verse form of any length consisting of alternating lines of five and seven syllables and concluding with a seven-syllable *envoi* or summary, as demonstrated by Lady Otomo's "Love's Complaint" (eighth century A.D.) and Japanese court poet Kakinomoto Hitomaro's "In Praise of Empress Jito," "I Loved Her Like the Leaves," and "In the Sea of Iwami," contained in the anthology *Manyoshu* or *Book of Ten Thou-*

sand Leaves (late seventh century A.D.) An unidentified choka model gives a glimpse of genteel court courtesy for an emperor:

> O palace maiden
> the daughter of my subject,
> Do you bring a wine holder?
> If you hold it up,
> Oh, hold it in your hands;
> oh, hold it firmly,
> ever firmly in your hands;
> O you wine-holding maiden.

chorus a group of unnamed singers posing as bystanders or elders who comment on and interpret the development, outcome, or theme of a dramatic scene, but remain out of the action. In the classical Greek tragedies of Euripides, Aeschylus, and Sophocles during the fifth and fourth centuries B.C., the chorus, who delivered serious opinions to the accompaniment of harp and flute, was the key to the meaning and purpose of a play. Composed of 12-15 masked participants divided into two groups, the first chorus chanted lyric odes as they danced in formation a sedate pattern of steps. An antiphonal chorus replied with epodes while dancing the same pattern in reverse. The chorus enhanced the psychological and emotional background of the text while it introduced characters, questioned newcomers, admonished wrongdoing, affirmed social restrictions, consoled victims, indicated passage of time, and explained events from the point of view of conservative community spokespersons.

Subsequent uses of a chorus include Seneca's tragedies (first century B.C.), Thomas Kyd's *Spanish Tragedy* (ca. 1585), John Milton's *Samson Agonistes* (1671), and T. S. Eliot's *Murder in the Cathedral* (1935).

An Elizabethan adaptation of the chorus was the single voice chorus or choral character, who spoke the prologue and epilogue, as in Christopher Marlowe's tragedy *Dr. Faustus* (1592) and William Shakespeare's chronicle *Henry V* (1599).

In the nineteenth and twentieth centuries, similar figures appear in drama— Eugene O'Neill's *Mourning Becomes Electra* (1931), Thornton Wilder's *Our Town* (1938), Jean Anouilh's *Antigone* (1944), Tennessee Williams's *The Glass Menagerie* (1945), Bertolt Brecht's *The Good Woman of Setzuan* (1940) and *The Caucasian Chalk Circle* (1948), Arthur Miller's *A View from the Bridge* (1955)—and in some novels: Nathaniel Hawthorne's *The Scarlet Letter* (1850), George Eliot's *Silas Marner* (1861), Thomas Hardy's *The Return of the Native* (1878), Zora Neale Hurston's "Spunk" (1925) and *Their Eyes Were Watching God* (1937), William Faulkner's *The Reivers* (1962), Ernest Gaines's *A Gathering of Old Men* (1983), and Toni Morrison's *Beloved* (1987).

chronicle a prose or verse reference work devoted to chronological events of historical eras or movements and compiled by a single author or group of writers; for example, the Chinese *Zuo Zhuan* (fourth century B.C.), Sima Qian's *Shiji* (90 B.C.), *Anglo-Saxon Chronicle* (ca. ninth century), Geoffrey of Monmouth's *History of the Kings of Britain* (ca. 1135), Layamon's *Brut* (ca. 1205), Raphael Holinshed's *Chronicles of England, Scotland and Ireland* (1587), Bernal Díaz del Castillo's account of Cortez's female translator Malinalli Tenepal in "The True History of the Conquest of New Spain" (1632), Dilue Rose Harris's *Reminiscences of Colonial Life in Texas* (1904), Dee Brown's *Bury My Heart at Wounded Knee* (1970), and Henk Tjon's Surinam history play *Stages*, which blends the events of slave times, colonialism, and modern independence and political corruption. Annals are a subset of the chronicle that list a year-by-year accounting of a period of reign.

In the twentieth century, chronicle novels or sagas depict a large cast of fictional and real characters whose lives demonstrate the attitudes and behaviors of a period, as found in John Dos Passos's *U. S. A.* (1938), Herman Wouk's *The Winds of War* (1971) and *War and Remembrance* (1978), and Edward Rutherfurd's *Sarum* (1988). In the American West, chronicles detail and analyze the nation's pioneer history, particularly Francis Parkman's *The Oregon Trail* (1846), William H. Prescott's *History of the Conquest of Mexico* (1856), Theodore Roosevelt's *The Winning of the West* (1889) and *Rough Riders* (1902), Frank E. Stevens's *The Black Hawk War* (1903), Mari Sandoz's *Cheyenne Autumn* (1953), Dee Brown's *Bury My Heart at Wounded Knee: An Indian History of the American West* (1970), and James Michener's *Centennial* (1974).

chronicle play   a dramatization of history common to the Elizabethan era, when alterations in the monarchy inspired writers to set on stage the strong feelings and heroic and ignoble acts that derive from intense or unprecedented political shifts. The focus of a chronicle is typically the chronological events of one monarch's reign and the influence of past history and social and moral expectations of the period, as found in William Shakespeare's *Richard II* (ca. 1595-1596).

In the twentieth century, the tradition of chronicle drama continued in Arthur Miller's *The Crucible* (1953) and Robert Bolt's *A Man for All Seasons* (1960). During the upsurge of outdoor dramas in the United States, dramatists Paul Green and Kermit Hunter centered their staged spectacles on periods of history, particularly Green's *The Lost Colony* (1937) and *The Highland Call* (1939) and Hunter's *Unto These Hills* (1950) and *Horn in the West* (1952), all reflecting political and economic forces impinging on North Carolina's frontier settlement.

circumlocution   an indirect method of discussing a topic without naming it, either to create irony or to avoid unpleasant or shocking terms; for example, Anna's insistence on privacy and her unstated horror of being mistaken as a member of the king's harem in Richard Rodgers and Oscar Hammerstein's *The King and I* (1951).

Pioneer diaries are rife with circumlocution, for instance, *Mollie: The Journal of Mollie Dorsey Sanford in Nebraska and Colorado Territories, 1857-1866* (1959), which conceals the writer's pregnancy until the birth of her son. Sanford is equally disinclined to discuss the infant's death, which she summarizes in one sentence, "God took ... to his fold, this one pet lamb."

The Colonel's Lady on the Western Frontier: The Correspondence of Alice Kirk Grierson (1989) demonstrates the author's delicacy in discussing a need for birth control to end her hard life of bearing and raising more children than she wants.

See also euphemism, Victorianism.

classic   an enduring or influential literary work that survives because of its high quality and because it addresses humanistic questions and issues, which apply to all people and all times. In a stricter definition, the term applies to works of ancient Greece and Rome, for example, Homer's epics, Sappho's verse, Aristophanes's comedies, Cicero's essays, or Pliny's letters.

cliché   overused, trite, tedious, or unoriginal terms and idioms, such as "the general public," "each and every one," "last but not least," "move forward" or "go forward," and "at this point in time." Quality literature avoids stale or unimaginative diction. However, classic lines take on a separate life, as with the timeworn phrase "to trip the light fantastic," from John Milton's "L'Allegro"(1632), and the warning, "When you call me that, *smile!*," an often-cited line from Owen Wister's prototypical Western, *The Virginian* (1902).

climax   the height of an action, a crisis or turning point from which all behaviors or attitudes are permanently altered and nothing can ever be what it once was. In William Shakespeare's *Othello* (ca. 1603-1604), the tragedy reaches its high point in Act III, Scene 3, when Othello admits that Iago has overpowered his reason.

In Edmond Rostand's *Cyrano de Bergerac* (1897), the tragedy reaches its peak in Act III, when a Capuchin monk unites Roxane with Christian. From that point on, Cyrano reverences the holy state of matrimony and supports his rival by writing love letters to Roxane in Christian's name.

A climactic point in Isabel Allende's historical novel *House of the Spirits* (1982) occurs after Senator Trueba's daughter is arrested and tortured. Realizing the menace of the militaristic regime his party helped to establish, Trueba relinquishes his conservative ideals and helps his daughter and her family flee the country.

Yoko Kawashima Watkins creates a turning point in *So Far from the Bamboo Grove* (1986) when the mother dies, leaving her two girls to fend for themselves in war-torn Japan.

See also Freytag diagram.

closet drama   a play or dramatic poem that is not intended for performance, for example, George Bernard Shaw's *Back to Methuselah* (1921), a complex study of human development over many centuries that is meant to be read. Other plays unsuited to the stage because of length, cumbrous author notes, or the absence of performable dialogue include John Milton's *Samson Agonistes* (1671), Percy Bysshe Shelley's *Prometheus Unbound* (1820), and Thomas Hardy's *The Dynasts* (1904).

code hero   a fictional type, essentially male, who exemplifies the standard qualities of the hero. The code hero as developed in Ernest Hemingway's novels and in the Westerns of Louis L'Amour and his imitators stresses the tight-lipped, two-fisted, hard-drinking loner who savors totally physical lovemaking, outdoor life, and challenging or violent sports. Like Jake Barnes in Hemingway's *The Sun Also Rises* (1926) and Lt. Frederic Henry in *A Farewell to Arms* (1929), the code hero says little about his private feelings and misgivings, both of which are detrimental to the macho image. Instead, his actions demonstrate cool control, grace under pressure, and courage in the face of death.

colloquialism   an informal, everyday expression used in speech, the military, the media, and advertising, including such contractions and abbreviations as didn't, won't, r & r, t.l.c., home ec., and p.e. Rudyard Kipling captured the easy exchange between colonial soldiers stationed in India during the late nineteenth century, just as Mark Twain and Bret Harte replicated the verbal mannerisms of the Mississippi River Delta and the American West. J. D. Salinger's *The Catcher in the Rye* (1951) is the American masterpiece depicting the slangy teenager. Other writers dependent on street lingo and day-to-day conversation include playwrights Lorraine Hansberry, August Wilson, and Alice Childress, short story writer Toni Cade Bambara, poets Robert Frost and Nikki Giovanni, and young adult novelists Paul Zindel, Walter Dean Myers, and S. E. Hinton.

comedy   any work that entertains and amuses and ends happily; also, a play that contains elements paralleling tragedy in that characters are overwhelmed by circumstance, as in Royall Tyler's *The Contrast* (1787), America's first original comedy, and Tom Taylor's *Our American Cousin* (1858), a perennial favorite of nineteenth-century touring companies, and the melancholy Pierrot comedies of France, which mime Marcel Marceau refined.

The characters of comedy undergo reversals of fortune, often of their own making or worsened by stupidity or gullibility. During the plot resolution, victims undergo a change of heart or alteration of behavior and attain sympathy, recognize their weaknesses and faults, and achieve contentment, discipline, forgiveness, reward, or elevation.

In William Shakespeare's *The Taming of the Shrew* (ca. 1589), the combined efforts of father and husband bring Katherine to the altar and into the power of Petruchio, who uses ridicule, torment, and coercion to mellow her. No longer the scold of her father's house, she becomes a dutiful wife.

In old comedy of the fifth century B.C., the earliest form of Greek comic drama, strict stage convention required a formal prologue to introduce the plot, followed by the *parados* or formal entrance of a chorus. The *agon* or conflict debated the subject of the drama, for example, a miser's greed or a father's inability to curb a wayward son. The chorus discussed the conflict in the *parabasis*, which is followed by the *anapest*, a choral debate of both sides of a social, theological, or political question. The debate ends in the *pnigos* or summation, which sober voices deliver with mock sincerity. An ode interrupts the drama to thank or propitiate deities. An *epirrhemia* digresses by comparing the fictional conflict to real events. An *antode*

echoes the themes of the ode. Comic drollery returns in the *antepirrhema*, a preface to more humorous or satiric episodes that comprise the falling action. A formal ode comments on the resolution of the problem. The comedy ends with a boisterous *exodos*, usually a procession, dance, wedding, or neighborhood festival or banquet.

comedy of humours   a realistic, satiric comedy in which characters reveal ridiculous domination by a single trait or psychological quirk, such as sloth or suspicion. Developed in George Chapman's *The Blind Beggar of Alexandria* (1596), Ben Johnson's *Every Man in His Humour* (1598) and its sequel, *Every Man Out of His Humour* (1599), and in William Shakespeare's *A Winter's Tale* (ca. 1610-1611), this popular, moralistic drama exposed the single peculiarity that possesses and rules a character beyond reason.

In general, the characters are never multi-dimensional because they lack a healthy balance of the four liquids (or humours)—black bile, yellow bile, blood, and phlegm—that course through the body. Characters tend to bear emblematic or tag names, as with Shakespeare's Shallow and Malvolio. Each models a single type of obsession or pattern of behavior, which requires broad acting to convey eccentricity.

comedy of manners   a drama that satirizes, ridicules, or mocks the artifice, duplicity, and pettiness of sophisticated or aristocratic society. Elements of comedy of manners include pretense, jealousy, or discontent in characters who war against conventions imposed by polite society. For instance, in Mary Chase's *Harvey* (1944), strong criticism of the genteel lifestyle comes from Dr. Sanderson, a psychiatrist who says of the protagonist, Elwood P. Dowd, a hallucinating alcoholic: "All he does is hang around bars. He doesn't work. All that corny bowing and getting up out of his chair every time a woman makes a move. Why he's as outdated as a cast-iron deer."

Other major examples include William Shakespeare's *Love's Labour's Lost* (ca. 1593-1595), Molière's *Les Précieuses Ridicules* (1659) and *Tartuffe* (1664), William Congreve's *The Way of the World* (1700), Oliver Goldsmith's *She Stoops to Conquer* (1773), Noel Coward's *Private Lives* (1930), Claire Booth's *The Women* (1936), Moss Hart and George S. Kaufman's *You Can't Take It With You* (1936), Thornton Wilder's *The Matchmaker* (1954), and Neil Simon's *Plaza Suite* (1968).

comic relief   a witty exchange, skit, interlude, or soliloquy that the writer deliberately inserts to ease tensions and lighten a dark or grim mood within a serious work, such as a tragedy, epic, or psychological novel. In Greek and Elizabethan drama, comic relief heightens a somber theme, as in the gravediggers' scene in William Shakespeare's *Hamlet* (ca. 1599-1600). In the twentieth century, Thomas Heggen and Joshua Logan's play *Mr. Roberts* (1948) counters the serious events of Pacific naval battles during World War II with the pranks of Ensign Frank Pulver.

command performance   a play performed at the request of a monarch or patron on a designated occasion, such as a birthday, marriage, military victory, or state visit. William Shakespeare's *A Midsummer Night's Dream* (ca. 1593-1595) celebrated an aristocratic nuptial; his *Henry VIII* (ca. 1612-1613) honored the marriage of the Princess Elizabeth.

commedia dell'arte   [kohm• MAY•dee•ah dehl AHR•tay]   a brilliant extemporaneous Italian drama of the Middle Ages that employs a skilled professional traveling troupe in comic performances of stock episodes, intrigues, and satiric foolery. The action calls for a set cast of caricatures—the bumbling rustic, swaggering soldier, gullible merchant, erudite doctor, humble wife, leading man and leading lady, bumptious maid, clowning trickster, dimwitted servant, and shameless moocher.

Begun in the mid-sixteenth century by Angelo Beolco, the *commedia dell'arte* departed from the era's high-toned morality plays and religious drama to interject zany *lazzo*, set pieces of comic scenario that formed the company's *canovacci*, or playbook. These professional comedies influenced the timing and characterization of works by playwrights Molière and Carlo Goldoni. Various combinations of prologue, complication, soliloquy, repartee, and resolution provided escapist entertainment that evolved into puppet plays, mime, minstrel shows, vaudeville, ballet, Keystone Cop movies, television sitcoms, and comic opera.

complication   the rising action; the beginning of a conflict or entanglement that is the focus of a fictional or dramatic action, as in Vinnie's announcement of out-of-town guests in Howard Lindsey and Russel Crouse's domestic comedy *Life with Father* (1939), the death of Grandma Blakeslee in Olive Anne Burns's novel *Cold Sassy Tree* (1984), and the return of the veteran Inman from the American Civil War in Charles Frazier's *Cold Mountain* (1997).

conceit   an elaborate comparison that bemuses or stretches the imagination to accommodate the logic or ingenuity of the image, as in the medieval lullaby, "Balulalo," a devout homage to the Christ Child that promises, "The knees of my heart shall I bow."

Conceits range over all literature: a statement by Queen Mary I of England, "When I am dead and opened, you shall find 'Calais' lying in my heart," Mark Twain's declaration that a human being is a "British Museum of infirmities and inferiorities," the geographical images in John Donne's "No Man Is an Island" (1633), Grace Paley's complaint, "I look like time boiled over" in *Enormous Changes at the Last Minute* (1974), and Nan Socolow's bold praise in "Riding into Battle, My Heart on Your Lance" (1989).

In Sandra Cisneros's *The House on Mango Street* (1989), the speaker demonstrates her youthful fancy when she hears an antique dealer's music box and remarks, "It's like all of a sudden he let go a million moths all over the dusty furniture and swan-neck shadows and in our bones."

See also pathetic fallacy, personification.

concrete a critical term characterizing themes, diction, and topics that focus on precise details about people, animals, and names of tangible objects rather than abstract ideas, beliefs, or aims. For example, the immediacy of natural settings is crucial to traditional haiku and the poetry of Gabriela Mistral, just as furniture, clothing, amenities, and the neighborhood dominate Tennessee Williams's play *A Streetcar Named Desire* (1940).

Corrie ten Boom stresses the gritty, uncompromising reality of a women's prison in her World War II memoir, *The Hiding Place* (1971). Incarcerated for smuggling Jews from Nazi-held Holland, the protagonist requests, "A Bible! Could you get me a Bible? And—a needle and thread! And a toothbrush! And soap!"

conflict the external physical struggle or internal emotional tension between opposing characters or forces in a dramatic action, as demonstrated by the yearnings that propel the protagonist to murder in Theodore Dreiser's novel *An American Tragedy* (1925) and the mental torment that drives the speaker to suicide in Sylvia Plath's autobiographical novel *The Bell Jar* (1963). Poetry also can demonstrate a clash of wills, as in the endangered wild animals killed by drivers in Margaret Atwood's "The Animals in That Country" (1968) and the frogs that get in the way of an exasperated driver in Joseph Bruchac's "Birdfoot's Grandpa" (1978).

connotation a range of implied associations, emotions, overtones, or shades of meaning suggested by a word that advances its use beyond the simple dictionary definition; for example, the emotional impact of the word "rest" in Horatio's benediction at the death of the title character in William Shakespeare's *Hamlet* (ca. 1599-1600). Horatio implies that rest is a pleasant demise when he says, "Good night, sweet prince, and flights of angels sing thee to thy rest."

In Carson McCullers's novel *The Heart Is a Lonely Hunter* (1940), the central character, Mr. Singer, is a compassionate deaf-mute whose name implies the joy that he brings to his close friends. In a subsequent novel, *The Member of the Wedding* (1946), the tomboyish character changes her name from Frankie to F. Jasmine to demonstrate her newfound femininity.

See also character name.

consonance the repetition of a pattern of stressed consonant sounds, but not of vowels, as in the placement of l and k in leek/lack/like, and s, m, and r in simmer/summer/swimmer. The subtlety of consonance is evident in the pairing of roads and wood in the opening line of Robert Frost's "The Road Not Taken" (1915), which begins, "Two roads diverged in a yellow wood." Robert Hayden's "Those Winter Sundays" (1962) applies consonance as an internal binding in the phrase "cracked hands that ached."

Consonance of end words may serve as an approximate or slant rhyme; for example, Lord Byron's linking of "mooring" and "lowering" in "Lines to Mr. Hodgson," Emily Dickinson's lines ending in "hid" and "head," and John Berryman's masculine rhyme of "mac" and "tech" in "American Lights Seen from Far Off" (1964).

context   the phrases preceding and following a given passage, which impinge on the meaning of the word as it applies to that particular situation. The use of context clues identifies and amplifies a usage, for example, Thomas Gray's "Elegy Written in a Country Churchyard" (1751), which refers to "rude forefathers" in a phrase that concludes "of the hamlet." The additional information indicates that the correct definition of rude should be "unrefined" rather than "discourteous."

contrast   the obvious difference or dissonance that appears when disparate objects, persons, statements, themes, or situations are compared, as found in literary foils, such as hero and villain, round and flat characters, or protagonist and antagonist. In *The Kitchen God's Wife* (1992), Amy Tan contrasts instances of powerlessness with moments of strength and self-sufficiency as she develops the main character, Winnie Louie, who flees Communist China and an abusive husband to remarry a kind Amerasian in California.

conventions   an accepted list of features or patterns or a code of rules, standards, or principles that readers and critics expect of a literary style or genre, as in the structure, length, development,

tone, and aim of a limerick, domestic comedy, haiku, literary epic, corrido, or vignette. In ancient Greece, tragedy adhered to a brief time and limited place and action, and, by the convention of decorum, relegated gruesome or violent scenes offstage.

In following convention, the author sticks to precedent or established practice; for example, Sir Arthur Conan Doyle's detective stories, Aesop's animal fables, Mary Stewart's Arthurian romances, Zane Grey's Western novels, and Seami's kabuki dramas.

corrido [cor•REE•doh]   the Hispanic term for a popular ballad, a melodic verse in colloquial language that tells a story, such as "The Corrido of Kansas" (ca. 1860), the earliest extant text, which tells of a cattle drive, and "Remembrance of General Zapata," a popular folk tribute from the early twentieth century. Corrido convention required a call for listeners' attention in the opening lines and a farewell at the end. Late twentieth-century literary corridos alter the essentially genial genre by stressing sensationalism and violence. A Mexican folk form, the corrido is sung to a simple melody played on guitar or accordion. A flexible structure, the corrido relies on an octosyllabic line, consonance for end rhyme, and a rhyme scheme of abcb. It is essentially anonymous except for the works of Marciano Silva and Arnulfo Castillo.

A derivation of Spanish couplets and romance ballads, the corrido is a blend of narrative and dialogue without a refrain. It served nineteenth-century peasants as poetry, newspaper, and propaganda by recording the daring of outlaws such as Heraclio Bernal, Joaquin Murrieta, Ignacio Parra, and Valentin Mancera. Epic-style corridos from 1910-1930 chronicled the acts of rebel leader Pancho Villa and the outcome of battles during the Mexican Revolution, the subject of corrido entertainment in John Reed's *Insurgent Mexico* (1914). The images stir the imagination and, like a news feature, supply names, dates, places, and brief quotations from the hero.

Updated versions from Texas-Mexican working class in the Rio Grande Valley in the 1970s champion Cesar Chavez, migrant campesinos or farmworkers, Chicano victims of Anglo racism, white heroes such as John and Robert Kennedy, and Martin Luther King, Jr.

See also ballad, quatrain.

counterpoint contrasting themes or diametrically opposite actions in a literary work, as in winning the revolution while destroying the countryside, a bitter irony for the soldiers and local peasants in Manuelo Azuelo's historical novel *The Underdogs* (1962). In Harper Lee's *To Kill a Mockingbird* (1960), the author counters the intertwined details and themes of two concerns of Atticus Finch's children—interest in his role as defender of a black man accused of raping a white woman and curiosity about the character and sufferings of Arthur "Boo" Radley, a reclusive next-door neighbor reputed to be insane. The interplay of the two interests elucidates the theme of bias.

couplet a pair of successive rhyming lines of poetry in the same meter. Once the favorite verse form, the couplet was a vehicle for the Arabic *ghazal* and the verse of Geoffrey Chaucer, William Shakespeare, John Donne, Jean de La Fontaine, John Dryden, and Alexander Pope, whose didactic mode required a constrictive verse form. Pope's neatly phrased aphorisms survive in couplet form, for example, from *An Essay on Criticism* (1711):

> True wit is nature to advantage dress'd,
> What oft was thought, but ne'er so well express'd.

Variations of the couplet include these:
- the heroic couplet, which pairs rhymed lines in iambic pentameter
- the closed couplet, a pair of rhymed lines that complete one thought
- the open couplet, a pair of lines that connects to other lines through enjambment, a spillover to the succeeding thought.

The rigidity of closed couplets dismayed the romantic poets, whose rebellion against conventions and constraints preceded the neglect of the couplet.

credo [CRAY•doh] a statement of beliefs or personal philosophy; for example, the singing of *Kimi ga yo*, the Japanese national anthem, in Jeanne Wakatsuki Houston and James Houston's *Farewell to Manzanar* (1973). The song becomes each singer's personal declaration of resilience during the incarceration of Japanese-Americans in internment camps during World War II.

criticism the reasoned analysis, classification, interpretation, and evaluation of artistic works and popular culture through the application of established principles of excellence, for example, Edgar Allan Poe's posthumous treatise *The Poetic Principle* (1850), Japanese critic Natsume Soseki's contemplation of Eastern and Western literary traditions in *Theory of Literature* (1907), Egyptian critic Taha-Husayn's *Principles of Literary Criticism* (ca. 1936), Lebanese critic Ghassan Kanafani's *The Literature of Resistance in Occupied Palestine 1948-1966* (1966), or Susan Sontag's "Notes on Camp" (1966). Criticism can derive from a variety of methods and points of view:
- Absolutist criticism, in opposition

to relativism, insists on universal laws governing assessment

• Biographical criticism studies motivation and details by connecting them to the life and conscious purpose of an author

• Comparative criticism groups works into genres or juxtaposes them alongside parallel works or dominant themes of a period

• Deconstruction is a method of dismantling, analyzing, or evaluating a text to challenge its clarity by disclosing hidden meanings, implications, contradictions, and alternate readings

• Didactic style evaluates the political, moral, and ethical issues that undergird a work

• Feminist criticism evaluates gender roles and the role of patriarchy in depicting male-female relationships

• Formal criticism explores how a work fits a particular genre, such as epic or drama

• Freudian analysis applies the precepts of neurologist Dr. Sigmund Freud, particularly the working of the subconscious mind on characters and their dilemmas

• Historical criticism sets a work in its era and explains how the attitudes and issues of the times influence character actions and values

• Impressionistic criticism focuses on the reader's personal response apart from any set theory or standard of literary excellence

• Judicial criticism applies a stringent body of evaluative standards or ethics

• Jungian analysis applies the concept of unconscious symbolism and associations to a literary motif

• Linguistic criticism studies the meaning and connotations of words at a particular time and place

• Marxist criticism focuses on the clash of social strata and the conditions that force an underclass to fight for personal and economic rights

• Mimetic analysis applies Aristotle's concept of the ideal by determining how well a work imitates nature

• New criticism insists on evaluating elements of the work itself without regard to external matters, such as the author's life or the period in which a work was written

• Pragmatic criticism focuses on aspects of a work that trigger the reader's emotions

• Reader-response analysis ponders the experiences that a reader brings to a work and the applicability of the work to the reader's life

• Relativistic criticism derives from the single personal evaluation of art and refrains from invoking universal laws of how and what a work may represent

• Romantic criticism determines what ideas, beliefs, emotions, or values a work expresses

• Structuralist analysis locates dual forces that impinge on characters of a work, such as the influence of the past and dreams of the future

• Textual criticism peruses the text of a work for accuracy and applicability to the author's canon, for example, the Dead Sea Scrolls or William Faulkner's "Rose of Lebanon," a short story that remained unpublished until 1996.

A frequently cited American critic, H. L. Mencken, produced a critical column, "The Free Lance," for the *Baltimore Sun*. In his skeptical, iconoclastic, and opinionated essays, he challenged national and world thinking, public issues, and objects of ridicule, ranging from censorship and Nazism to religious fundamentalism, the Ku Klux Klan, and popular idols. Concerning attorney Clarence Darrow's attempt to strike down the Tennessee law against teaching evolution in public schools, Mencken commented, "On the one side was bigotry, ignorance, hatred, superstition, every sort of blackness that the human mind is capable of. On the other side was sense."

cruelty joke   a humorous, but implicitly hard-handed or vicious form of folly literature that derides race and gender differences, illiteracy, spouse or animal abuse, bad luck, and physical flaws or freakish conditions in humans and beasts, especially dowager's hump, tics, stammers, harelip, and squints. By offsetting the foolish against the wise, the cruelty joke implies that females, retarded people, evangelicals, dark-skinned races, homosexuals, nonreaders, or handicapped people are, by nature of their condition, slow-witted.

In folly literature, these objects of fun become the dupes of the trickster, as in Mark Twain's anecdotal story "The Celebrated Jumping Frog of Calaveras County" (1867), "The Preacher Who Couldn't Read" in Langston Hughes and Arna Bontemps's *The Book of Negro Folklore* (1958), and the episode of Reverend Thomas and Sister Monroe in Maya Angelou's *I Know Why the Caged Bird Sings* (1970).

cue   the last two or three words an actor speaks, which readies other actors to begin their responses or movements. Actors listen for their own individual cues. When necessary, off-stage prompters remind participants to begin performing by mouthing the next phrases.

cycle   a body of poems, stories, novels, sagas, epics, or dramas by a single author or several authors that reflect a unifying subject or theme; for example, Paula Gunn Allen's Keres stories in *The Woman Who Owned the Shadows* (1983) and Rita

Dove's interlocking verse romance, *Thomas and Beulah* (1986). Early cycles include:
- the classical epic cycle by Homer and Virgil, who derived subjects, themes, settings, and characters from the Trojan War
- the Frankish legends of the Charlemagne Cycle
- the Arthurian cycle, a collection of works that reflect the legend of King Arthur, the knights of the Round Table, the quest for the Holy Grail, and the philosophies of chivalry and courtly love
- fourteenth-century English mystery play cycles that survive from York, Chester, Wakefield, Towneley, and one unnamed town.

cyclorama   [sy•kloh•RAH•muh] curved walls enclosing a room on which are painted or projected landscapes, galloping forces, fleeing armies. A cyclorama production encases the audience in an engrossing, multifaceted spectacle or tourist attraction, such as the burning of Atlanta or the Battle of Manassas during the American Civil War.

D

dactyl   a metrical foot or unit that contains three syllables, a stressed syllable followed by two unstressed syllables (), as in Vachel Lindsay's ode "The Ghost of the Buffaloes" (1934), which describes the movement of burly animals:

> Ghost-kings came headlong, row upon row,
> Gods of the Indians, torches aglow.

The language during Homer's time, the classical Greek period, falls naturally into dactylic hexameter, or six dactyls per line. Henry Wadsworth Longfellow imitates the Greek epic line in *Evangeline* (1857):

Now through rushing chutes, among
   green islands, where plumelike,
Cotton-trees nodded their shadowy
   crests, they swept with the current,
Then emerged into broad lagoons,
   where silvery sandbars
Lay in the stream, and along the wim-
   pling waves of their margin,
Shining with snow-white plumes, large
   flocks of pelicans waded.

denotation   the literal or dictionary meaning of a word without its accompanying emotional implications. Denotation
is the opposite of connotation, which
allies the limited meaning with attitudes
and psychological associations, for example, colorful or denigrating synonyms for
thin—lean, wispy, thin, frail, gaunt, and
skinny, each of which carries hidden bag-
gage, which can be positive or negative.

dénouement   [day•noo•MAH]
the falling action or unraveling of the suspenseful elements of a dramatic plot, for
example, an explanation of the worldwide
unrest of hostile robots in Karel Capek's
dystopic play, *R. U. R.* (1920). Beginning
after the climax, the dénouement clears up
questions, often by revelation of hidden
facts or misconceptions, unmasking of
falsehoods, explanation of mysteries, or
the resolution of a problem, for example,
the undisclosed parentage at the heart of
Michael Dorris's *Yellow Raft on Blue Water*
(1987). In Amy Tan's *The Joy Luck Club*
(1989), characters from pre–World War II
China enlighten the younger generation
about the wartime crises that forced people to make difficult choices, such as a
mother who abandons her twin daughters
because she is too ill to save herself and
the children.

detective fiction   a short story,
novella, or novel that offers a solution to
a mystery or crime, usually murder or
theft, in which the protagonist employs
observation and keen deductive logic to
unravel a mysterious or baffling situation
or to right a wrong, as in the works of
Edgar Allan Poe, Sir Arthur Conan
Doyle, Ellery Queen, Raymond Chandler,
Dashiell Hammett, Erle Stanley Gardner,
Patricia Cornwell, John Le Carré, and
Agatha Christie. In Ellen Raskin's young
adult novel *The Westing Game* (1975), a
young protagonist unearths a complicated
ruse based on the lyrics of "America the
Beautiful" and discloses links among families living in an apartment building. *See
also* spy thriller.

deus ex machina   [DAY•oos eks
MAH•kee•nah]   an unforeseen or improbable solution to a problem, often an
unlikely coincidence such as the identification of a long-lost sibling by a birth-
mark, physical resemblance, article of
jewelry, or clothing. Derived from the
Greek "god from a machine," the stage
convention of lowering a deity by crane to
stage level to intercede in human affairs,
the use of unexpected retribution or rescue in the falling action occurs in Charles
Dickens's *Oliver Twist* (1839) when the
protagonist is identified as the child of a
wealthy woman, and in Alfred, Lord Tennyson's "Gareth and Lynette," an episode
of *Idylls of the King* (1885) in which the
warrior faces certain death in a duel with
a huge, menacing knight who suddenly
turns out to be a small boy in disguise.

dialect   a nonstandard or informal
speech pattern of a minority group or section of a country, as found in Scottish poet
Robert Burns's toast in song, "We'll tak a
cup o' kindness yet/For auld lang syne!,"
Sojourner Truth's stirring speech, "Ain't I
a Woman?" (1851), the Jamaican patois in
twentieth-century storyteller Louise Bennett's story-poem, "Dryfoot Boy," and a
spoken passage from Harriette Arnow's
The Dollmaker (1972):

My people back home … they hated Catholics frum away back—an they ain't never heard a commies; but boy, if anybody went around a callen my people commies on account of they don't like Catholics they'd git their heads knocked in, and nobody ud wait to round up bedsheets fer to do th job in—they'd do it onu spot … without waiten tu mess around with a lot a KKK's.

Dialect, such as the Elizabethan English that became Southern Appalachian or the Hispanic-English blend called Spanglish or Tex-Mex, evolves from isolation or separation from a majority group or from a group's deliberate attempt to establish identity through words and terms known to only a limited number of insiders. Dialect varies from a major language by omitting sounds, altering grammatical forms, creating separate vocabulary, or eliding, the loss of letters and syllables that produces Maya Angelou's "powhitetrash" in *I Know Why the Caged Bird Sings* (1970) and James Weldon Johnson and John Rosamund Johnson's "Lift Ev'ry Voice and Sing" (1900), the original title of the Negro National Anthem. In the cowboy song "Whoopee-ti-yi-yo, Git Along, Little Dogies," the Southwestern pronunciation of "get" becomes "git" and the term "dogies" replaces "calves." For *Nights with Uncle Remus* (1883), Joel Chandler Harris couches in dialect his warning, "Watch out w'en youer gittin' all you want. Fattenin' hogs ain't in luck." In the folk song "The Wearin' o' the Green," the apostrophes indicate the absence of final sounds in "Wearing of," a characteristic of Irish brogue.

A literary use of dialogue comes from Harriet Beecher Stowe when she conveys Southern slave dialect in her protest novel, *Uncle Tom's Cabin* (1852), with an alteration of standard diction and verb forms, for example, Topsy's statement, "I 'spect I growed," for "I guess I grew." In the mid-twentieth century, Lorraine Hansberry applied subtler dialect to enhance the social drama of *A Raisin in the Sun* (1959). Mama Younger, on meeting her daughter's Nigerian boyfriend, creates humor by commenting to an African guest, "I think it's so sad the way our American Negroes don't know nothing about Africa 'cept Tarzan and all that. All that money they pour into these churches when they ought to be helping your people over there drive out them French and Englishmen done taken away your land."

dialogue the expression of the exact words exchanged between two or more conversants in a narrative, as used in Plato's *Symposium* (416 B.C.), the Chinese *Zhanguoce* (ca. 8 B.C.), Luigi Pirandello's one-act play of the 1920s, *The Man with the Flower in His Mouth*, Samuel Beckett's absurdist drama, *Waiting for Godot* (1952), *I Do, I Do* (1966), a two-person reflection on marriage by Harvey Schmidt and Tom Jones, and Derek Walcott's *Pantomime* (1980), a quick-witted discussion of local and foreign values. In *True Grit* (1968), Charles Portis furthers the caricature of Rooster Cogburn with a courtroom exchange between the marshal and Mr. Goudy, a prosecuting attorney, about the number of people Rooster has gunned down:

> Mr. Cogburn: I never shot nobody I didn't have to.
> Mr. Goudy: That was not the question. How many?
> Mr. Cogburn: Shot or killed?
> Mr. Goudy: Let us restrict it to "killed" so that we have a manageable figure … Twenty-three dead men in four years. That comes to about six men a year.
> Mr. Cogburn: It is dangerous work.

diary a single writer's day-by-day record of thoughts, experiences, and musings, as in the personal narrative of Anaïs Nin (1967). Diaries range across the literary spectrum, including the writings of Michitsuma's mother in *Kagero Diary* (ca. 971); the anonymous Japanese daybook *Sarashina Diary* (ca. 1050); *Winter Quarters, The 1846–1848 Life Writings of Mary Haskin Parker Richards* (1996), a testimonial to the courage of Mormon pioneers; and the World War II *Diary of a Young Girl* by Anne Frank (1952). Diaries give an invaluable account of daily details and commonalties, such as dress, diet, manners, attitudes, worship, work, and family life.

Mary Boykin Chesnut's dozen detailed journals from 1861 to 1865, published as *Mary Chesnut's Civil War* (1981), offer daily accounts of the era; for example, her terror during the bombardment on the night of April 12, 1861:

> I do not pretend to go to sleep. How can I? If Anderson does not accept terms— at four—the orders are he shall be fired upon. I count four—St. Michael chimes. I begin to hope. At half-past four, the heavy booming of a cannon. I sprang out of bed. And on my knees—prostrate—I prayed as I never prayed before.

diatribe   a denunciation, tirade, ultimatum, or other humorless expostulation or verbal abuse, as in the caustic criticism of Frederick Douglass's speech "What to the Slave Is the Fourth of July?" (1852), Donald Davidson's *The Attack on Leviathan* (1938), which lambasted the social, political, educational, and economic mongrelization of the United States, and the speaker's condemnation of Southern racism and violence against blacks in Maya Angelou's autobiography *I Know Why the Caged Bird Sings* (1970).

Originally an ethical or moral sermon, diatribe reached its height in the writings of Greek stoics and rose to new occasions for complaint or mockery in Rome with the works of poets Virgil,

Horace, Lucan, and Persius, the satirist Juvenal, orator Cicero, teacher Epictetus, and dramatist Seneca, whose name evolved into the adjective "senecan," a description of fervid, overblown oratory, stage posturing, and rant.

In more recent times, diatribe has degenerated into angry retort, snide irony, mean-spirited vituperation, or rationalization, the vehicle of Huck Finn's father in Chapter 5 of Mark Twain's *The Adventures of Huckleberry Finn* (1884), the knight's berating of his squire Sancho Panza in Miguel de Cervantes's *Don Quixote* (1615), or the hectoring and bombast of the envious Sir Kay against Sir Lancelot in Alfred, Lord Tennyson's "Gareth and Lynette" in *Idylls of the King* (1885), where retort lapses into a surly personal vendetta with Kay's remark, "Sir Fine-face, Sir Fair-hands? but see thou to it that thine own fineness, Lancelot, some fine day undo thee not."

In the mid-twentieth century, the famous stage bluster of populist attorney Matthew Harrison Brady against his opponent Henry Drummond in Jerome Lawrence and Robert E. Lee's historical drama *Inherit the Wind* (1955) epitomizes the use of diatribe as a courtroom maneuver of the famous Scopes Monkey Trial of 1925, when Clarence Darrow lost to William Jennings Bryan, prosecutor of the case against John T. Scopes for teaching evolution in defiance of Tennessee state law.

A frequently revived tirade by a female speaker occurs in Lillian Hellman's *The Little Foxes* (1939), in which both Regina Giddens and her maid Addie spout personal animosity. Addie, who has watched the underhanded maneuvers of the Giddens family, regrets that black victims must suffer white manipulation. Of her white masters, she complains, "Well, there are people who eat the earth and eat all the people on it like in the Bible with the locusts. And other people who stand around and watch them eat it."

diction the choice of words and syntax used in expressions; for example, the slave era references and biblical references in Martin Luther King, Jr.'s "I Have a Dream" speech delivered to protesters of racism and segregation, and the elevated language and refined style of a presidential State of the Union address.

The style and substance of diction exists on several levels: formal, informal, colloquial, dialect, archaic, neologism, cliché, euphemism, and slang. The diction that is acceptable to the majority of English-speaking people is called standard English. The diction that an author chooses for a character becomes a part of the personality, as with Long John Silver's brusque, salty retorts in Robert Louis Stevenson's sea adventure, *Treasure Island* (1883), and the frail, defensive replies of Laura Wingfield in Tennessee Williams's drama *The Glass Menagerie* (1945). *See also* archaism, cliché, colloquialism, euphemism, inversion.

didacticism the intent of a literary work or passage to convey instruction, religious dogma, persuasion, or social or moral guidance, an obvious trait of Booker T. Washington's autobiography, *Up from Slavery* (1901); Harold Wright Bell's sentimental novel *The Shepherd of the Hills* (1907); Julius Lester's compendium of slave narratives, *To Be a Slave* (1968); Ann Zwinger's pro-ecology treatise, *Run, River, Run* (1975); Richard Brautigan's poem "All Watched Over by Machines of Loving Grace"; and Michael Blake's frontier novel, *Dances with Wolves* (1988).

Although found in all genres, didacticism is common to fable, sermon, lecture, homily, diatribe, tract, and aphorism; for example, Benjamin Franklin's adages in *Poor Richard's Almanack* (1733-1758). In his pithy admonitions, he warns, "He that lies down with dogs shall rise up with fleas," and promises, "He that hath a trade hath an estate."

digression a temporary cessation of a narrative to accommodate the insertion of a distantly related or unrelated topic or issue, an element in Laurence Sterne's *Tristram Shandy* (1767), Doris Lessing's *The Golden Notebook* (1962), and John Fowles's *The French Lieutenant's Woman* (1969). There are two major purposes for digression: comic effect and the inclusion of data or vital information; for example, a contrast of war weapons, strategies, or modes of transportation in Thucydides's *History of the Peloponnesian War* (ca. 405 B.C.) and John Milton's extended description of Satan in *Paradise Lost* (1674).

As a method of connecting themes and morals to the central subject, digression is useful to the orator and writer; for example, John Steinbeck's intercalary chapters in *The Grapes of Wrath* (1939), which stray from the hardships of dispossessed Midwestern farmers to study the effects of economic downturn on truckers, waitresses, and bankers.

dilemma tale an open-ended moral folk tale or enigma tale intended to spark discussion and debate. The African dilemma tale presents human characters, often in dire predicaments, and stops short of a resolution to ask listeners to select from a variety of alternatives. Group consideration of humanistic issues—such as the welfare of an individual as opposed to the welfare of a group—promotes ethical behavior and compassion for serious human situations that have no clear-cut solutions; for example, the endings of the Togo tale "The Five Helpers" and the Nigerian tale "The Talking Skull."

dirge a song of mourning or honor to the dead; for example, David's lyric dirge for Jonathan and Saul in II Samuel 1:19-27. Less structured than the elegy, the dirge is more melodious, as found in the Irish keen or funeral solo, or in native American funereal verse intended for presentation with flute accompaniment. Hal Borland incorporates the traditional plains Indian hunter's death chant for a slaughtered buck into the rituals of Tom Black Bull, protagonist of *When the Legends Die* (1963), who sings, "Earth, drink this blood that now belongs to you."

dithyramb [DIHTH•ram] an emotional Greek choral ode, hymn, ceremonial anthem, passionate chant, or seasonal song performed in honor of the god Dionysus. Because he presided over grapes and wine, his hymns reflect on the passage of the seasons, a cycle that became a metaphor for human life, growth, death, and rebirth. Types of dithyrambs varied from chant to paean, choral recitation, and a form of call-and-response, which evolved into dramatic dialogue. Around 534 B.C., Thespis is credited with introducing the first actor, who took different roles and conversed with the choral leader.

documentary an historical work derived from the arrangement and presentation of nonfiction, such as data, graphs, news articles, editorials, government reports, maps, eyewitness reports, interviews, political cartoons, and trial transcripts. Because Dee Brown chooses to write *Bury My Heart at Wounded Knee* (1970) as a documentary, he avoids fictional dialogue. For example, as an introduction, he cites a speech by the Shawnee chief Tecumseh:

> Where today are the Pequot? Where are the Narragansett, the Mohican, the Pokanoket, and many other once powerful tribes of our people? They have

vanished before the avarice and the oppression of the White Man, as snow before a summer sun.

Brown forms his analysis from description, time lines, speeches, photographs, and footnotes, all of which support his point of view.

Straying from Brown's pure documentary, Thomas Keneally blends fiction with documentary data in *Schindler's List* (1982), which avoids the conventions of fiction to relate world events that initiate and shape the struggle of a Gentile factory owner to save a group of Jewish workers from extermination by Nazi invaders.

dog drama drama that features well-trained dogs in leading roles. This type of drama rose to popularity during the 1900s in Great Britain, particularly in London. Oddly, there are hardly any extant British-written dog dramas. Most surviving examples are French. The eccentric genre failed to interest U.S. theatergoers, but movies and television series attest to the genre's continuing popularity. Lassie is an American icon, as are Rin Tin Tin, Benjy, Walt Disney's 101 Dalmatians, Lady and the Tramp, and Jack London's Buck and White Fang.

doggerel a trivial or crude attempt at verse, common to children's alphabet or counting games, advertising slogans, crude rap, and topical burlesque; for example, the riddling rhyme in George Bernard Shaw's *Pygmalion* (1912) and Touchstone's galloping rhymes in William Shakespeare's *As You Like It* (ca. 1599):

> Sweetest nut hath sourest rind,
> Such a nut is Rosalind.
> He that sweetest rose will find
> Must find love's prick and Rosalind.

Shallow and derogatory, doggerel tends toward heavy-handed rhythm, forced or slant rhyme, and couplet form, either humorous, satiric, or mock-serious in intent, the aim of Mark Twain's "The Aged Pilot Man" in *Roughing It* (1872), a canal boat jingle that rises to action with the pilot's cry:

> Hurray! hurray!
> Avast! belay!
> Take in more sail!
> Lord, what a gale!
> How, boy, haul taut on the hind mule's tail!

As a demonstration of the stress of battle, Stephen Crane has a soldier in *The Red Badge of Courage* (1895) sing a witless parody of "Sing a Song of Sixpence":

> Sing a song 'a vic'try,
> A pocketful 'a bullets,
> Five an' twenty dead men
> Baked in a—pie.

Twentieth-century doggerel can provide an incidental shift in mood, for example, the persistent jump rope rhymes coming from neighborhood children in Sandra Cisneros's *The House on Mango Street* (1989) and the memoir of Sadie and Bessie Delany, *Having Our Say: The Delany Sisters' First 100 Years* (1993), in which Bessie cites a racist ditty from a late nineteenth-century minstrel show that mocks the notion of a black U.S. president. Journalist Charles Kuralt's whimsical epitaph, taken from Clarence Day's *Scenes from the Mesozoic and Other Drawings* (1932), bubbles with upbeat optimism and the nonsense line "Tiddlely-widdlely tootle-oo."

See also jingle, macaronic verse, rap.

doppelgänger [DAHP•p'l•gang•uhr] a motif that stresses a pairing of characters, as with the two sides of human nature depicted by Robert Louis Stevenson's *Dr. Jekyll and Mr. Hyde* (1886) and by the unnamed captain and Legatt, his stowaway, in Joseph Conrad's novella *The Secret Sharer* (1912). In Southern literature, the concept of duality dominates works

about siblings fathered by a single father on white wives and black slave concubines, for example, George Washington Cable's plantation novel *The Grandissimes* (1880), Mark Twain's *Pudd'nhead Wilson* (1895), and Robert Penn Warren's *Band of Angels* (1955), a romance about a woman who is brought up among privileged whites until her father's death, when she learns that her mother was an octoroon.

In Amy Tan's *The Kitchen God's Wife* (1992), the *doppelgänger* marks the villain Wen Fu as clever enough to deceive but not smart enough to pass an entrance exam into pilot's school. He becomes a Jekyll and Hyde as he poses as his dead brother Wen Chen; by posturing, bluffing, and bullying to cover his weaknesses, Wen Fu manages a skillful juggling act until the crash of his plane costs him an eye. Like a man deprived of two ways of seeing, from this period on, Wen Fu looks through the evil eye and reasons with a damaged brain.

double entendre [DOOB•luh ahn•TAHND] a ribald form of pun containing a deliberate ambiguity implying risqué or sexual meaning. Typically, this verbal ambiguity conceals vulgar wordplay or repartee and pretends to notice no impropriety or insult. A favorite of the stage, smutty implication colors William Shakespeare's humor in the comedy *The Taming of the Shrew* (ca. 1589), in which Petruchio turns a jest about a wasp into a sexual quip, and in the tragedy *Othello* (ca. 1603-1604), in which the villain Iago refers to a coital position as "making the beast with two backs." Margaret Atwood uses *double entendre* in her title *The Handmaid's Tale* (1986). The homophone tale/tail alludes to the sexual themes of her dystopic novel, which is a recorded tale told by a victim of sexual slavery.

the dozens   a pattern of repartee or argument that consists of exchanging exaggerated or fanciful insults, a favorite element in the dialect writings of Zora Neale Hurston. One of the elements of modern rap poetry, the dozens—a corruption of the "doesn'ts"—enhances African-American conversation and appears in twentieth-century American writings: Langston Hughes *Ask Your Mama* (1961), Terri McMillan's *Waiting to Exhale* (1992), and the fiction of Richard Wright, August Wilson, and Ralph Ellison. *See also* rap.

drama   a literary work that recreates actions that tell a story, for example, Pauline Hopkins's historical play *Slaves' Escape: The Underground Railroad* (1880), twentieth-century Barbadian playwright Kamau Brathwaite's adapted Greek drama *Odale's Choice*, Reginald Rose's *Twelve Angry Men* (1954), and Trevor Rhone's *Smile Orange* (1981), one of the longest-running plays in the Caribbean. Drama requires actors to impersonate human, animal, and fantastic characters onstage through word, expression, and gesture, as in Guan Hanqing's courtroom drama *Injustice to Don E* (ca. 1275) and Lillian Hellman's intense play about gossip and homosexuality, *The Children's Hour* (1934). Drama advances from the exposition or introduction of characters and situations to the rising action or complication, climax or crisis, falling action or dénouement, and resolution or catastrophe. Both comedy and tragedy follow the same pattern of action up to the final stage. In comedy, the action ends with a joyous or positive resolution of difficulties; in tragedy, the plot leads to destruction, loss, death, or family or national disgrace.

dramatic conventions   the traditional arrangement of characters on a stage who appear before sets to speak and act out a series of events that form the play. A necessary convention for drama is the audience's acceptance that the fictional characters are real and that the fourth wall of the setting is absent so that viewers may witness the action. The compression of time and the inclusion of incidental music and lighting are additional variances from reality.

In *Our Town* (1938), dramatist Thornton Wilder alludes to the origins of Western drama, which were less tied to sets, costumes, and props and more attuned to the words of the chorus and the actors with whom the chorus interacted. Because Wilder confers important tasks on the Stage Manager, he departs from contemporary dramatic conventions and presents a play that is more like classical Greek drama than plays typical of the early twentieth century.

dramatic monologue   a poem, prayer, or soliloquy with or without an audience that depicts the speech, attitudes, and values of a single character. The dramatic monologue is a vehicle for Robert Browning's "My Last Duchess" (1842), William Butler Yeats's *Crazy Jane* (1932), and Czeslaw Milosz's "Song of a Citizen" (1943). Stephen Vincent Benét's epic ballad *John Brown's Body* (1929) contains a young soldier's commentary on glimpsing General Robert E. Lee alone in his tent:

> His hands are lying there
> Quiet as stones or shadows in his lap.
> But there is nothing ruined in his face,
> And nothing beaten in those steady eyes.
> If he's grown old, it isn't like a man,
> It's more the way a river might grow old.

dream vision (also dream allegory) an imaginative, impressionistic literary motif or framework through which the author presents a dreamscape, imagined journey, vision quest, supernatural visitation, or allegorical utopia, as in Enkidu's dream in *Gilgamesh* (1200 B.C.), Dante's *Divine Comedy* (ca. 1320), Lewis Carroll's *Alice in Wonderland* (1865), Virginia Woolf's *Orlando* (1928), supernatural voices in *Black Elk Speaks: The Life Story of a Holy Man of the Oglala Sioux* (1932), and Isaac Bashevis Singer's *Gimpel the Fool* (1957). By escaping the confines of reality, the author is able to probe feelings and subconscious longings to give depth to a character study, for example, the nature and causes of Ebenezer Scrooge's greed in Charles Dickens's *A Christmas Carol* (1843).

dystopia   an imaginary or futuristic world in which the desire for perfection produces wretched or tortuous consequences, as depicted in the repressive environments of Jack London's *The Iron Heel* (1907), Karel Capek's *R. U. R.* (1920), Evgeny Zamyatin's *We* (1921), Aldous Huxley's *Brave New World* (1932), Ayn Rand's *Anthem* (1937), George Orwell's *1984* (1949), Ray Bradbury's *Fahrenheit 451* (1951), William Golding's *Lord of the Flies* (1954), Anthony Burgess's *A Clockwork Orange* (1962), Ursula Le Guin's *The Dispossessed* (1974), Marge Piercy's *Woman on the Edge of Time* (1976), Margaret Atwood's *The Handmaid's Tale* (1985), and Lois Lowry's *The Giver* (1993).

In Mark Twain's *A Connecticut Yankee in King Arthur's Court* (1886), a nineteenth-century metal worker from the Colt Arms factory is propelled from Hartford, Connecticut to King Arthur's Camelot in sixth-century England. His idealism and swagger lead the medieval kingdom to adopt such advanced concepts as insurance agencies, baseball, capitalism, newspapers, and industrialism. The revolt of the established Church demonstrates a social and economic backlash, which reclaims the power base by once more subjecting medieval English citizens to slavery, patriarchy, and feudal law.
See also utopia.

E

eclogue [EHK•log] a short bucolic or pastoral verse, idyll, or dialogue reflecting rustic themes, such as a shepherd's songs honoring the passage of the seasons. The eclogue typically presents rural themes and lush description to the exclusion of extensive dialogue and characterization, as displayed in Virgil's *Eclogues* (37 B.C.), Edmund Spenser's *The Shepherd's Calendar* (1579), Aphra Behn's "The Willing Mistress" (1673), and the agrarian poetry of Robert Frost and Mary Hunter Austin. *See also* pastoral.

editorial   a critical or personal essay written to express views of a newspaper, journal, or magazine. Editorial collections from American literature include Washington Irving's *Salmagundi* (1808), H. L. Mencken's *The Vintage Mencken* (1983), and Molly Ivins's *Molly Ivins Can't Say That, Can She?* (1991). In the 1940s and 1950s, Harry Golden produced salient commentary on American attitudes and behaviors in *The Carolina Israelite*, a liberal paper published in Charlotte, North Carolina. His collected editorials appeared as *Only in America* (1958), *For Two Cents Plain* (1959), and *Enjoy, Enjoy* (1971).

elegy   stately, serene verse. An elegy is a praise poem, sustained lament or consolation, or meditation on loss, war, love, death, or other serious subject, as in "On Her Brother" (seventh century A.D.) by the Arabian poet al-Khansa, Garcilaso de la Vega's *First Eclogue* (ca. 1535), "A Woman's Sorrow" (ca. 1585) by Korea's foremost female elegist, Ho Nansorhon, John Milton's *Lycidas* (1637), Thomas Gray's "Elegy Written in a Country Churchyard" (1751), Percy Bysshe Shelley's *Adonais* (1821), Alfred, Lord Tennyson's *In Memoriam* (1850), Walt Whitman's "When Lilacs Last in the Dooryard Bloom'd" (1866), Juan Ramón Jiménez's *Elegías lamentables* (1910), William Butler Yeats's "In Memory of Major Robert Gregory" (1919), Rainer Maria Rilke's *Duino Elegies* (1922), Allen Tate's "Ode to the Confederate Dead" (1922), Allen Ginsberg's "Kaddish" (1961), Anne Sexton's "Sylvia's Death" (1963), and Adrienne Rich's *Charleston in the 1860s: Derived from the Diaries of Mary Boykin Chesnut* (1975).

The *naga uta*, a rare example of long Japanese verse, is an elegiac revery from the classical era, demonstrated by Hitómaro's cantos on nature and human relations. A pensive segment recalls:

> Just as the sea tangle sways and floats
> At one with the waves,
> So my girl clung to me
> As she lay by my side.

elision the omission or slurring of a word or syllable, for example, dropping the end of a word in "even[ing] song" or through syncope, which omits a central consonant, as in "ne'er so well." The purpose of elision is to force a phrase to conform to a metrical count or to give the impression of speed, familiarity, or vernacular speech, as in Robert Burns's "wee, sleekit, cow'rin, tim'rous beastie" in "To a Mouse" (1785) and Sterling A. Brown's "Slim in Hell" (1932):

> You been a travelin' rascal
>   In yo' day.
> You kin roam once mo';
>   Den you comes to stay.

ellipsis the omission of a word that may be supplied from context. Ellipsis produces a compact phrase, as in Ruth Pitter's "Yorkshire Wife's Saga" (1968), which notes that "Men [went] down the mine, and mother did the rest."

emblem poem (also concrete poetry) a shaped poem arranged in an identifiable figure or object that is the theme or topic described; also, a pattern produced by typographic distortion or distinct layout to suggest movement or emotion, as in India's *bandhas*, Chinese *hui-wen* of the second century, Sanskrit *citra-kavyas* from the seventh century, and Japanese *ashide-e* from the sixteenth century. George Herbert's "Easter Wings" (1633) demonstrates the alliance of theme, subject, and physical shape. (See next page.) Taking an opposite pattern is Dylan Thomas's "Vision and Prayer" (1952), which begins with a narrow line, widens gradually to the center, then recedes to a small conclusion. The overall shape resembles a diamond.

Other examples cover the literary spectrum: George Herbert's "The Altar" (1633), Lewis Carroll's sinuous rat tail in "A Long Tale" from *Alice in Wonderland* (1865), e. e. cummings's "Your Little Voice" (1938), John Updike's "Pendulum," and May Swenson's wave-like poems, "Women" (1968) and "How Everything Happens" (1989).

empathy the oneness produced by projecting the self into a literary character or object. An intense psychological and emotional identification is inherent in Richard Wright's poem "Between the World and Me" (1935), in which a witness's view of the site of a lynching mesmerizes him into experiencing the victim's terror, pain, and emotions.

encomium an elaborate or stately eulogy, ode, elegy, epitaph, paean, or praise in prose or verse, as found in Pindar's odes in tribute to Greek athletes (fifth century B.C.) and the tomb scene in William Shakespeare's *Much Ado About Nothing* (ca. 1598), in which Claudio reads a eulogy glorifying Hero, the woman whom he slandered. Elizabeth Barrett Browning employs the dignified, sonorous form for

Lord, who createdst man in wealth and store,
Though foolishly he lost the same,
Decaying more and more,
Till he became
Most poor:
With thee
O let me rise
As larks, harmoniously,
And sing this day thy victories:
Then shall the fall further the flight in me.

Emblem poem "Easter Wings" by George Herbert.

"To George Sand: A Recognition" (1844), a praise sonnet that concludes:

> We see thy woman-heart beat evermore
> Through the large flame. Beat purer, heart, and higher,
> Till God unsex thee on the heavenly shore
> Where incarnate spirits purely aspire!

In Robert Hayden's verse encomium "Frederick Douglass" (1967), the poet lauds "this man, this Douglass, this former slave, this Negro."

See also ode, paean, panegyric.

end-stopped   the completion of a thought or sentence coinciding with the end of a line of verse. As opposed to the more romantic or impressionistic result of run-on thoughts, the preference for end-stopped lines denotes a need for tidiness and closure, for example, in Anne Bradstreet's "The Prologue" (1650):

> Let poets and historians set these forth;
> My obscure lines shall not so dim their worth.

enjambment   a continuation of thought and grammatical structure in one or more lines of poetry. An element of romantic verse, run-on lines suggest unfettered thought, motion, and feeling, essentials in Japanese haiku and choka, for example, Kakinomoto Hitomaro's one-sentence complaint:

> The autumn moon
> We saw last year
> Shines again: but she
> Who was with me then
> The years separate forever.

In "The Other Side of a Mirror" (1908), Mary Elizabeth Coleridge's description of a viewer separates subject and verb:

> Her lips were open—not a sound
> Came through the parted lines of red.

Syrian poet Khalil Gibran's lyric verse "Song of Man" (1951) contains a confessional flow, separating preposition and object: "I was here from the moment of the/Beginning, and here I am still."

epic   a long formal poem narrating the story of a race or nation facing a threat to its existence or value system, for example, the enslavement of the Hebrew people and their rescue by Moses in Exodus, the Jewish epic found in the Torah. The epic focuses on the interplay between gods or divinities and human agents, most of whom are male leaders, princes, kings, warriors, priests, seers, or statesmen. Derived from scraps of folk stories, visions, tales, hymns, myths, legends, rituals, sagas, song lyrics, genealogies, or poems, the segments of action in an epic form a unified history told in one of two major styles:

• chronological sequence or event by event in time order, as with the seven plagues that conclude in the killing of Egyptian firstborns in Exodus

• *in medias res* , a Latin term meaning "in the middle of things," hooking the reader with an episode of high, cataclysmic adventure, then employing a type of flashback that retells significant events that led to a major cataclysm, such as the fall of Troy in Virgil's *Aeneid*.

The written composition of an epic may follow centuries of oral or folk tradition derived from the repeated—and varied—performances of wandering singers or chanters known as scops, griots, bards, rhapsodists, cantors, troubadours, minstrels, harpers, or gleemen. An example from Africa, the Mandingan epic *Sundiata*, existed orally in Mali from the late thirteenth century until the griot Djeli Mamoudou Kouyaté told it to a folklorist, who wrote it down in the 1950s. Other African epics that are primarily oral are the Soninkan *The Dausi* and the Bambaran *Monzon and the King of Kore*.

Another type of epic writing is the literary epic, which is the work of a single author who imitates the style, tone, and focus of a folk epic, for instance, Henry Wadsworth Longfellow's *The Song of Hiawatha* (1855) and Robert Holland's *The Song of Tekakwitha* (1942), the story of a female convert to Catholicism who became the first North American Indian saint. Both of these epics adapt the metrical style and idealized characterization common to European verse, but the subject is native American lore.

Epics are written to epic convention, a tradition of traits and stylistic devices that set them apart from histories, chronicles, verse narratives, legends, and sagas. An epic usually includes these elements:

• a great hero, such as Beowulf, Finn Mac Cool, or Rama, dedicated to the salvation of a threatened nation or to the religious and moral principles of a people. In Holland's *The Song of Tekakwitha*, the focal character is a Mohawk Indian woman, one of the few heroines in the epic canon. The epic hero Shaka, a Zulu chieftain, founded a south African empire in the eighteenth century

• a series of journeys or adventures that require courage and a test of the hero's dedication and of the devotion of followers, as in Daniel Bryan's *The Mountain Muse: Comprising the Adventures of Daniel Boone; and the Power of Virtuous and Refined Beauty* (1813). The journey motif dominates the actions of Qayaq, hero of the Inupiac epic, who travels along the Arctic Ocean to Barrow, Herschel Island, and south into a Tlingit Indian village in Canada

• superhuman strength, vision, or perception, a quality found in Homer's Odysseus, who survives storms stirred up by the gods of the seas and winds and who realizes the need for caution as he draws near his palace, which a cadre of suitors overrun while seeking to marry his prestigious wife, Penelope, queen of Ithaca

• supernatural influences, whether gods or goddesses, unidentified spirits of the air, earth, or underworld, such as the akua or cannibal spirits in the Hawaiian epic of Pele, goddess of the volcano, Manitou, the nature god of Hiawatha and his people, or Yahweh, the source of leadership and moral guidance to Moses, Aaron, and the Children of Israel in Exodus

• a lengthy catalog of details, for example, lists of warriors, fighters, ships, cities, tribes, or topographical elements, as found in descriptive passages of the German epic, the *Niebelungelied* (1200) and in the Balinese *Bhima Swarga* (400 A.D.)

• lofty speeches or harangues to restore flagging spirits or convince weak or doubting followers that the task they aspire to is attainable and worthy of effort, as in Joel Barlow's *The Vision of Columbus* (1787)

• epic simile, an extended comparison so freighted with detail that the figure becomes a fanciful digression, for example, John Milton's extended description of Satan in *Paradise Lost* (1674)

• epic epithet, a standard phrase used to identify a character, as in Homer's repeated descriptions of grey-eyed Athena and white-armed Penelope.

Many nations have one or more works that fit all or most of these characteristics. Among the folk epics are these:

Sumerian *Gilgamesh* (1200 B.C.)
Finnish *Kalevala* (1100 B.C.)
Greek *Iliad* and *Odyssey* (ca. 850 B.C.)
Hebrew *Exodus* (ca. 600 B.C.)
Apollonius's *Argonautica* (235 B.C.)
Indian *Ramayana* (300 B.C.) and *Mahabharata* (200 B.C.)
Balinese *Bhima Swarga* (400 A.D.)
Anglo-Saxon *Widsith* (ca. 450)
Anglo-Saxon *Beowulf* (600)
Russian *Lay of the Host of Igor* (ca. 870)
Japanese *The Tale of Heike* (ca. 1225)
Persian *Shahnamah* (1000), collected by Firdausi
French *Chanson de Roland [The Song of Roland]* (1080)
Irish epic tale, "The Destruction of Dá Derga's Hostel" (ca. 1100)
Spanish *El Cid* (1150)
Slavic *Edda* (1150-1250)
Hungarian romantic epic, *Berta of Hungary* (ca. 1270)
Mali *Sundiata* (ca. 1275)
Zulu *Shaka* (late eighteenth century)
Delaware pictographic *Walum Olum* (1820)

Literary epics—those that result largely from the work of a single author—include these:

Naevius's *Annales* (ca. 265 B.C.)
Virgil's *Aeneid* (19 B.C.)
Lucan's *Pharsalia* (A.D. 65)
Ossian's *Fingal* (ca. 300)
Dante's *Divina Commedia [The Divine Comedy]* (1314-1317)

John Barbour's *Bruce* (1375)
Ariosto's *Orlando Furioso* (1516)
Luis Vaz de Camoëns's *Os Lusiadas [The Luciad]* (1572)
Torquato Tasso's *Jerusalem Delivered* (1575)
Edmund Spenser's *Faerie Queene* (1590-1596)
Tulsidas's *Ramcaritmanas* (ca. 1620)
John Milton's *Paradise Lost* (1667)
Joel Barlow's *The Vision of Columbus* (1787) and *The Columbiad* (1807)
Adam Kidd's *The Huron Chief* (1830)
Henry Wadsworth Longfellow's *The Song of Hiawatha* (1855)
Alfred, Lord Tennyson's *Idylls of the King* (1859-1885)
Frances Ellen Watkins Harper's *Moses: A Story of the Nile* (1869)
Stephen Vincent Benét's *John Brown's Body* (1928)
Jaishankar Prasad's *Kamayani* (1930s)
John Dos Passos's *USA* (1936)
Richard Adams's *Watership Down* (1972)
Derek Walcott's *Omeros* (1990)
Lela Kiana Oman's *The Epic of Qayaq: The Longest Story Ever Told by My People* (1995), a rare epic written by a woman, a native of Kobuk Valley, Alaska.

Note that Virgil, Dante, Tasso, Walcott, and others reflect the style, motifs, tone, and purpose used by Homer, the eighth-century B.C. epic poet who is credited with both the *Iliad* and the *Odyssey*. Scholars question whether the two works were composed by the same author. Some critics surmise that the author of the *Odyssey* may have been female, perhaps Nausicaa, the princess who welcomes Odysseus to Alcinoos's kingdom.

epigram a terse observation, comment, or didactic adage that expresses a witty, ponderous, pious, or waggish thought in few words. A form common to philosophers Confucius, Lao Tzu, Mohammed, David the Psalmist, and Jesus, the epigram was also a favorite of the playwright Aristophanes, philosopher Plato, orators Demosthenes and Cicero, epistle writer Pliny the Younger, satirists Martial and Juvenal, and poets Horace, Sappho, and Virgil. During the Renaissance, Miguel de Cervantes salted his romantic epic on Don Quixote with numerous epigrams: "Forewarned forearmed," "Between jest and earnest," "Why do you lead me a wild-goose chase?" and "Can we ever have too much of a good thing?"

epigraph   a short motto, Bible verse, or literary quotation on a coin or monument, on a title page, or at the beginning of a canto or chapter, as found at the beginning of Eleanor Ross Taylor's poem *Welcome Eumenides* (1972). A common inclusion in Victorian novels, epigraphs were intended to comment on the action or give moral instruction to the reader. A worthy example is George Eliot's *Middlemarch* (1872), in which she cites lines from William Shakespeare, Dante, Blaise Pascal, Geoffrey Chaucer, Miguel de Cervantes, John Milton, Oliver Goldsmith, and Edmund Spenser before chapters to append pithy wisdom, smatterings of humor, prophecy, thematic parallels, or assessments of the plot or characters.

epilogue   a concluding section, moral tag, or closing speech or peroration that summarizes theme or action, as found in Puck's wishes for happy marriages at the close of William Shakespeare's *A Midsummer Night's Dream* (ca. 1593-1595), Voltaire's didactic fantasy *Candide* (1759), in which the hero gives up adventures and seeks happiness in tending his garden, John Irving's summary statements about each character at the end of *The World*

According to Garp (1978), and Donna Cross's reflection on the era that saw the rise of a legendary female pope in *Pope Joan* (1996).

epiphany [eh•PIH•fuh•nee]   a revelation or an appearance or manifestation of a divinity; also, a sudden insight, enlightenment, or intuitive grasp of a truth experienced by a character at a climactic moment, as in the defining moment in Mary Stewart's *The Hollow Hills* (1973) when young Arthur realizes that he is the prophesied king and rescuer of England. In *The Sound and the Fury* (1929), William Faulkner ennobles Dilsey, maid and cook to a crumbling Southern household, by describing her response to an Easter service. On her way home, she weeps unashamedly and declares, "I've seed de first en de last," a reference to the moral, economic, and social demise of the Compson family.

episode   a coherent event, digression, or incident in a narrative or serial that stands out on its own merit, for example, sixteenth-century Hawaiian stories of knight errantry in "The Adventures of Iwikauikaua," loose scenarios in Wu Chengen's *Journey to the West* (ca. 1570), and individual stops on a cross-country journey in John Steinbeck's *Travels with Charley* (1962).

Episodic literature such as the romantic epic, historical fiction, and picaresque novel contains a string of identifiable events loosely connected by commentary or descriptions, for example, in Miguel de Cervantes's *Don Quixote* (1615), Mark Twain's Western memoir, *Roughing It* (1872), Willa Cather's prairie romance, *O Pioneers!* (1913), William Faulkner's episodic trilogy—*The Hamlet* (1957), *The Town* (1957), and *The Mansion* (1959), Ernest Gaines's *The Autobiography of Miss Jane Pittman* (1971), and Allan Gurganus's

Oldest Living Confederate Widow Tells All (1984).

epistle a formal instructive letter, poem, or composition written to a particular person or group, for example, Paul's letter to the Corinthians, in which he describes the importance of love, and Anne Bradstreet's poem "A Letter to Her Husband, Absent upon Public Employment" (1678), in which she longs for his return and declares,

> I wish my Sun may never set, but burn
> Within the Cancer of my glowing breast,
> The welcome house of him my dearest guest.

Thornton Wilder uses the epistle as a means of connecting characters living on separate continents in *The Bridge of San Luis Rey* (1927).

epistolary novel a stylized novel told through letters, as demonstrated in Aphra Behn's *Love Letters Between a Nobleman and His Sister* (1684), Samuel Richardson's *Pamela* (1740) and *Clarissa Harlowe* (1748), Fanny Burney's *Evelina* (1778), Choderlos de Laclos's *Dangerous Liaisons* (1782), Johann Goethe's *The Sorrows of Young Werther* (1787), J. P. Marquand's *The Late George Apley* (1937), Saul Bellow's *Herzog* (1964), John Barth's *Letters* (1979), and Alice Walker's *The Color Purple* (1982).

A unique feature of epistolary fiction is the implied intimacy between writer and receiver of letters, a valuable feature of *The Color Purple*, which unites in writing Celie and Nettie, sisters who are parted in their teens. The separation is amplified after Celie's vengeful husband hides Nettie's letters for thirty years. Celie, who writes to God in the absence of her sister, devours three decades' worth of Nettie's narratives in a short period and catches up on events at Nettie's home in Africa.

epitaph a prose, verse inscription, or valediction on a burial slab, tomb, or memorial appealing to passersby—in Roman style—to enjoy life while they still can, or describing the life span, character, achievements, or virtues of a deceased person, for instance, Thomas Jefferson's burial marker, which names his most prized achievements:

> Thomas Jefferson
> Author of the
> Declaration
> of
> American Independence
> of the
> Statute of Virginia
> for
> Religious Freedom
> And Father of the
> University of Virginia.

William Butler Yeats chose a pithy remark for himself:

> Cast a cold eye
> On life, on death.
> Horseman, pass by! (1939)

As a vehicle for humor in a ghost story, "The Haunted Valley" (ca. 1867), Ambrose Bierce composed a punning echo on a grave marker—JO. DUNFER. DONE FER.—and follows with a salty inscription (see next page).

An epitaph may deliver a humorous or pungent bit of wit, as in John Dryden's wry couplet, "Here lies my wife: here let her lie!/Now she's at rest, and so am I." Robert Louis Stevenson wrote the poem "Requiem" (1887) in the form of an epitaph, which concludes,

> Here he lies where he longed to be;
> Home is the sailor, home from sea,
>   And the hunter home from the hill.

See also encomium, ode, paean, panegyric.

eponym a word or place name derived from a person's name, as with the

> AH WEE—CHINAMAN.
> Age unknown. Worked for Jo. Dunfer.
> This monument is erected by him to keep the Chink's
> memory green. Likewise as a warning to Celestials
> not to take on airs. Devil take 'em!
> She Was a Good Egg.

Epitaph by Ambrose Bierce.

Ferris wheel, teddy bear, graham cracker, Constantinople, bloomers, sandwich, alexandrine, and quisling. An eponymous character name is also the title of a literary work, either directly, as is the case with Anna Karenina, Little Big Man, and Ajax, or indirectly, as in *Native Son* and *El Cid*. Jumbo, P. T. Barnum's elephant, is one of the few terms associated with an animal; grog derives from a nickname—"Old Grog"—given to an admiral who began the custom of watering down his sailors' daily ration of rum.

Some eponyms derive from literature, the Bible, and mythology, for instance, mephistophelian, onanism, scrooge, pollyanna, Caspar Milquetoast, Samson, Delilah, Judas, Jonah, doubting thomas, romeo, casanova, don juan, hector, satanic, hygiene, hypnosis, iridescent, martial, saturnine, odyssey, panic, ocean, mercurial, and thespian.

essay   a brief prose composition that contains a unified theme and methodical, tightly constructed development of ideas, as in the Chinese historical miscellany *Shujing* (sixth century B.C.), al-Jahiz's "Flies and Mosquitoes" from *The Book of Animals* (ninth century), the ethical disquisitions of Han Yu (ca. 820 A.D.), Ouyang Hsiu's expository essays on politics (ca. 1070), Kamo no Chomei's contemplative "Account of a Ten-Foot Square Hut" (1212), and D. H. Lawrence's reflective piece "The Spirit of Place" in *Studies in Classic American Literature* (1923).

The essay may be objective, for example, a formal, logical statement on a single topic delivered from an unbiased, unemotional point of view, as is found in a treatise, editorial, sermon, exegesis, or pamphlet. The essay may take a subjective or personal approach, as in an anecdote account, chronicle, speech, opinion, memoir, or eulogy, or may present one side of an issue, as in Jonathan Swift's "A Modest Proposal" (1729) and George Washington Cable's polemical essays, *The Silent South* (1885) and *The Negro Question* (1890).

The collection of essays entitled *I'll Take My Stand* (1930) became the literary manifesto of a coterie of Southern authors known as the Fugitive Agrarians. Other outstanding models include Richard Wright's reflective essay, "How 'Bigger' Was Born" (1940), individual chapters on aspects of poverty in James Agee's *Let Us Now Praise Famous Men* (1941), the exhortation of Martin Luther King, Jr.'s "Letter from a Birmingham Jail" (1963), and Nikki Giovanni's polemical essays in *Racism 101* (1994).

Light essays, such as Joseph Glover Baldwin's *The Flush Times of California* (1853), may recount a tall tale or jab a satiric finger, the aim of the chapters in Florence King's *Southern Ladies and Gentlemen* (1975). Nostalgic glimpses of the past color Truman Capote's "A Christmas Memory" (1956), a popular holiday essay. An anecdote may be formatted to entertain as well as provoke thought, a common thread in Harry Golden's *Only in*

America (1958) and *For Two Cents Plain* (1959), composed of articles he published as editor of *The Carolina Israelite*.

eulogy [YOO•luh•gee] a funeral speech, tribute, or commendation in praise of a person of worthy character and behavior, usually composed after the subject's death, as found in the scholarly ancestor worship of the 125 cantos of the Korean cycle *Songs of Flying Dragons* (ca. 1447), which extol the virtues of a Confucian monarch:

> May your sons and grandsons reign unbroken,
> But you can secure the dynasty only
> When you worship Heaven and benefit the people.

A memorable speech from William Shakespeare's *Julius Caesar* (ca. 1599) is Mark Antony's public oration over Caesar's remains, which he uncovers and displays to mourners to stir them to vengeance.

See also encomium, paean, panegyric.

euphemism [YOO•fuh•mizm] an inoffensive or indirect term substituted for a blunt, coarse, or shocking expression; for example, Frank B. Gilbreath and Ernestine Gilbreath Carey's *Cheaper by the Dozen* (1963) cites as synonyms for urinate either "visiting Mrs. Murphy" or "examining the rear tire." In Olive Ann Burns's *Cold Sassy Tree* (1984), a Southern pastor avoids direct mention of death in his eulogy of Grandma Blakeslee: "Asleep in Jesus, blessed sleep from which none ever wake to weep ... a sacred mother of Israel, has gone to receive the cross of righteousness which God has promised to all those who love His appearing." In Amy Tan's *The Kitchen God's Wife* (1992), Chinese speakers call prostitutes "roadside wives" and refer to a ghost when they are socially forbidden to say that something is wrong.

euphony [YOO•fuh•nee] a pattern or grouping of soft, soothing, pleasant sounds to create a positive effect. Euphony may stress letters shaped by the lips (p, b, l), breathy sounds (wh, h, th, f), nasal sounds (m, n), or vowels (a, e, i, o, u, y). Willa Cather stresses harmonious sounds in *My Antonia* (1926) when she describes the prairie: "As I looked about me I felt that the grass was the country, as the water is the sea. The red of the grass made all the great prairie the colour of wine-stains, or of certain seaweeds when they are first washed up." A year later, O. E. Rölvaag produced a similarly euphonious reflection on the prairie, *Giants in the Earth* (1927), by imitating the soft sibilance of waving grass:

> "Tish-ah!" said the grass.... "Tish-ah, tish-ah!" ... Never had it said anything else—never would it say anything else, but it complained aloud every time—for nothing like this had ever happened to it before.... "Tish-ah, tish-ah!" it cried, and rose up in surprise to look at this rough, hard thing that had crushed it to the ground so rudely, and then moved on.

euphuism [YOO•fyoo•izm] elaborately artificial, pedantic diction. Derived from John Lyly's prose romance *Euphues: The Anatomy of Wit* (1578) and its sequel, *Euphues and His England* (1580), the term describes the effusive speeches in William Shakespeare's *Love's Labour's Lost* (ca. 1593-1595). It applies to outmoded expressions and ornate phrasing for comic effect or characterization, as spoken by the title character in Molière's *Tartuffe* (1664) and by Doctor Pangloss in Voltaire's *Candide* (1755).

exegesis [ek•suh•JEE•sihs] an interpretation, analysis, or explanation of a scriptural passage or of an essay, elucidating a difficult literary passage or unraveling the symbolism in an allegory, for instance, the religious purpose of Christian's journey to heaven in John Bunyan's *The Pilgrim's Progress* (1678). Exegesis is the equivalent of the French term *explication de texte*, which names a formal explanation of ambiguities, figures of speech, and themes in a literary work, for example, a discussion of racial memory in Toni Morrison's *Beloved* (1987).

exemplum (also exemplary tale), pl. exempla   a brief moral tale or anecdote in a sermon, speech, or didactic treatise that teaches by allegory or illustrative example, as found in Geoffrey Chaucer's "The Pardoner's Tale" (1385) and Maxine Hong Kingston's *The Woman Warrior* (1975). The exemplum expresses a doctrine or illustrates a stern moral code, often through gentle self-mockery or humbling experience, for instance, Phaedrus's fables and the Sufist Rumi's story of the blind men examining the elephant. In general, characters remain nameless and one-dimensional. Action displays the relationships of peasants, townspeople, and animals.

A twentieth-century exemplary tale, Isak Dinesen's "Babette's Feast" (1949), describes the culinary skill of a clever outsider, who invites members of an isolated, conservative Lutheran colony to share an epiphany of food, which treats typically parsimonious diners to sensual foods—red Amontillado, turtle soup, grapes, peaches, and fresh figs.

The exemplary tale is common to religious texts, for example, "Al-kahf" [The Cave] in Sura 18 from the Koran (613 A.D.), a dervish manuscript, *Kitasb-i-Amu Daria* [The Book of the River Oxur], Jonathan Edwards's sermon, "Sinners in the Hands of an Angry God" (1741), and Yiddish *mesholim*. A modern moral tale often compared to Zen Buddhist lore is Richard Bach's fable, *Jonathan Livingston Seagull* (1970), which tells of an ambitious seagull who dreams of expressing himself in exuberant flight.

existentialism   a loosely defined philosophy that contrasts the random nature of the universe with the inadequacy of human control or intelligence, for example, the dejected protagonist's cry, "Then who is my father?" in Conrad Richter's *The Light in the Forest* (1953) and the marooned woman's isolation in Scott O'Dell's *Island of the Blue Dolphins* (1960). The existentialist hero accepts his/her fate of insignificance and creates meaning by rising to the challenge of events and situations.

Meursault, the jailed protagonist of Albert Camus's *The Stranger* (1946), achieves nobility by maintaining his self-respect and facing down a hostile environment that insists on his guilt based on trivial findings from a handful of witnesses, none of whom viewed the crime. Unable to halt an ignoble and undeserved execution in the public square, Meursault can only hope for a jeering mob to attend his decapitation.

An influential satire and cult classic of the 1960s, Joseph Heller's *Catch-22* (1961) echoes images of death in the personal war of the introspective anti-hero Yossarian against combat and the military. In an intense coming-to-knowledge, he remarks on the fragility of a human life: "Drop him out of a window and he'll fall. Set fire to him and he'll burn. Bury him and he'll rot like other kinds of garbage. The spirit gone, man is garbage."

exposition   the presentation of characters, tone, mood, setting, and status quo in a literary work, for example, the introduction to amoral residents of a mining camp in Bret Harte's "The Luck of Roaring Camp" (1868), the description of a poor couple shortly before Christmas in

O. Henry's "The Gift of the Magi" (1905), the arrival of revolution to a farming village in Mariano Azuela's *The Underdogs* (1915), and the social demarcation between English aristocrats and the servant class in Kazuo Ishiguro's *Remains of the Day* (1990). Modern literature often lacks a formal exposition, for instance, the absence of explanation and objectives of Estragon and Vladimir, the two characters in Samuel Beckett's absurdist drama, *Waiting for Godot* (1954).

expressionism   an artistic style reflected in nightmarish montage or fantasy that moves beyond realism to recreate feeling and emotion, as found in August Strindberg's *Dream Play* (1902), Karel Capek's robot play *R.U.R.* (1921), the anti-realism in T. S. Eliot's poem *The Waste Land* (1922), and the timelessness of Jean-Paul Sartre's hellish drama *No Exit* (1944).

Expressionistic style may develop through oversimplification of detail and gesture, stream-of-consciousness, or distortions of spatial relations and action. In *One Day in the Life of Ivan Denisovich* (1963), Alexander Solzhenitsyn stresses spare, intensified landscape, bursts of dialogue, disjointed scenes, and elongated moments in the main character's life. The author studies each moment as though to illuminate it with one brief flash of light. Thus, expressionism highlights acts of rising, eating, marching, relaxing, and laboring as though to present them on a movie screen in slow motion.

extempo   improvisational street verse or occasional verse in the Caribbean dialect and calypso style. Extempo is usually satiric or insulting and is composed in irregular quatrains blending iambic and anapestic tetrameter and rhyming aabb, often concluding in feminine rhyme or slant rhyme, for example:

Hey John, your woman be worse than lazy;
The way she walks, I think she crazy.

See also dozens.

fable   a brief, elementary moral story in verse or prose in which the characters are usually animals demonstrating human foibles, for example, the Kikuyu folk tale "The Girl Who Was Sacrificed by Her Kin and Whom Her Lover Brought Back from Below," translated by anthropologist Paul Radin in 1952, and the polished short story "The Rocking Horse Winner" (1926) by D. H. Lawrence. The genre extends worldwide: Hesiod's story "The Hawk and the Nightingale" (eighth century B.C.), Aesop's "The Goose that Laid the Golden Egg" (ca. 600 B.C.), the Indian classic *Panchatantra* (ca. second century A.D.), Phaedrus's fables (first century A.D.), Marie de France's fables (ca. 1200), Robert Henryson's *Morall Fabillis of Esope* (ca. 1500), Jean de la Fontaine's Reynard the Fox stories (1668), Bernard de Mandeville's "The Fable of the Bees" (1714), John Gay's *Fifty-One Fables in Verse* (1727), Rudyard Kipling's *Just-So Stories* (1902), Joel Chandler Harris's Uncle Remus stories (late nineteenth century), and James Thurber's *Fables of Our Time* (1940) and *Further Fables of Our Time* (1956).

The term also applies to longer works of illustrative fiction, for example, Mary Hunter Austin's Southwestern animal lore in *The Trail Book* (1918), Amy Lowell's humorous *A Critical Fable* (1922), T. S. Eliot's *Old Possum's Book of Practical Cats* (1939), Eudora Welty's jocular tale *The Robber Bridegroom* (1942), Antoine de Saint-Exupéry's *The Little Prince* (1943), George Orwell's political satire, *Animal*

Farm (1945), James Russell Lowell's *A Fable for Critics* (1848), Anne Bodart's *The Blue Dog* (1956), *99 Fables of William March* (1960), and Katha Pollitt's verse fable, "A Turkish Story" (1989).

A classic beast fable, Horace's "The City Mouse and the Country Mouse" (30 B.C.), which Jan Brett reprised in 1995 as "Town Mouse, Country Mouse," lampoons the knowing, ostentatious city dweller who overwhelms the country bumpkin with lavish dishes on an ample banquet table. The story winds down rapidly as the country mouse flees an invasive cat and retreats to the safety of his humble rural table.

fabliau, pl. fabliaux (both pronounced [fab•lee•OH]) a short earthy or risqué tale that stresses vengeance, racy details, scatology, personal indignity, irreverence, *double entendre*, and scurrilous humor. An outgrowth of the Roman *fabula*, the fabliau is a cynical, unsophisticated parallel to trickster lore in that it stresses sly plots, human weaknesses, and poetic justice to cranks and villains, particularly pinchpenny husbands, sour-faced preachers, and pompous know-it-alls. Raw and comedic, the fabliau is prominent in world folklore, whether a part of the village jests of West Africa, Asian storytalk, native American clown ritual, or European lore of the Middle Ages.

Favorite compendia of fabliaux include the anonymous scholiast anthology known as *Carmina Burana* (thirteenth century), Giovanni Boccaccio's *Decameron* (1353), and Geoffrey Chaucer's *The Canterbury Tales* (1387), particularly "The Miller's Tale," "The Reeve's Tale," "The Merchant's Tale," and "The Shipman's Tale." A nineteenth-century favorite is Anton Chekhov's tale "A Slander," which ridicules a bumbling host who makes a to-do while explaining away a smack of his lips over a jellied sturgeon and thus ruins his reputation.

fairy tale a component of oral folklore that describes shrewd, good-hearted human victors fighting evil in a world governed by enchantment or magic in the form of witches, ogres, giants, fairies, elves, ravenous forest animals, and other supernatural agents, as demonstrated by the ninth-century Japanese story "The Bamboo Cutter and the Moon Child" and Richard Burton's translation of the Arabic compendium *The Book of the Thousand Nights and a Night* (1880). Common to the Western fairy tale tradition are "Little Red Riding Hood," "Rapunzel," "Cinderella," "Puss in Boots," and "Snow White." Hallmarks of literary fairy tale collections include Jacob and Wilhelm Grimm's *Kinder-and Hausmärchen* (1822), Charles Perrault's *Mother Goose Stories* (1697), and Hans Christian Andersen's original *Tales* (1835), the most famous of which are "The Ugly Duckling," "The Princess and the Pea," and "The Little Mermaid." Other literary fairy tales were written by John Ruskin, Charles Kingsley, Rudyard Kipling, Jean Ingelow, Mark Twain, and Oscar Wilde, who composed *The Happy Prince and Other Tales* (1888) for his own two sons. A modern example of the "good-triumphs-over-evil" plot is Robin McKinley's *Beauty* (1978), a retelling of "Beauty and the Beast."

fantasy a dimension of imaginative literature that blends the real world with incredible characters, talking beasts, and unreal beings, and may be interpreted as allegory or symbolism, for instance, Edgar Allan Poe's "The Masque of the Red Death" (1842), a surreal story about the terrors of the bubonic plague. Fantasy literature incorporates numerous subgenres: dream vision, fable, fairy tale, romance, and science fiction.

Fantasy titles include Nathaniel Hawthorne's "Dr. Heidegger's Experiment" (1837), Christina Rossetti's "Goblin Market" (1849), South Carolina storyteller Caesar Grant's "All God's Chillen Had Wings" (1860s), Lewis Carroll's *Alice in Wonderland* (1865), Robert Browning's "The Pied Piper of Hamelin" (1879), L. Frank Baum's *The Wizard of Oz* (1900), J. M. Barrie's *Peter Pan* (1904), Franz Kafka's "The Metamorphosis" (1915), Maurice Maeterlinck's "The Blue Bird" (1909), Stephen Vincent Benét's "The Devil and Daniel Webster" (1937), Irani novelist Sadeq Hedayat's *The Blind Owl* (1937), J. R. R. Tolkien's Ring Trilogy (1955), and Julio Cortázar's *Bestiary* (1951).

farce low, amoral comedy that includes situation comedy, camp, burlesque, and slapstick. Punctuated with raucous, energetic fun, knockabout confrontations, harmless fights, mugging, bizarre coincidences, and horseplay, farce evolved from improvisational comedy, particularly Greek satyr plays and medieval miracle plays. An early model is the phylax of ancient Greece, mastered by Rhinthon of Tarentum in the fourth century B.C. and depicted on Greek and Italian vase painting. Adapted from Middle Comedy, the phylax rose to popularity in southern Italy during the third and fourth centuries.

Developed through the fast-paced humor of *commedia dell'arte*, Roman comedy, and vaudeville, farce invigorates Aristophanes's *Wasps* (422 B.C.), Plautus's *Menaechmi* (ca. 186 B.C.), and William Shakespeare's *The Taming of the Shrew* (ca. 1589), *The Merry Wives of Windsor* (ca. 1597), *Much Ado about Nothing* (ca. 1598), and most notably *The Comedy of Errors* (ca. 1580s-1594), which Shakespeare adapted from *Menaechmi*. Favorite stage

revivals include Brandon Thomas's *Charley's Aunt* (1892), Moss Hart and George S. Kaufman's *You Can't Take It with You* (1936), Joe Orton's *What the Butler Saw* (1969), and Neil Simon's *The Last of the Red Hot Lovers* (1972). A hit on stage and in film, Burt Shevelove and Larry Gelbart's *A Funny Thing Happened on the Way to the Forum* (1962) is a wacky comedy that ridicules the strictures of slavery, marriage, and the military with death jokes, misplaced bodies, and a couple longing to be together.

See also bedroom farce.

Fastnachtspiel [FAHST·nakt·shpeel] a medieval German comedy featuring the Fool as central character. The fastnachtspiel was often performed outdoors on wagons. Often lewd and ribald, the genre attracted a popular following because it incorporated elements of mystery and morality plays.

Feast of the Fool a mock religious ceremony climaxing in the ritual crowning of the fool. Originating in European churches around the eleventh or twelfth century, the Feast of the Fool involved musical entertainment, wine drinking, and merrymaking. A time of hedonistic abandon, the fool ritual flourished until the late 1700s, when the church disdained religious mockery.

feminine rhyme a pattern of syllabic stress that ends with an unaccented syllable, as in Dorothy Parker's famous assertion (1927) that

> Men seldom make passes
> At girls who wear glasses

or in the anonymous jingle

> Fools' names and fools' faces
> Are often seen in public places.

See also masculine rhyme.

fiction imaginative, inventive prose

narrative in the form of fable, fairy tale, fantasy, myth, legend, folklore, short story, vignette, novella, or novel. The elements of fiction include plot, character, point of view, tone, setting, theme, and mood.

figurative language   an expression or trope that departs from literal reality and normal syntax, for example, antithesis, apostrophe, circumlocution, conceit, hyperbole, inversion, irony, metaphor, metonymy, personification, simile, and synecdoche.

flashback   an abrupt return to an earlier time to fill in background details or scenes pertinent to a plot or to the evaluation of a character's actions or attitudes, for instance, memories of the protagonists' sons in childhood in Arthur Miller's play *Death of a Salesman* (1949), in Heinrich Böll's character novel *The Clown* (1963), in the explanation of Jeanne Wakatsuki Houston's return to the prison site of her childhood in *Farewell to Manzanar* (1973), and in the circular narrative of Michael Ondaatje's *The English Patient* (1992).

In Victor Hugo's *Les Misérables* (1862), the author opens the story with Jean Valjean the convict, then returns to a glimpse of Valjean's sister and her seven hungry children. The flashback explains why Valjean breaks a window to steal bread and why a court sentences him to a prison galley.

Another author who depends on flashback is N. Scott Momaday, who reflects on his childhood memories of the Kiowa in *The Way to Rainy Mountain* (1969). Frequent references to historical events intersperse Momaday's memories of his grandparents, whose reflections helped the boy to understand the history of the Kiowa. Of the summer of 1879, he recalls the "horse-eating sun dance," a fearful event when the starving tribe members are forced to kill and eat their ponies.

foil   a character whose presence in a literary work enhances the contrasting traits of another character. The foil serves as an opposite or as a standard by which another character is measured, as with the turtle and hare in Aesop's fables, Prince Hal and Hotspur in William Shakespeare's history plays, the attitudes and behaviors of Becky and Amelia in William Makepeace Thackeray's social novel *Vanity Fair* (1848), and the title character and Elijah Muhammad in Alex Haley's *The Autobiography of Malcolm X* (1965).

In Suzanne Fisher Staples's young adult novel *Shabanu, Daughter of the Wind* (1989), the compliance with custom and religion in the older sister, Phulan, contrasts the independence of Shabanu, her rebellious younger sister.

Some contrasting characters are so significant to a fictional work that they pose an antithesis in the title, as with Matthew Arnold's verse epic, "Sohrab and Rustum" (1853) and Stephen Vincent Benét's story "The Devil and Daniel Webster" (1939).

folklore   stories and verse passed orally to preserve semi-historic or fanciful accounts; a narration that folklorist Zora Neale Hurston termed "the potlikker of human living." Folklore takes numerous shapes in its replication of folk customs and interests, for example:
• Chinese verses anthologized in *Shih Ching* or *The Book of Songs* (sixth century B.C.)
• the Korean tale *The Song of a Faithful Wife*, a popular narrative first set down in 1754
• the anonymous blues, country, slave, and cowboy lore of "De Midnight Special," "Down in the Valley," "Shortenin' Bread," and "Home on the Range" (1917), folk lyrics collected by American folklorist John Lomax

• Paul Green's earth-based lore from Southern sharecroppers for *In Abraham's Bosom* (1927)

• refined Hispanic lore in Victoria Moreno's 1980 version of La Llorona, the Weeping Woman, and varied settings of appearances of the Mexican deity, the Virgin of Guadalupe

• the comic patter of rivals in Langston Hughes and Zora Neal Hurston's play, *Mule Bone*, which was first performed in 1991.

Folk tales typically center on a crisis overcome by a hero or heroine who is the only fully developed character in the text, as found in the actions of the title character in DuBose Heyward's folk novel *Porgy* (1925), which composer George Gershwin adapted into America's first folk opera, *Porgy and Bess* (1935). N. Scott Momaday employs the tale of Changing Bear Maiden in *House Made of Dawn* (1968) as an extension of bear imagery and a model of animal power in nature. Laura Esquivel's romantic fable *Like Water for Chocolate* (1992) expresses as family lore the history of an ancestor who was forbidden to marry.

folktheater an indigenous expression of community or tribal ritual, whether combined with religious festivities, hunting celebrations, or harvest thanksgiving. Typically, the text of European folk plays gloried in the universal wisdom of fools and jesters. Scenery and props were few; street clothes served as costumes. Troupes performed on boards laid across trestles.

In the Western world, these productions evolved into miracle and mystery plays and, from there, into mutations that were less grandiose and/or spiritual. The characters were people who could be citizens of any community and who spoke the vernacular. Musical accompaniment

often anticipated the entrances of key characters with clanking copper pots, wooden rattles, and cowbells.

Folktheater remains a staple in Asia. The Bhavai of Gujarat, India, employs folk drama as social commentary on village life. Originally played by troupes of itinerant males, the theater survives in Darpana, where a training school for traditional artists provides actors to perform new material on social evils. Karala culture in southwestern India derives from the village grove arts of the first century B.C., when local artists painted topographical and thematic motifs on the ground, on which choreographers led dancers. Dressed in immense headdresses and gorgeous costumes, they performed to timed rhythms on drums and acted out the strife between menacing demons and the Mother Goddess. These village festivals were the forerunner of *jatra* or folktheater.

After colonial English influence virtually stripped the theater of music and dance, a demand for *jatra* returned traditional plays to the stage. In Turkey, the influence of Turks from Anatolia and Seljuks and Ottomans produced a hybrid of East and West. Still performed, the village plays from ancient times are less common, but elements of traditional folktheater from the sixteenth century survive in modern drama.

In Europe, the Neihardt plays from the Austrian alps were written as folktheater, connected particularly with customs and celebrations involving the summer and winter solstices and the rites of spring. In fourteenth-century France, folktheater incorporated social criticism in farce mocking trial scenes and absurd judgments. The dialogue was snappy and humorous. The mascarade popular in the Soule region of southern France incorporated mumming, including lively dancing and the entrance of a hobbyhorse.

A favorite date for folktheater productions, particularly among the Dutch, was Shrove Tuesday, the Tuesday preceding Ash Wednesday. Objects of ridicule were often local magistrates, whose pomposity and bumbling leadership contrasted the holiday celebration of common sense and merriment.

Italian folktheater, called "peasant plays," was so popular that Pope Leo X ordered a command performance by Angelo Beolco's troupe from Siena.

foot   a unit of rhythm or meter. *See* anapest, dactyl, iamb, meter, scansion, spondee, trochee.

foreshadowing   an object, statement, action, or motif that anticipates, prefigures, or predicts a significant event, as in the revelations of character that appear in the expositions of Edith Wharton's *The House of Mirth* (1905) and Flannery O'Connor's "A Good Man Is Hard to Find" (1955).

In *The Underdogs* (1915), novelist Mariano Azuela depicts a Mexican soldier aiming his gun at a mirror image of himself and shattering the glass, which reflects his whole body. Later, a letter from a comrade indicates that the soldier killed himself after his company's victory.

In William Gibson's *The Miracle Worker* (1959), Helen Keller dashes a pitcher on the floor during her initial encounter with her teacher, Annie Sullivan. In the pivotal scene, Helen pumps water into a pitcher and recalls saying "wah wah" in babyhood, thus linking an abstract word with the tangible feeling of water flowing over her hand.

foreword   a brief essay, preface, or introduction explaining some aspect of the main text of a literary work, for instance, Mark Twain's explanation of Missouri dialect preceding *The Adventures of Huckleberry Finn* (1884) and Dalton Trumbo's introduction to World War I preceding *Johnny Got His Gun* (1939). *See also* preface, prologue.

framework narrative   an outer story or setting that encases and supports a story, which may be told in flashback, as in Harry Bailly's suggestion of a series of stories at the beginning of Geoffrey Chaucer's *Canterbury Tales* (1385), musings on the past that begin Mary Shelley's *Frankenstein* (1818) and Emily Brontë's *Wuthering Heights* (1847), and Marlow's introduction to Joseph Conrad's *The Heart of Darkness* (1902). Ralph Ellison's *Invisible Man* (1947) begins with a prologue that describes the anonymous protagonist's bizarre intent to withdraw from society and live unseen in a brightly lighted Harlem cellar. Following the framework introduction to abnormal behavior, paranoia, and delusion, the text justifies and explains the protagonist's unusual lifestyle.

free verse   (also vers libre)   poetry written in a loose, vernacular, or unpatterned rhythm that suits its style and language, for instance, "The earth is your mother," the reassuring nature hymn that ends Leslie Marmon Silko's short story "Lullaby" (1981). Natural word clusters, irregular line lengths, and unpredictable caesura of modern verse and some translated verse indicate that diction, phrasing, and rhetorical intent provide more than a simple metrical pattern, as is the case with the works of T. S. Eliot, Ezra Pound, William Carlos Williams, Hilda Doolittle, Walt Whitman, e. e. cummings, Sonia Sanchez, and Nikki Giovanni.

Freytag diagram   [FRY•tahg] a triangular framework described in German critic Gustav Freytag's *Die Technik des Dramas* (1863) as the standard for a five-

（

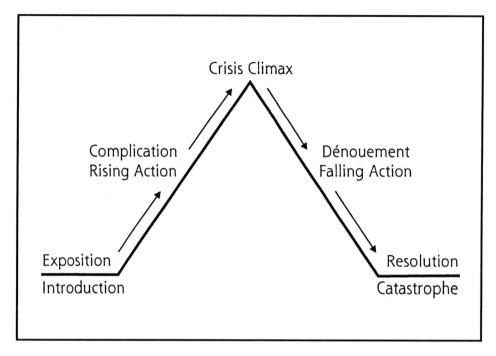

Freytag diagram. (Raymond M. Barrett, Jr.)

act drama, beginning with the introduction or exposition, moving upward with the rising action or complication to a peak or climax, which is the turning point in the action. The dramatic thrust then descends through the falling action or dénouement to a catastrophe or conclusion.

genre [ZHAHN•ruh]   a broad, descriptive literary heading or classification that typifies the style or form of a piece of writing—as in drama, essay, fiction, nonfiction, satire, fable, or verse—and establishes the characteristics—subject, length, meter, rhyme scheme, intent, or effect—that set it apart from other literary works. As an example, rap is a subset of poetry that relies on rhythmic chant about political and social ills; in contrast,

limerick is a subset of poetry that imparts light, humorous, ribald, or taunting events or characterization through a tightly constructed verse form.

ghazal [GAH•z'l]   a constrictive, 10- or 12-verse love lyric, a genre consisting of couplets in monorhyme—aa, ba, ca, da, etc. The ghazal, which is rooted in classic Arabic poetry of the tenth century A.D., evolved from the *qasida*, a lengthy ode or eulogy praising an emperor or his court, which begins with a *nasib* or prelude and mounts to 100 couplets or more. The opening couplet sets the poem's style, rhyme, and mood, for example, Omar ibn Abi Rabi'a's seventh-century rhapsody that begins:

> Ah for the throes of a heart sorely wounded!
> Ah for the eyes that have struck me with madness!

The final couplet may make a show of skill

or offer a personal remark under the poet's pen name. The couplets in the body of the poem are separate epigrams, unbound by unity or consistency of subject matter but dealing generally with love.

Relished by Persian court poets, the ghazal was a specialty of Saadi and Hafiz and continues to influence poets of other countries. Hasrat, Iqbal, and Josh evolved a more unified ghazal that centered on one theme or subject, for example, mystical reflection on the divine or unrequited love. In Muslim tradition, the ghazal could be performed in a public reading or chanted as a devotional in a shrine. Interpretive readings stressed melody, improvisation, and accompaniment by drum or strings. The master of the ghazal in nineteenth-century India, Asadullah Khan Ghalib, is still quoted widely in Urdu and Persian.

In the early twentieth century, popularity passed to the middle class as the ghazal became a light-classical, romantic focus of Hindi movie music. By the 1970s, rock and disco film scores replaced the sweeter, more delicate cinema ghazal. Nevertheless, the Urdu ghazal in North India and Pakistan remains popular.

gothic   romantic writing, such as the *roman noir*, that highlights isolated or ominous locales; large, rambling structures; implied danger to an isolated or vulnerable character; and horrific distress or menace, such as mysterious disappearances or deaths, supernatural manifestations, omens, unexplained events, or an atmosphere of terror and suspense, as described on board the *San Dominick* in Herman Melville's novella *Benito Cereno* (1857).

In Charlotte Brontë's *Jane Eyre* (1847), the ghostly trappings of Thornfield, including Rochester's menacing dog Pilot and the appearance of Mother Bunches, hint at gothic atmosphere before yielding to realism. At the novel's climax, Brontë dispels the mystery of the gypsy's fortune-telling and has Rochester introduce Jane and their wedding party to Bertha, whose demonic laughter and eccentric caprices have disrupted sleep and caused a fire and a torn wedding veil.

A hybridized form of gothic is Southern gothic. Examples include the early novels of William Faulkner, the wry wit of Eudora Welty's stories, Flannery O'Connor's two novellas, *Wise Blood* (1952) and *The Violent Bear It Away* (1960), and Carson McCullers's *The Ballad of the Sad Café* (1951). A witty play, Beth Henley's *Crimes of the Heart* (1979), reveals a family's strength in traumatic times through the jailing of Babe, one of the McGrath daughters, who shot her husband in the stomach. The girls' eccentricities follow the style of their mother, who plotted suicide because she was having "a very bad day." The daughters conclude that she hanged her cat and herself so she wouldn't have to die alone.

Grand Guignol [grahn gee·NYOHL]   short plays performed at the Théâtre du Grand Guignol and Paris cabarets in nineteenth-century France. The name derives from a popular puppet character, Guignol, a peasant dupe named for a real silk worker from Lyons. The works emphasized sadistic violence, horror, and rape and colored the scandalous absurdist drama *Ubu Roi* (1896) by Alfred Jarry, a forerunner of surrealism. The play opened with unrealistic settings and grotesque costumes and featured mock-tragic buffoonery and stylized acting parodying traditional tragedy. The opening line was the single word *"merde"* [excrement]. Ingenious stage devices simulated the flow of blood.

Beginning in 1908, the Grand Guignol genre became popular in Great

Britain, perhaps because of the enormous curiosity about the infamous Jack the Ripper, who murdered and flayed prostitutes. France's Grand Guignol remained in production until 1962.

See also cabaret.

green man an animistic woodland figure from Celtic folklore, often depicted emerging from foliage or entwined in leaves and greenery on wood carvings and intricate paintings, stained glass, architectural detail, columns, statues, arrases, and pro-ecology advertisements. Dating to prehistory, the green man—also called Jack in the Green, the Old Man of the Woods, and, in Russia, Green George—is a counterpart to Gaia, the earth mother. Like the Greek Dionysus, the green man is a powerful archetype representing pantheism, the laws of nature, and irrepressible life. His ambiguous mystique reflects renewal and rebirth, a tie that kept him viable when Christianity replaced paganism. In the Middle Ages, he evolved into a symbol of science and technology.

A common character in British Mayday processions, mummers' plays, morris dance, and folktheater, the green man was an icon of spring and fertility. He is connected with the sanctity of St. George and may have been the inspiration for the folk hero Robin Hood. Sir James G. Frazer's *The Golden Bough* (1915) allies the green man of Russia, Switzerland, Germany, and England with tree worship.

J. R. R. Tolkien expresses the spirit of the green man in the merry character of Tom Bombadil. In *The Fellowship of the Ring* (1965), he captures the mystic presence: "Tom Bombadil is the Master. No one has ever caught old Tom walking in the forest, wading in the water, leaping on the hill-tops under light and shadow. He has no fear. Tom Bombadil is master."

green room a backstage room where actors gather for costume adjustment, snacks, drinks, and last-minute cue rehearsals. Derived from the Greek masking room, the green room is a launching spot for the next entrance onstage. The room is also used after a performance for receptions and visits from friends and wellwishers.

griot [GREE•oh] an African storyteller or tribal genealogist and historian, who holds an honored position among villagers, a guise that Virginia Hamilton adopts for *The People Could Fly* (1985), a collection of black folktales. Similar to the master of ceremonies at the Kwakiutl potlatch in Margaret Craven's *I Heard the Owl Call My Name* (1973), the griot is central to folk tradition. The griot's style of storytelling may employ African instruments and chants to educate, enlighten, or preserve history, ritual, morals, or family and dynastic lineage. In *Their Eyes Were Watching God* (1937), novelist Zora Neale Hurston employs the tradition of the enlightener for the character Janey, who explains to the character Pheoby the need for physical and spiritual fulfillment.

In the decades following the American Civil War, Joel Chandler Harris analyzed the oral traditions, literary style, and moral purpose of the griot in "Negro Folklore: The Story of Mr. Rabbit and Mr. Fox, as Told by Uncle Remus" (1879), an article that preceded *Uncle Remus: His Songs and His Sayings* (1880) and the classic trickster story, "Br'er Rabbit and the Tarbaby."

Twentieth-century griots include Algerian griot Marguerite Amrouche, Boston storyteller Brother Blue, Caribbean tellers Grace Hallworth and Ken Corbsie, and Mary Carter Smith, a preserver of the stories and songs of the African diaspora.

grotesque a shocking, unforeseen, dehumanizing, distorted, or ridiculous motif or situation characterized by fantasy, diabolic shapes, caricature, absurdity, ugliness, and freakishness, elements contained in the works of Edgar Allan Poe, Sherwood Anderson, Emile Zola, Franz Kafka, Jean Genet, Flannery O'Connor, Eudora Welty, William Faulkner, and T. Coraghessan Boyle. In "The Metamorphosis" (1915), Franz Kafka describes a bizarre and unforeseen transfiguration of Gregor Samsa into a loathsome beetle. The grotesqueness of the sudden change forces the reader to examine the character in terms of who he was, what he has become, and what his family expects of him.

groundlings members of a theater audience during the English Renaissance who stood in an area between the apron of the stage and the covered seating area. Admittance to the theater was inexpensive for those who preferred to stand. The groundlings' jostling and loud commentary intimidated some actors and influenced the opening of plays.

As a means of getting the audience's attention, William Shakespeare opened with the allegorical figure of Prologue or a dramatic flourish. For example, *Romeo and Juliet* (ca. 1593–1595), *Henry V* (1599), *Troilus and Cressida* (ca. 1602), *Pericles* (ca. 1606–1608), and *Henry VIII* (ca. 1612–1613) begin with prologues; *Julius Caesar* (ca. 1599) opens on a military procession before the appearance of the focal characters. More dramatic is the first scene of *Macbeth* (ca. 1603–1606), which reveals three witches conferring during a fierce storm.

In the Elizabethan tradition, German and Austrian opera houses maintain a section of the ground floor behind the last row of seats for *stehplatz*, or attendees who wish to hear a performance for the lowest price.

H

haiku [hy•KOO] a traditional Japanese form of untitled, unrhymed verse creating an intense image, suggestion, mood, or impression. Dating to the thirteenth century, it was originally called hokku and derives from songs, eulogies, and prayers from Shinto or Buddhist rituals anthologized in the mid-eighth century. It takes shape in three lines of seventeen syllables. The first line contains five syllables, the second seven, and the last five. Haiku was the favorite form of poets Kobayashi Issa, Sokan, Masaoka Shiki, and Yosa Buson and reached its height in the seventeenth century with the lyrics of Matsuo Basho, the objectivist master of the genre.

Haiku is influenced by Zen philosophy and tends toward seasonal observation featuring details of weather or time of year. Subject and theme stress the fleeting quality of natural beauty, as in petals, views of the moon, and human loveliness. The "aha!" experience in the last line illustrates the zen concept of *satori*, or enlightenment, by revealing some aspect of reality, particularly transience or evanescence.

Western poets are drawn to the accessible, flexible haiku form, as are writers in Africa, Asia, South America, and the Middle East. American masters are numerous: Mieko Yoshikami, Amy Lowell, Ezra Pound, Conrad Aiken, Richard Wright, Wallace Stevens, W. B. Yeats, and Robert Frost. Ernest Gaines creates an impromptu haiku in the parting journal of a semi-literate condemned man in *A Lesson Before Dying* (1993):

day breakin
sun comin up
the bird in the tre soun like a blu bird
sky blu blu mr wigin.

See also imagism.

ham   a performer displaying outrageously amateurish overacting marked by exaggerated emotions and gestures.

hamartia [hah•mahr•TEE•uh] the fatal character flaw, error in judgment, or moral weakness in a tragic hero. *See also* tragedy.

happening   a performance incorporating poetry readings, darkly ironic skits, spontaneous singing, and interruptions by the audience. During the heyday of happenings in the 1960s, verbal vulgarity and nudity were frequent elements. Often, happenings were staged in inexpensive empty stores or lofts or on the street. A part of the Beat scene, happenings tended toward black turtlenecks, beards, scruffy poets, and arch expressions of despair.

heroic couplet   a rhymed pair of lines composed in iambic pentameter, a common form in English poetry dating to Geoffrey Chaucer in the fourteenth century and reaching its height in the eighteenth century with the works of John Dryden and Alexander Pope. *See also* couplet.

hexameter   a poetic line containing six feet, often broken into two trimeters, the standard verse length in classic Greek and Roman poetry. Phaedrus, author of *Phaedri Augusti Liberti Fabularum Aesopiarum* [The Aesopic Fables of Phaedrus the Freedman of Augustus] (ca. 37 B.C.), employed polished senarian verses, a description of the six-foot meter ($\cup/\cup/\cup/\cup/\cup/\cup/$) common to the stage. The thirteenth line of Phaedrus's "The Frogs

Asked for a King" demonstrates the tendency of hexameter lines to break into halves after the third beat: *Pater deorum risit atque illis dedit* [The father of the gods laughed and granted them (a sliver of wood)]. To the English-speaker, hexameter is long, ponderous, and somewhat awkward and tends to fall into more readable ranks of threes. Henry Wadsworth Longfellow revived the classic tradition in his poems *Evangeline* (1847) and *The Courtship of Miles Standish* (1858). *See also* alexandrine.

high comedy   a subtle satire that appeals to the intellect rather than the emotions by stressing humorous situations that have serious overtones, as in William Shakespeare's *Much Ado About Nothing* (ca. 1598), Molière's *Tartuffe* (1664), William Congreve's *The Way of the World* (1700), Jane Austen's *Pride and Prejudice* (1813), Oscar Wilde's *A Woman of No Importance* (1893), George Bernard Shaw's *Pygmalion* (1913) and *Androcles and the Lion* (1916), and Evelyn Waugh's *The Loved One* (1948).

historical fiction   a fictional representation of an historical era, as in Nathaniel Hawthorne's *The Scarlet Letter* (1850), Stephen Crane's *The Red Badge of Courage* (1895), Caribbean playwright Lewis Osborn Innis's *Carmelita, the Belle of San Jose* (1897), Johan Bojer's *The Emigrants* (1924), Margaret Mitchell's *Gone with the Wind* (1936), Ibuse Masuji's *Waves: A War Diary* (1938), James Michener's *Hawaii* (1959) and *Centennial* (1974), Lawrence Yep's *Dragonwings* (1975), and Toni Morrison's *Paradise* (1997).

Drama and poetry are also the vehicle of historical fiction, for example, Crocker Howard's classic Civil War drama, *Shenandoah* (1888), Walter Woods's four-act play, *Billy the Kid* (1906), and Rosemary Benét and Stephen Vincent Benét's verse collection *The Book of Americans* (1933), which lauds such legendary figures as Daniel Boone and John Chapman, better known as Johnny Appleseed.

In Amy Tan's *The Kitchen God's Wife* (1992), the main character's oral narrative blends her life story with facts surrounding China's turbulent twentieth century. References to Formosa's new name (Taiwan), Madame Chiang, Claire Chennault, Flying Tigers, Burma Road, propaganda leaflets, Nanking massacre, Emperor Hirohito, intervention of the British and American military, and Mr. Roosevelt and Mr. Churchill indicate the national and international events that impinge on the characters' choices as they flee the invading Japanese and move into makeshift quarters in Kunming.

In *No Promises in the Wind* (1970), young adult novelist Irene Hunt blends the story of two runaways with the Depression, the fall preceding Franklin Roosevelt's first term in office, and the March day on which he was sworn in as United States President. In addition to his inaugural speech, Hunt mentions Charles Evans Hughes, Herbert Spence, organized labor, gangsters, Chicago's west side, bank closures, and bread lines.

See also biography.

historic milieu   the historical, political, or geographic setting of events in a period of history, as in the violent background of Francis Scott Key's "The Star-Spangled Banner" (1814), Louisiana politics in Robert Penn Warren's *All the King's Men* (1946), Reconstruction and subsequent violence in Margaret Walker's *Jubilee* (1966), the Mexican Revolution in Carlos Fuentes's *The Old Gringo* (1985), and Sonia Sanchez's verse collection, *Does Your House Have Lions?* (1997). The last two volumes describe personal sufferings

and loss at the height of the AIDS epidemic.

A thorough understanding of Alexander Solzhenitsyn's *One Day in the Life of Ivan Denisovich* (1962) requires some background knowledge of historical milieu—the two world wars, formation of the Russian state, and iron-handed Communist rule. Likewise, Albert Camus's *The Stranger* (1942) reflects the anti-colonialism that permeates Algeria in the decades following World War II, when the smoldering hostility in the Arabs who stalk the protagonist demonstrates an unspoken anger at the French presence in northern Africa.

From more recent events, the race prejudice and genocide in Latin American countries cast an ominous shadow over Barbara Kingsolver's *The Bean Trees* (1988), which draws on the working of Sanctuary, an underground program helping people to flee political persecution. Likewise, the background of Mark Mathabane's *Kaffir Boy* (1986) reflects the political turmoil during the period of South African history known as apartheid. *See also* milieu.

homophones   words that are pronounced alike but are spelled differently, as in principal/principle, main/mane, and tailor/Taylor. Homophones are often the source of puns, for example, the play on all/awl in the opening scene of William Shakespeare's *Julius Caesar* (ca. 1599). Robert Newton Peck uses homophones to create humor in the somber young adult classic, *A Day No Pigs Would Die* (1972). In a scene describing the protagonist's poor performance in school, his Aunt Matty declares that he needs a tutor. Rob is relieved that he knows what a "tooter" is.

hubris   [HYOO•brihs]   excessive pride, insolence, or conceit. Hubris is the major sin or character flaw in ancient Greek philosophy and the cause of the downfall of a tragic hero, such as the title character in *Omeros* (1990), Derek Walcott's Caribbean epic. Zora Neale Hurston's *Their Eyes Were Watching God* (1937) demonstrates the destruction of a marriage between her heroine, Janie, and Joe "Jody" Starks, the arrogant mayor of Apopka, Florida. Starks makes himself the big man by showing off his glossy-haired wife at a town meeting, where other wives cover their hair with headrags of calico and percale. *See also* hamartia, tragedy.

humanism   an artistic focus on ennobling, civilizing, or uplifting human qualities, values, aims, and interests, as found in Chilean short story writer Manuel Rojas's "The Glass of Milk" (1956) and Chief Dan George's poem "There Is a Longing." Humanistic themes highlight the ability of human characters to achieve their best through self-improvement, reason, and enlightenment rather than dependence on social or supernatural intervention, as in Bette Greene's young adult novel *Summer of My German Soldier* (1973), in which a battered Jewish girl risks punishment and ostracism by sheltering an escapee from a German prisoner of war camp. James Agee's *Let Us Now Praise Famous Men* (1941) is a journalistic tribute to common labor. The author describes poor farm workers readying themselves for sleep and another day of toil:

> and when the women are through, they may or may not come out too, with their dresses wet in front with the dishwashing and their hard hands softened and seamed as if withered with water, and sit a little while with the man or the men: and if they do, it is not for long, for everyone is much too tired, and has been awake and at work since daylight whitened a little behind the trees on the hill, and it is now very close to dark,

with daylight scarcely more than a sort of tincture on the air …

humor   a gentle, affirmative emphasis on human nature, foibles, and idiosyncrasies, for example, greed, meddling, and talkativeness, as displayed by the trial of a lusty fox accused of raping a noblewoman in the beast epic *Roman de Renart* (ca. 1250 B.C.), Lao She's short story about social hypocrisy, "The Grand Opening" (1933), and Paul Keens-Douglas's Jamaican peasant stories, "Tanti at the Oval" and "When Moon Shine" (1992). Mark Twain demonstrates an agreeable chiding of humanity in *Roughing It* (1872), in which he reports:

> During the preceding night an ambushed savage had sent a bullet through the pony rider's jacket, but he had ridden on, just the same, because pony riders were not allowed to stop and inquire into such things except when killed.

A world-wise epigram from Margaret Mitchell's *Gone with the Wind* (1936) notes, "Until you've lost your reputation, you never realize what burden it was or what freedom really is."

A more rollicking form of humor comes from the rabelaisian style, derived from the episodic novels of François Rabelais, a mid-sixteenth-century rebel and idealist whose *Gargantua and Pantagruel* (1564) set the tone and style for an inventive satire that exceeds the normal limits of comedy with exaggeration, grotesqueness, and impudent ridicule of scholasticism and the corrupt practices of the Catholic church. The term "rabelaisian humor" implies a robustness and extravagance of style and plotting, marked by crude jests, exhibitionism, caricature, and coarse parody.

hyperbole   bold exaggeration to draw attention to an idea or to create humor, as in Florence King's *Confessions of* *a Failed Southern Lady* (1985), in which she suddenly discovers that, when she was young, she was a child, just like other children. She comments, "I hadn't known that before; I thought I was just short." Depending on the author's control of intentional overstatement, the result may be greater emphasis, an outsized image, or comic or bitter effect, as found in Pat Conroy's introduction to Mary Edwards Wertsch's *Military Brats* (1991), in which he claims, "The sound of gunfire on rifle ranges strikes an authentic chord of home in me even now." Signal words often precede hyperbole—for example, always and never, both demonstrating the extremes of the comparison.

The extravagance of hyperbole can heighten either comedy or tragedy, as is the case with Charles Dickens's *Oliver Twist* (1839), in which the directors of the workhouse conclude that

> the poor people liked it! It was a regular place of public entertainment for the poorer classes; a tavern where there was nothing to pay; a public breakfast, dinner, tea, and supper all the year round; a brick and mortar elysium, where it was all play and no work.

On the other extreme, a whimsical bit of hyperbole in Isak Dinesen's culinary fable, "Babette's Feast" (1953), declares that the protagonist's multicourse supper alters a grim religious colony with "one glorious radiance. Taciturn old people received the gift of tongues; ears that for years had been almost deaf were opened to it. Time itself had merged into eternity."

A protracted line of hyperboles flavors Laura Esquivel's feminist fable *Like Water for Chocolate* (1992), in which a seriosymbolic birthing produces a baby girl who weeps from the fumes of chopped onion. Nacha, the cook/midwife, "swept up the residue the tears had left on the red stone floor. There was enough salt to fill a ten-pound sack—it was used for cooking and lasted a long time."

I

iamb   a metrical foot or unit that contains two syllables, an unstressed syllable followed by a stressed syllable ($\smile\,'$), the dominant metrical rhythm in Elizabeth Barrett Browning's "The Cry of the Children" (1844), in which she mourns:

> Alas, alas, the children! they are seeking
>   Death in life, as best to have:
> They are binding up their hearts away
>   from breaking,
> With a cerement from the grave.

English tends toward iambic pentameter, a metrical pattern of five iambic units per line, the verse meter favored by Renaissance playwrights Christopher Marlowe and William Shakespeare. *See also* blank verse, heroic couplet.

idiom   a phrase, grammatical construction, or expression that contains more meaning than the simple sum of its words; for example, in Toni Cade Bambara's folksy story "Blues Ain't No Mockin' Bird," "to talk him out of it" is a phrase meaning to dissuade in Granny's description of an effort to stop a man from jumping off a bridge.

Folklorist Zora Neale Hurston was an expert on black idiom. Her posthumous "Harlem Slanguage" contains phrases such as "I'm cracking but I'm facking" and a description of black skin tones, from "yaller" to "yaller, high brown, vaseline brown, seal brown, and low brown" to dark black. In a description of her mother's death, Hurston inserts a Southern term for courtesy in an allegorical section of her autobiography, *Dust Tracks on a Road* (1942):

Just then, Death finished his prowling through the house on his padded feet and entered the room. He bowed to Mama in his way, and she made her manners and left us to act out our ceremonies over unimportant things.

idyll [I•d'l]   originally a brief picturesque verse or prose description, as found in the short form of Robert Browning's *Dramatic Idyls* (1880). An idyll often pictures a rustic scene suggesting idealized contentment and serenity, as in William Wordsworth's "The Solitary Reaper" (1807). The term also applies to longer narrative poems, as in the chivalric episodes that make up Alfred, Lord Tennyson's *Idylls of the King* (1885). Mark Twain's *The Adventures of Tom Sawyer* (1876), Robert Frost's "Birches" (1916), and Mary Hunter Austin's collection of nature verse, *Children Sing in the Far West* (1928), have been classified as childhood idylls.

imagery   a pattern or series of interconnected word pictures that make an object or feeling come alive in the mind by evoking a single unified sense impression—sight, sound, taste, touch, or smell, as found in the keen observations of Su Shi's poetry (ca. 1100), D. H. Lawrence's verse collection, *Birds, Beasts and Flowers* (1923), German poet Nelly Sachs's vision of "The Swan," and Toni Morrison's novel *Beloved* (1987), in which she describes friendship in visual, tactile glimpses:

> She is a friend to my mind. She gathers me. The pieces I am, she gathers them and gives them back to me in all the right order. It's good when you got a woman who is a friend of your mind.

Imagery is a literary method of helping the reader or listener to see, hear, taste, smell, or feel an object, situation, attitude, or emotion, a contributing factor to the flow of the Nebraska scenery in Willa Cather's *My Antonia* (1926):

> As I looked about me I felt that the grass

was the country, as the water is the sea. The red of the grass made all the great prairie the colour of wine-stains, or of certain seaweeds when they are first washed up. And there was so much motion in it; the whole country seemed, somehow, to be running.

Authors often tie abstract words to a concrete mental picture by using a metaphor, simile, allegory, allusion, metonomy, or personification that appeals directly to the senses. The poet Edna St. Vincent Millay expresses a lack of commitment to love in terms of segments of the year in "I Know I Am But Summer" (1923) by claiming, "I know I am but summer to your heart,/And not the full four seasons of the year." In *Letters from the Earth* (1963), Mark Twain sums up human frailties by comparing them to faults in a machine: "Man seems to be a rickety poor sort of a thing, any way you take him; a kind of British Museum of infirmities and inferiorities. He is always undergoing repairs. A machine that was as unreliable as he is would have no market."

In *Invisible Man* (1947), novelist Ralph Ellison creates impressive color and action pictures, for example, an explosion in a paint factory that coats the narrator with white, fascination with a blues song entitled "What Did I Do to Be So Black and Blue," a jumping-jack doll that epitomizes servility, and a retreat into a coal cellar where the unnamed narrator disappears from the light like an animal seeking protection in the forest. Sophie Trupin's frontier memoir, *Dakota Diaspora: Memoirs of a Jewish Homesteader* (1984), expresses imagery through allusion in which a family of Russian Jews move to "Nordokota," where each becomes a Moses leading people out of the bondage of czarist Russia.

imagism   a direct study of a single object through controlled free-verse statements that impinge on the object's purpose or use, as found in the bold clarity and conciseness of William Carlos Williams's poem "The Red Wheelbarrow" (1934), the exactness of Hilda Doolittle's "The Pear Tree" (1940), and the tight construction of Uruguayan poet Gaston Figueira's "The Pineapple" (1963). Imagism was the favorite mode of expression for the Chinese poet Li Po in the mid-eighth century A.D. and for the Arab poet Ma'arri in *Meditations* (ca. 1050 A.D.). The method influenced Edgar Allan Poe's "To Helen" (1831), Charles Baudelaire's *Les Fleurs du Mal* (1857), and Giuseppe Ungaretti's "Morning." American imagists Amy Lowell and Ezra Pound revived the Japanese haiku as a vehicle for imagism, for instance, Pound's "In a Station of the Metro" (1916) and Lowell's "Autumn Haze" (1919).

impressionism   a style of the late nineteenth and early twentieth centuries that is rooted in the personal reactions to a situation or object, for example, James Agee's "Knoxville: Summer 1915," a gentle reverie recalling a secure moment in the speaker's childhood. In contrast are the fierce memories of the Auschwitz death camp in Ka-Tzetnik's *The Clock Overhead* (1968).

In opposition to strict realism, literary impressionism stresses the subjective interpretation of stimuli. The purpose of this focus is to provide clues to the emotional makeup of the character. A model of perception through the senses is James Joyce's *A Portrait of the Artist as a Young Man* (1916), which concentrates on the protagonist's inner landscape rather than lingering on descriptions of setting, lesser characters, and actions. Other proponents of impressionism include the French symbolists, Marcel Proust, Henry James, Oscar Wilde, Ford Madox Ford, Stephen Crane, and Virginia Woolf.

in medias res   Latin phrase meaning "in the middle of things," a reference to the literary approach to time that begins at the height of action, then recounts or flashes back to past action or motivation. *See* epic.

incantation   a systematized ritual chant or song that summons intense emotions and allies worshippers with supernatural spirits or powers, as in the altar prayer to Laka in Hawaiian lore:

> This spoil and rape of the wildwood,
> This plucking of wilderness maile—
> Collect of garlands, Laka, for you.
> Hiiaka, the prophet, heals our diseases.
> Enter, possess, inspire your altar;
> Heed our prayer, 'tis for life'
> Our petition to you is for life.
> *Chorus*: Give us life, save from transgression!

The incantation of the three witches in William Shakespeare's *Macbeth* (ca. 1603–1606)—"Double, double, toil and trouble"—is one of the most familiar word formulas from English literature. In a chapter on hoodoo in Zora Neale Hurston's *Mules and Men* (1935), she employs incantation and ritual to initiate herself into Caribbean voodoo.

incongruity   an unlikely or unseemly contrast of situations or language, for example, flower girl Eliza Doolittle's failure at small talk in George Bernard Shaw's *Pygmalion* (1912), King Mongut's attempt to prove himself enlightened and sophisticated in Richard Rodgers and Oscar Hammerstein's *The King and I* (1951), and mismated roommates in Neil Simon's *The Odd Couple* (1965).

In incongruity, the author or speaker leaves expectations unsatisfied, for example, by putting something ludicrous in place of a serious subject, as with Ralph Waldo Emerson's declaration, "The louder he talked of his honor, the faster we counted our spoons." Irish playwright Hugh Leonard enhances the comedy of his ghost play, *Da* (1973), by interjecting the grudges and persistent complaints of a dead father's apparition as his son makes a farewell visit to his childhood home.

Jessamyn West makes repeated use of incongruity as a source of the gentle humor of *Except for Me and Thee* (1949), a social novel reflecting the difficulties of Quakers during the early years of the American Civil War. When Eliza Bird-well's husband Jess involves himself in the Underground Railroad, he replaces his plain farm clothes with the finery of Enoch, his hired man. Eliza labels Jess a "sheep in wolf's clothing." In reply, he notes, "This is the first, and I hope the last, time, Eliza, thee's ever going to be kissed by a man of fashion. Best make the most of it."

interior monologue   the random and often illogical flow of unspoken thoughts, memories, images, and impressions that serves as narrative in stream-of-consciousness writing, for example, the confusion and blended details of past and present in a dying woman's thoughts, the subject of Katherine Anne Porter's "The Jilting of Granny Weatherall" (1965). An example from Kaye Gibbons's *Ellen Foster* (1987) expresses an abused child's thinking about death:

> They put her [mother] in a box too and him in a box oh shut the lid down hard on this one and nail it, nail it with the strongest nails. Do all you can to keep it shut and him in it always. Time would make him meaner to me if he could get out and grab me again.

intermezzo [in•tuhr•MEDZ•zoh], pl. intermezzi   short, usually comic passages or ornate complements pantomimed in fifteenth and sixteenth century Italian theater productions during scenery changes or between acts of more serious drama or opera. Forerunners of comic opera, intermezzi were forms of spectacle linked to the main production by similar themes, motifs, and settings. They were performed on pageant wagons or portable set pieces on platforms. The most elaborate featured dazzling special effects, such as movable ships, castles, thunder, smoke and fire, and stage machinery that made mythical creatures appear from the sea or air, as in Giacomo Torelli's *The Marriage of Thetis* (1654) and *The Battle of the Argonauts* (1608), a naval engagement staged in Florence on the Arno River. The genre derives from the Italian *mascherata* and from entertainments performed for court banquets, state visits, and weddings. The allegorical characters derived from mythology or classical literature, much like classic Greek satyr plays and British interludes and masques. A Spanish variation, the seventeenth-century *sainete*, consists of comic stories of saints' lives produced for amusement rather than enlightenment. These interludes reveal urban concerns and employ risqué, even bawdy situations.

internal rhyme   rhyming within a line, as found in the alliance of vowel sounds that grace Countee Cullen's lyric "Heritage" (1925), in which he broaches his national background with the question "What is Africa to me: copper sun or scarlet sea." Internal rhyme may serve a poet in various ways, for example:

• as stress or highlight of some significant detail, as found in the narrator's introductory comment in Lord Byron's *The Prison of Chillon* (1816):

> My hair is gray, but not with years,
> Nor grew it white in a single night …

• as a unifying factor in Edgar Allan Poe's "Annabel Lee" (1849), a favorite nineteenth-century recitation piece:

And the stars never rise, but I feel the
    bright eyes
        Of the beautiful Annabel Lee;
And so, all the night-tide, I lie down by
    the side
Of my darling—my darling—my life
    and my bride,
        In her sepulcher there by the sea,
    In her tomb by the sounding sea.

• as an adjunct to humor, as in Edith Sitwell's "Sir Beelzebub" (1922), which declares:

Nobody comes to give him his rum but
    the
Rim of the sky hippopotamus-glum
Enhances the chances to bless with a
    benison
Alfred Lord Tennyson crossing the
    bar....

interpolation   a passage or added material inserted into a text, for example, a new prologue added to the beginning of a play to tie the plot to current events or contemporary values, morals, or situations. Early Christian philosophy was imposed on the text of *Beowulf* through interpolation.

invective   hurtful, cruel sarcasm, stinging rejoinder, or humiliating verbal abuse intended to belittle or to weaken a threat, as in Florence King's personal vituperation against feminist Andrea Dworkin in *Lump It or Leave It* (1991). The derogatory style of invective tinges the satire of Roman poets Martial and Catullus and of social critics Alexander Pope, Samuel Butler, Charles Dickens, and George Bernard Shaw.

Jonathan Swift's *Gulliver's Travels* (1726) loses its control when the author lambastes England's venality. He claims that

vast numbers of our people are compelled to seek their livelihood by begging, robbing, stealing, cheating, pimping, forswearing, flattering, suborning, forging, gaming, lying, fawning, hectoring, vot-

ing, scribbling, stargazing, poysoning, whoring, canting, libelling, free-thinking, and the like occupations.

inversion   a rearrangement of the standard subject-verb-complement or subject-verb-object pattern in English sentences, for example, Aphra Behn's "Love Armed" (1676), which declares of personified Love: "fresh pains he did create/And strange tyrannic power he showed." Inversion—also called anastrophe—makes for tedious reading and unnatural flow in prose but often serves poetic style and sentiment, as in Robert Frost's opening line in "Mending Wall" (1914), "Something there is that doesn't love a wall." The inversion here places the predicate nominative ahead of subject and verb. In Herman Melville's short story "Bartleby, the Scrivener" (1856), the unnamed lawyer chafes at the annoyance of an incompetent and troublesome clerk and hopes that "departed he was."

invocation   an appeal or direct address to a deity or muse or the summoning of divine or supernatural powers, as in the title of Adah Menken's poem "Hear, O Israel" (ca. 1860), a citation of the Jewish call to worship. Invocation takes a patterned form in call and response, for example, the dialect appeal to Jesus led by Serena in Dubose Heyward's folk novel *Porgy* (1925):

"Oh, Jedus, who done trouble de wateh
    in de sea ob Gallerie-"
"Amen!" came the chorus, led by Porgy.
"An' likewise who done cas' de Debbil
    out ob de afflicted, time an' time
    agin,"
"Oh, Jedus!"
"Wut mek yu ain't lay yo' han' on dis sister' head?"

Another example is John G. Neihardt's *Black Elk Speaks* (1932), in which the pious Sioux prays, "In sorrow I am sending a feeble voice, O Six powers of the World.

Hear me in my sorrow, for I may never call again. O make my people live!"

In Paul Green's history play, *The Lost Colony* (1937), the playwright imitates English hymnody in the minister's prayer and a salute to the New World settler, whom he describes as the "lusty singer, dreamer, pioneer."

A masterful use of dialect, Alice Walker's *The Color Purple* (1982) features the protagonist's private talks with God: "Dear God. Dear stars, dear trees, dear sky, dear peoples. Dear Everything. Dear God. Thank you for bringing my sister Nettie and our children home."

See also litany.

irony   an implied discrepancy between what is said or done and what is meant, as in dual meaning of the love letter in Act IV of Edmond Rostand's *Cyrano de Bergerac* (1897), Brazilian poet Monteiro Lobato's short story, "The Farm Magnate" (1934), the religious setting of Argentine poet Alfonsina Storni's "She Who Understands" (1937), and the folkloric quality of Egyptian playwright Tawfiq al-Hakim's *The River of Madness* (1963). A comic display of pantaloons creates irony in Richard Rodgers and Oscar Hammerstein's *The King and I* (1951) after the newly refined Siamese women hoist their skirts to flee a diplomat wearing a monocle. O. Henry achieves humor through irony in "The Ransom of Red Chief" (1910), the tale of kidnappers who are terrorized by their mischievous young victim. Thomas Berger employs humorous irony in *Little Big Man* (1964), a whimsical Western novel that places the orphan Jack Crabb in the home of a pious minister, whose young wife debauches the boy while pretending to save his soul. A poignant example of situational irony, Charlie Gordon, protagonist of Daniel Keyes's *Flowers for Algernon* (1959), suffers the backlash of a pious supervisor of the handicapped, who observes, "What do you know about being shut out from every human experience as our patients have been?" without knowing that Charlie was born mentally retarded and will soon return to that state after regressing from improvements made by experimental surgery.

Irony is capable of heightening tragedy as well as comedy and whimsy. In tragic mode, irony stalks Okonkwo, the high-minded protagonist of Chinua Achebe's *Things Fall Apart* (1959). Failing to halt the advance of cultural change to his African tribe, Okonkwo hangs himself and recedes into anonymity.

Frequently described as tongue-in-cheek humor, irony heightens the effect of fireside entertainment on the lurking eavesdropper in John Gardner's *Grendel* (1971). The protagonist laughs in the darkness at the uncouth humor and vulgarity of the carousing Danes, then withdraws with his sack of human victims to a woodland lard to "eat and laugh and eat until I can barely walk."

O. Henry applies a masterly touch of dramatic irony to "The Cabellero's Way," one of the stories in *Heart of the West* (1907). The Cisco Kid discovers that his girlfriend has betrayed him to a pursuer. He tricks the lawman into shooting the girl, then departs at a casual trot, singing "Don't you monkey with my Lulu girl."

More lethal than dramatic irony is verbal irony, a situation that overloads words with the opposite of their message, as in Mark Antony's strongly worded funeral oration that labels as assassins the noble Marcus Brutus and a coterie of plotters in William Shakespeare's *Julius Caesar* (ca. 1599). Antony pauses at regular intervals to note, "For Brutus is an honourable man: So are they all, all honourable men." After eight repetitions of the claim of honor, Antony turns the word into a damning diatribe that prefaces civil chaos. Similarly virulent, a touch of historical irony concludes Dee Brown's *Bury My Heart at Wounded Knee* (1970), which describes the return of massacred and dying Indians to a church that flaunts a banner reading, "PEACE ON EARTH, GOOD WILL TO MEN."

A third classification, tragic irony, displays actions that lead characters to their own downfall. The most famous is Sophocles's *Oedipus Rex* (409 B.C.), in which the title character calls down the gods' wrath as a way to end the plague of Thebes. When the king discovers the truth of his birth and his role in killing his royal predecessor, he scratches out his eyes as recompense for seeing the villainy of his actions. A similar reckoning punishes Pao-yu, protagonist of Tsao Hsueh-chin's classic Chinese court novel *The Dream of the Red Chamber* (1791). At the height of a charmed life as court ladies' man, Pao-yu loses the one maiden he longs to win and withdraws to a Buddhist cell to counter the worldly lusts that colored his rise to power and influence.

jargon   words that derive from an industry, profession, sports, or the media, as with conference-calling, e-mail, voice mail, RAM, DOS, and CD-ROM from business, electronics, and computers. Jargon is often the *lingua franca* of science fiction and futurism, as in the technical verbiage of "Bokanovsky's Process" in Aldous Huxley's *Brave New World* (1939), the electronic bard in Stanislaw Lem's "The First Sally (A) OR Trurl's Electronic Bard" (1974), and the creation and manipulation of dinosaurs in Michael Crichton's *Jurassic Park* (1990).

jingle   a melodic verse cadence stressing sound over meaning, as in the onomatopoetic refrain in William Shakespeare's *Much Ado About Nothing* (ca. 1598), which repeats, "Be you blithe and bonny; converting all your sounds of woe into Hey nonny, nonny," and a similar melodic outburst in the anonymous cowboy song "Whoopee-ti-yi-yo, Git Along, Little Dogies." Akin to doggerel, jingle can also express literary themes in a bouncy verse style, the method of Lewis Carroll for his mock-epic "Jabberwocky" (1872). In a folk play, *Quare Medicine* (1925), playwright Paul Green created Doctor Immanuel, seller of Universal Remedy, which he advertises with a jingle beginning, "Two dollars a bottle, two dollars."

As an adjunct to satire, Aldous Huxley's *Brave New World* (1932) parodies noisy, choplogic advertising rhymes and sleep-teaching aphorisms: "Streptocock-Gee to Banbury T," "A, B, C, vitamin D: The fat's in the liver, the cod's in the sea," "Euphoric, narcotic, pleasantly hallucinant," and "a gramme is better than a damn." In similar satire of advertising, Ray Bradbury's *Fahrenheit 451* (1951) uses the maddeningly alliterated product name "Denham's Dandy Dental Detergent" and the "Click, Pic, Look, Eye, Now, Flick, Here, There, Swift, Pace, Up, Down, In, Out, Why, How, Who, What, Where, Eh? Uh! Bang! Smack! Wallop, Bing, Bong, Boom!" of film to stress the brainlessness and casual violence of a repressive society.

journal   a first-person narrative, diary, daybook, or log filled with authentic details, as found in Julius Caesar's *Gallic Commentaries* (58–52 B.C.). Frontier literature is rich with these personal commentaries, for example, Catherine Parr Traill's *The Backwoods of Canada* (1871), which outlines practical data on pickling, raising dough, and making sugar, soap, tapers, and candles.

Personalized views color *The Explorations of Captain James Cook in the Pacific As Told by Selections of His Own Journals, 1768–1779* (1779), Charles Darwin's *Voyage of the Beagle* (1839), *Original Journals of the Lewis and Clark Expedition* (1905), Georgia Eliza Frances "Fanny" Andrews's *The Wartime Journal of a Georgia Girl* (1908), Elinore Pruitt Stewart's *Letters of a Woman Homesteader* (1914), Henry Lewis Morgan's *The Indian Journals, 1859–1862* (1959), Eldridge Cleaver's prison journal, *Soul on Ice* (1965), and Basil H. Johnston's Ojibway memoir, *Indian School Days* (1989), which recalls a coed Jesuit boarding school near Lake Huron where Indian children learned trades valued by the white world. An edited journal, *A Midwife's Tale: The Life of Martha Ballard, Based on Her Diary, 1785–1812* (1990), preserves in the original phrasing, grammar, and spelling the writer's description of the daily tasks of a New England nurse.

A journal is also a narrative device, as demonstrated by Isabel Allende's *The House of the Spirits* (1982), which examines a South American family's actions by retelling events as described in her Grandmother Clara's journal, which covers a span of fifty years in the Trueba family's affairs.

juvenilia   immature literature or apprentice works composed by a young author, for example, Anne Frank's *The Diary of a Young Girl* (1945) and Zlata Filipovich's *Zlata's Diary* (1994). Critics sometimes peruse the juvenilia of great writers for clues to their development, as is the case with the Brontë children, who produced very small, hand-lettered volumes of imaginative adventure stories from 1825 to 1831. Richard Wright men-

tions an amateurish story, "The Voodoo of Hell's Half-Acre," in his autobiography, *Black Boy* (1945). By limiting the vocabulary and depth of her autobiographical *Little House on the Prairie* (1935), Laura Ingalls Wilder produces literary juvenilia by giving the impression that the work was composed by a young author.

juxtaposition   a form of incongruity derived from the placement or close alliance of unusual images, characters, or ideas, for example, the setting of Moss Hart and George S. Kaufman's *You Can't Take It with You* (1936), which displays a collection of snakes, typewriter, xylophone, and skull-shaped candy dish, and a cast of characters whose hobbies impel them to print leftist pamphlets, dance classical ballet, write novels, serve watermelon and corn flakes for dinner, paint portraits, attend commencement addresses, wrestle, play the saxophone, and contrive new forms of fireworks. O. Henry makes subtly humorous jabs at a sanctimonious banker in "The Ransom of Red Chief" (1910) by describing Ebenezer Dorset as a "mortgage financier and a stern, upright collection-plate passer and forecloser."

kabuki   [kuh•BOO•kee]   a Japanese drama or spectacle dating to 1600, involving music and dance to traditional instruments and melodies, brilliantly colored settings and costumes, heavy, mask-like makeup applied over a white base, and rigidly stylized acting that emulates the jerky motions and gestures of puppets. An outgrowth of the rising middle class, kabuki evolved from the Buddhist *odori*, or shocking dances, and demonstrated an ebullient renaissance that called for drums, flutes, three-string samisen, and wooden batabata, or clappers. Literary form varied from comedy and satire to domestic drama, history play, and dance spectacle and was punctuated by *chariba*, or comic relief. Acting style tended toward exaggerated expressions, improvisation, melodrama, violence, and the camp elements of *onnagata*, or stylized female impersonators, one of kabuki's most popular elements.

The master of seventeenth-century kabuki, Chikamatsu Monzaemon, produced over 150 plays. His successor, Takedo Izumo, wrote a landmark eleven-act drama, *The Treasury of Loyal Retainers* (1748), a vengeance play. In the nineteenth century, playwrights Tsuruya Namboku and Mokuami Kawatake both added realism to kabuki dramas.

katauta [kah•tuh•OO•tah] a primitive verse form and the basic unit of Japanese poetry intended to be one breath in length. Spontaneous and intuitive in texture, it is written as a tightly condensed question or answer and consists of nineteen syllables—three lines of five, seven, and seven syllables each. The third line harmonizes the rhythm by mimicking the cadence of the previous line. Evolving from spring fertility ritual and planting rites, the *katauta* may be paired, question with answer, as in this model, the first half by Takeru Yamato and the second by an unidentified poet:

> Passing across
> The new land of Tsukuba,
> How many nights did we sleep?
>
> Counting on my fingers,
> It has been nine times by night
> And will be ten times by day.

When written as a six-line question with answer, the poem is called a mondo.

keen an Irish lament or funeral dirge, for instance, Paul Muldoon's "Keen" (1987). Keening is also a term describing an instinctive cry or dramatic response to loss or death, as in Maurya's mourning of dead sons in John Millington Synge's play *Riders to the Sea* (1904). A dramatic keening marks the biblical biography of King David in II Samuel 18-33, when the father cries out for his dead son, "O my son Absalom, my son, my son Absalom! would God I had died for thee, O Absalom, my son, my son!"

kenning a metaphoric form of circumlocution, the substitution of a figurative noun phrase for a single term, for example, the term "shape-shifter" to name a wily supernatural adversary. Old German and Anglo-Saxon combinations produced "swan road" and "whale path" for ocean, "bone house" for body, and "ring giver" for king. The term is comparable to the epithets of classical literature, in which noun compounds identify characters, as with "swollen-foot" for Oedipus and "the far-seer" for the clairvoyant Teiresias.

künstlerroman [KUHN•stluhr•roh•mahn] a form of *bildungsroman* that details the apprenticeship or maturation of a young artist through struggle and attainment of understanding, which is applied to a mission or goal, as found in James Joyce's impressionistic novel *A Portrait of the Artist as a Young Man* (1916).

Hermann Hesse allies autobiographical insights with facts about the historical Gautama Buddha to create *Siddhartha* (1922), an historical novel about a spiritual quest. The title character begins with a naive concept of worldliness, allies himself with an idealistic cult, then loses sight of his original aim. After freeing himself from sensual desires, he returns to the quest, this time fortified with experience.

kyogen [KYOH•gin] farcical interludes common to the Japanese theater of the early seventeenth century that parallel the improvisation of Italian *commedia dell'arte. Kyogen* influenced early twentieth-century drama, as in James R. Brandon and Tamako Niwa's *The Zen Substitute* (1910), a comic plot adapted from the Japanese farce *Hanago*. The story, based on disguise motifs and mix-ups in identity, turns on the standard pairing of the overbearing wife with a weak husband.

L

lament   a poem expressing deep regret, grievous loss, or sorrow, for example, the ancient Lanai poem "Where are You, O Puupehe?" from Hawaiian lore, plaintive poems of twentieth-century Spanish poet Federico García Lorca, and "The Crime Was in Granada" (1939), Antonio Machado's lament for Lorca. Other examples include Catullus's lyric farewell to his dead brother in "Ave atque Vale" (57 B.C.), Rory Dall O'Cahan's "The Derry Air" (1600s), later published as "The Londonderry Air" and "Danny Boy," Caroline Augusta Ball's Civil War-era poem "The Jacket of Gray" (1866), and Dylan Thomas's "Do Not Go Gentle into That Good Night" (1946). *See also* dirge, elegy, keen.

lampoon   a brief but pointed insult or satiric jab at an object of ridicule or enemy, as in Catullus's bitter two-line attack on Julius Caesar, which concludes, "I don't care whether you are white or black." A malicious, destructive element akin to diatribe, caricature, and political cartoon, lampoon flourished in the eighteenth century, particularly in "An Epistle from Mr. Pope, to Dr. Arbuthnot" (1735), Alexander Pope's lethal attack on a personal enemy.

lauda or **laude** [LAW•dah], pl. laude or laudi traditional rhythmic recitations, songs, or hymns praising the Virgin Mary and the saints and sung at religious and dramatic celebrations. An early Italian genre that preceded the oratorio, the lauda was immensely popular from the thirteenth century until well into the sixteenth. The first and most famous of these praise hymns is the *Canticle of the Sun* of St. Francis d'Assisi, composed around 1225. The work contains the praise of "Brother Sun," "Sister Moon," "Brother Wind," "Sister Water," "Brother Fire," and "Mother Earth."

One of the early masters of the spiritual lauda was the thirteenth-century Franciscan poet and mystic Jacopone da Todi, reputed composer of the Latin lauda "Stabat mater dolorosa," which joins the anonymous "Dies Irae" to form traditional parts of Catholic liturgy. His contemporary, Tuscan poet Guittone d'Arezzo, created sacred ballads along with sonnets and love lyrics. Like Dante, da Todi and d'Arezzo chose vernacular Italian over Latin.

In the fourteenth and fifteenth centuries, lauda evolved into a dialogue form, similar to call-and-response, becoming increasingly elaborate and gaining new popularity until late in the nineteenth century. A parallel hybrid, the secular ballata or song, added vocal ornamentation, syncopation, and romantic emotion, as in the love lyrics of Francesco Landini, a blind Florentine poet of the fourteenth century. Contemporary poet Lucille Clifton reprises the style and tone of the lauda in "Mary's Dream," a segment of *Admonitions* (1980).

lay or **lai**   a romantic, supernatural, or fanciful adventure tale or short narrative poem performed as a song, for example, Marie de France's "The Honeysuckle: Chevrefoil" from *Contes* (ca. 1175), Sir Walter Scott's *The Lay of the Last Minstrel* (1805), and Thomas Babington Macaulay's *Lays of Ancient Rome* (1842), which recount famous episodes from

Livy's first-century *Histories* (14 A.D.), such as "Horatius at the Bridge."

lazzo [LATZ•zoh], pl. lazzi a standardized comic bit, set routine, or predictable exchange, as in "the slow burn *lazzo,*" "the lost hat *lazzo,*" "the wooing *lazzo,*" "the lying witness *lazzo,*" and "the *lazzo* of fear." Like building blocks in a wall, these elements of spontaneous comeback and improvisational theater were valuable tools of acting families. They became prized signature repertory passed from generation to generation like heirlooms.

Lazzi featured the precise word, *bon mot*, or quip, which professional actors stored up in notebooks for insertion into typical scenes. They filled the notebooks of Flaminio Scala, who, in 1611, published 50 of the 700 known *lazzi*. The popularity of this genre invigorated the Italian *commedia dell'arte* and became a key ingredient in comic opera and the stage comedies of Molière and William Shakespeare.

legend an historical or traditional component of folklore that relates the rise and fall of rulers, heroes, and heroines in preliterate times, for instance, Thomas Malory's *Le Morte d'Arthur* (1450), the seventeenth-century Hawaiian story "Cannibals of Halmanu," Irwin Russell's "The First Banjo" (1878), Walter Noble Burns's *The Saga of Billy the Kid* (1926), J. Frank Dobie's *The Ben Lilly Legend* (1950), T. H. White's "The Sword in the Stone" in *The Once and Future King* (1958), Glenn Shirley's *Belle Starr and Her Times: The Literature, the Facts, and the Legends* (1982), and Velma Wallis's *Two Old Women: An Alaska Legend of Betrayal, Courage and Survival* (1993).

In Washington Irving's ghost tale, "The Legend of Sleepy Hollow" (1822), the bony antihero, Ichabod Crane, falls prey to a legend about a headless horse-

man. The author uses the conventions of legend to write "Rip Van Winkle: The Posthumous Writing of Diedrich Knickerbocker" (1819), a fanciful tale laced with the supernatural.

leitmotiv [LYT•moh•teef] a recurring phrase, situation, controlling metaphor, idea, or theme providing unity and coherence in a literary work, as in repeated references to the vein of gold that precedes a family's rise to prominence in Victor Villaseñor's Mexican saga, *Rain of Gold* (1991).

limerick [LIHM•uh•rihk] occasional or light-spirited verse, doggerel, jest, or unsigned barb, usually strung together with jouncing meter and forced or slant rhyme. Limerick follows a five-line pattern that takes a familiar shape on the page:

An apostate whom grudges o'erweighed
Proud clergymen oft did degrade.
But at his demise,
His soul failed to rise,
And sank to stoke coal with a spade.

Verses one, two, and five carry three beats blending anapaestic (‿‿') and iambic (‿') rhythm. Lines three and four drop one of the beats, thus producing a pair of strong beats at a significant, climactic, or humorous moment in the action. The rhyme scheme rarely varies from the standard aabba, as demonstrated by o'erweighed/ degrade/demise/to rise/a spade. Victims of the limerick's wicked, sometimes obscene wit include the clergy, women, the aged or handicapped, homosexuals, royalty, police, and various minority races, nationalities, and religions.

litany [LIHT•uh•nee] a ritualistic prayer, liturgical supplication, series of petitions or invocations, or prolonged list of items chanted or intoned, for example, Grandmother Henderson's stoic early morning prayer in Maya Angelou's autobiography, *I Know Why the Caged Bird Sings* (1970), and Bruce St. John's "Bajan Litany" (1975), a call-and-response poem that reflects religious ecstasy. *See also* call and response, incantation.

litotes [LY•toh•teez] a form of understatement or denial that creates a positive statement by canceling an opposite adjective with a negative, as in "not a little," "not a bad sort of soldier," "no small matter," and "I am not unhappy here." Federico García Lorca stresses change with litotes in "Somnambule Ballad" (1928), which declares, "But I am no more I,/nor is my house now my house." *See* understatement.

liturgy an established ceremony or ritualistic form of worship, as found in anthropologist Joseph Epes Brown's expansion on Black Elk's Sioux lore in *The Sacred Pipe* (1953). The liturgical chant and dithyramb of Greek worship of the god Dionysus was the forerunner of Greek drama. In *The Handmaid's Tale* (1986), author Margaret Atwood satirizes a bastardized liturgy consisting of the reading of the biblical account of Leah's desire for children, which the antagonist reads to sanctify his monthly sexual union with a handmaid. The passage begins, *"Give me children, or else I die. Am I in God's stead, who hath withheld from thee the fruit of the womb? Behold my maid Bilhah. She shall bear upon my knees, that I may also have children by her.* And so on and so forth. We had it read to us every breakfast."

local color the use of geographic, linguistic, and social exotica or detail to establish the authenticity of a realistic narrative, as embodied by the picturesque settings of James Vance Marshall's Australian landscapes in *Walkabout* (1959) and the customs and attitudes of

India and its people in Ruth Prawer Jhabvala's *Heat and Dust* (1975). Examples from North America include John Pendleton Kennedy's *Swallow Barn, or A Sojourn in the Old Dominion* (1832), George Washington Cable's collection of stories, *Old Creole Days* (1879), Mary Hunter Austin's immersion in native American life on the Southwestern desert in *The Basket Woman* (1904), and Marjorie Kinnan Rawlings's *When a Whippoorwill* (1930) and *The Yearling* (1938), which reflects on Florida's harsh landscape and abundant vegetation:

> The peace of the vast aloof scrub had drawn him with the beneficence of its silence. Something in him was raw and tender. The touch of men was hurtful upon it, but the touch of the pines was healing. Making a living came harder there, distances were troublesome in the buying of supplies and the marketing of crops.

low comedy a coarse, raucous drama featuring transparent acts of trickery, posturing, drinking, dirty jokes, mockery, disorder, and fighting that entertain by distracting the audience from more serious matters, as in bawdy scenes from Boccaccio's *Decameron* (1348), Chaucer's *Canterbury Tales* (1385), the Italian *commedia dell'arte*, Miguel de Cervantes's *Don Quixote* (1615), William Shakespeare's *The Merry Wives of Windsor* (ca. 1597), and "The King's Cameleopard," the stage show concocted by the King and Duke in Mark Twain's *The Adventures of Huckleberry Finn* (1886). Twentieth-century versions of low comedy are common to minstrel shows, vaudeville, circus acts, the films of Mack Sennett and Charlie Chaplin, and television sitcoms of the Marx brothers, Red Skelton, and Lucille Ball.

lyricism a style of writing that focuses on intense emotion and stresses flowing, melodic verse such as that found in songs, odes, ballads, psalms, or hymns. Lyricism permeates Sidney Lanier's ode "Song of the Chattahoochee" (1877) and A. B. Paterson's dialect traveler's ballad "Waltzing Matilda" (1895), often called the Australian national anthem. Originally referring only to lines sung to the accompaniment of a lyre, lyricism may also describe prose, for example, the majestic paeans to nature in John Muir's essays on the Sierra Mountain range in *The Mountains of California* (1894), in which he exults:

> How deep our sleep last night in the mountain's heart, beneath the trees and stars, hushed by solemn-sounding waterfalls and many small soothing voices in sweet accord whispering peace!

M

macaronic verse humorous poetry, doggerel, or nonsense rhyme that applies the grammar of one language to the vocabulary of another, for example, the Latinization of modern languages in the *Carmina Burana* (thirteenth century), witty nonsense in Molière's *The Imaginary Invalid* (1673), and the vernacular blend of language in the World War I song "Hinky Dinky Parlez-Voo."

In an ominous scene in *The Name of the Rose* (1980), Umberto Eco places in the effusive rhyming of a witless hunchback a hellish spiel of English doggerel blended with pulpit Latin: "Penitenziagite! Watch out for the drago who cometh in futurum to gnaw your anima! Death is super now! Pray the Santo Pater come to liberar nos a malo and all our sin." Uncertain of the effect, the hunchback winds down uncertainly with "not worth excrement. Amen. No?"

See also doggerel, jingle.

magical realism an innovative free association of whimsy, fantasy, folklore, myth, surrealism, religious ritual, and realistic detail derived from a juxtaposition of ideas from the conscious and subconscious minds. A mid-twentieth-century innovation from Latin America, the style is anticipated in numerous innovative works, including Korean novelist Kim Man-jung's *The Cloud Dream of the Nine* (ca. 1690).

Magical realism was first described in 1949 by Cuban novelist Alejo Carpentier and influenced the fiction of Jorge Luis Borges, Günter Grass, Italo Calvino, Mikhail Bulgakov, Salman Rushdie, Milan Kundera, Bernard Malamud, and Umberto Eco. The energetic style of magical realism invigorates Enchi Fumiko's *Masks* (1958), Gabriel García Márquez's *One Hundred Years of Solitude* (1967), the short stories of Mexican writer Gerardo María, and Isabel Allende's novel *The Infinite Plan* (1991).

makta [MAHK•tah] in Turkish poetry, the concluding couplet in a ghazal, at which point the poet may identify a pen name, state a personal opinion, or demonstrate skill in versification. *See also* ghazal.

malapropism inappropriate use of diction, usually the substitution of a word for a similar term, as in "I deny the allegation and refute the alligator" and "comparisons are odorous [odious]." Examples from literature include Launce's twisted words in William Shakespeare's *Two Gentlemen of Verona* (ca. 1594), the mixups of Mrs. Malaprop in Richard Sheridan's *The Rivals* (1775), the confusion of deceased/diseased and orgies/obsequies in Mark Twain's *The Adventures of Huckleberry Finn* (1886), and the humorous substitution of "Catch Her in the Ride" for J. D. Salinger's title *The Catcher in the Rye* in Amy Tan's *The Kitchen God's Wife* (1992).

maqam [mah•KAM] or **maqama** [mah•KAH•ma], pl. maqamat an Arabic genre derived from the eloquent rhymed dialogue of an assembly of male dignitaries or a seemly address of a humble speaker to his betters. Similar to Greek dialogues, maqamat reached prominence with Abu al-Fadl Ahmad's *Maqamat Al-Hamadhani* (ca. 1005) and Abu Muhammad al-Qasim's *Maqamat al-Hariri* (ca. 1120).

masculine rhyme a pattern of syllabic stress that ends with an accented syllable, particularly an iamb, spondee, or anapest, as in Aphra Behn's jolly love rhyme "The Willing Mistress" (1673), which rhymes round/ground and express/rest to conclude:

> He did but kiss and clasp me round,
> Whilst those his thoughts express:
> And laid me gently on the ground;
> Ah who can guess the rest?

masque a light, imaginative court comedy, tableau, or skit composed to divert the audience through mummery and pantomime, holiday pageantry, music, dancing, costumes, masks, floats, and ingenious backdrops and sets, often composed of intricate moving parts. The text tends toward sober verse drama, sometimes countered by an antimasque or rollicking satire of serious themes and allegory.

Founded in folk festival, the Jacobean masque rose to become the preferred entertainment for aristocracy and royalty, as demonstrated by Ben Jonson's *Masque of Blackness* (1605) and *Masque of Beauty* (1608) and Thomas Campion's *Masque in Honor of the Marriage of Lord Hayes* (1607). During the English Renaissance, actors in tableaus and spectacles frequently included members of the royal court.

Three favorite masques appear in witty plays by William Shakespeare—*Much Ado About Nothing* (ca. 1598), *As You Like It* (ca. 1599), and *The Tempest* (ca. 1610–1611). A mythological masque, Shakespeare's most famous, provides closure at the wedding scene in *A Midsummer Night's Dream* (ca. 1593–1594).

Modern examples include pre-Lenten parades and tableaux at the New Orleans Mardi Gras celebration and seasonal carnivals throughout South America and the Caribbean.

matinee an afternoon theatrical performance. An American innovation, the matinee is less formal than night performances and attracts children's groups, clubs, tourists, and people seeking a daytime diversion. Prices are lower, but the cast is usually the same as in the evening. The first American matinee occurred in 1843 at the Olympic theater in New York City.

maxim [MAK•sihm] a terse, practical aphorism or memorable epigram offering advice, criticism, or a truism about human behavior, for instance, François La Rochefoucauld's *Maximes* (1665), Benjamin Franklin's saliant adages collected in *Poor Richard's Almanack* (1758), and the coinages of Sappho, Miguel de Cervantes, Oscar Wilde, Joel Chandler Harris, and Gertrude Stein. *See also* aphorism, epigram.

melodrama a romantic or sensational plot carried to the extremes of emotion through weeping, consternation, dismay, disillusion, or resignation to circumstance, as in Joaquin Miller's suspenseful *The Danites in the Sierras* (1876), an overreaction to the supposed crimes of Mormon immigrants to the frontier, and John Fowles's revelation of the seduction and abandonment of Sarah, locally known as Tragedy, in *The French Lieutenant's Woman* (1969). In Jane Austen's *Pride and*

Prejudice (1813), the Bennet family reacts excessively to their daughter's elopement with a cad. The family's energies carom from disbelief and embarrassment to welcoming the couple with optimism and wishes for happiness.

Melodramatic elements color other literary genres, for example, the title of Richard Wright's first short story, "The Voodoo of Hell's Half-Acre," which he mentions in *Black Boy* (1945).

memoir   a short recollection of personal observations and experiences composed as autobiography or biography or historical fiction, as in Lady Dabu's *The Poetic Memoirs* (ca. 1190), the epistolary memoir, *A Record of Sorrowful Days* (ca. 1806), by Lady Hong of Hyegyong Palace, Mark Twain's *Life on the Mississippi* (1883), Oliver Otis Howard's *Famous Indian Chiefs I Have Known* (1906), Hsiao Hung's *Market Street* (1935), a fictional account of the Battle of Little Big Horn in Thomas Berger's *Little Big Man* (1964), Anne E. Moody's eyewitness account of pre-integration sit-ins in *Coming of Age in Mississippi* (1968), Jeanne Wakatsuki Houston and James Houston's autobiographical *Farewell to Manzanar* (1973), Gary Soto's "Like Mexicans" (1982), and Alice Kirk Grierson's *The Colonel's Lady on the Western Frontier: The Correspondence of Alice Kirk Grierson* (1989).

metaphor   an implied analogy or comparison of unlike things, such as Hermann Hesse's straightforward description of his hero in *Siddhartha* (1922), a goal-driven seeker who moves toward his aim like the relentless tumble of a stone falling to the bottom of a pool.

In a speech by Wovoka in *The Story of the American Indian* (1934), anthropologist Paul Radin records an impassioned extended metaphor common to native American lore:

You ask me to plow the ground. Shall I take a knife and tear my mother's bosom? Then when I die she will not take me to her bosom to rest. You ask me to dig for stones! Shall I dig under her skin for her bones? Then when I die I cannot enter her body to be born again. You ask me to cut grass and make hay and sell it, and be rich like white men but how dare I cut my mother's hair?

See also image, synesthesia.

meter   the pattern of stressed and unstressed syllables in poetry to form a cadence. The five patterns are iambic (.'), trochaic ('.), dactylic ('..), anapestic (..'), and spondaic ("). The number of metrical feet in a line gives a name to the cadence, as in monometer for one foot, dimeter for two, trimeter for three, and so on through tetrameter, pentameter, hexameter, heptameter, and octameter. Innes Randolph's comic anti–Reconstruction Era ballad, "I'm a Good Old Rebel," summarizes rebel complaints in crisp iambic trimeter:

I hate the Constitution,
    This great republic too;
I hate the freedman's buro,
    In uniforms of blue.
I hate the nasty eagle,
    With all his brags and fuss;
The lyin' thievin' Yankees,
    I hate 'em wuss and wuss.

metonymy   a substitution of a word for another word closely associated with it, as in "over the waves" to mean on the sea, "bowing to the sceptered isle," a reference to Great Britain, the "Big Apple" for New York City, "academe" for the staff of colleges and universities, the "White House" for the American President, the "Kremlin" for the Russian government, the "Stars and Stripes" for the American flag, "the crown" for a king or queen, "Uncle Sam" for the United States government, or the "wearing of the green" for a celebration of St. Patrick's Day.

milieu   a historical or geographic

setting that influences character action or attitudes. Edmond Rostand's romantic drama *Cyrano de Bergerac* (1897) reflects the turmoil that besets Europe as the Spanish defend Arras and precipitates a hasty wartime wedding between Roxane and Christian.

In Scott O'Dell's historical novel *Streams to the River, River to the Sea* (1986), which takes place during the presidency of Thomas Jefferson, Lewis and Clark hire Sacajawea to translate and trade for horses during their party's exploration of the American Northwest. Similarly, in Chaim Potok's *The Chosen* (1967), events reflect the atmosphere and tensions of World War II, particularly those connected with the fall of Nazi Germany, the revelation of the Holocaust, and the United Nations' vote to sanction a Jewish state in Palestine. The inclusion of President Franklin Roosevelt's death dramatizes the love that Americans feel for their leader, who dies before the war's end. *See also* historic milieu.

minstrel show   a traveling variety show offering singing, tap dancing, skits, castanets, tambourine, and comic patter. In the eleventh century, these stage entertainments were popular with Europe's clergy and nobility, who maintained their own troupes; popularity rose among the middle classes by the fourteenth century, when minstrel performances left the estates of aristocrats and migrated to cities. Programming included music, acting, and skits performed by the fool. The term applied only to musicians in the fifteenth century.

Originally conceived as family entertainment in the United States, minstrel shows were the innovation of nineteenth-century vaudeville comedian Thomas D. Rice, creator of the benign dancing caricature known as Jim Crow, introduced November 12, 1833, at the Bowery Theatre in Louisville. His black-face joviality became so popular that he was drafted for the lead role in George L. Aiken's play *Uncle Tom's Cabin* (1852).

Developed by Dan Emmett and E. P. Christy, the minstrel show became the rage between 1850 and 1870. Performers were white men and women who used burnt corks to blacken their faces and hands. They poked fun at black racist stereotypes, particularly the happy darky and the superstitious fieldhand.

The performance divided into two segments: a semicircle with Tambo the tambourine player at one end and "Mr. Bones" the bones player at the other. The interlocutor at the center served as master of ceremonies and joked with the end performers. Common ingredients included straw hats, banjos, and overalls. In the second half, an olio of specialty acts and songs deemphasized wisecracks and patter.

The American Civil War helped to quell the jubilant racism of minstrel shows, but the figure of Jim Crow remained as a symbol of the denigration of blacks. In his autobiography, *Black Boy* (1937), Richard Wright comments on his teen years: "I learned new modes of behavior, new rules in how to live the Jim Crow life."

miracle play   a nonscriptural secular or nonbiblical religious drama from the Middle Ages composed about a saint's life or martyrdom, divine miracles or intervention in human affairs, or supernatural events connected with appearances of the Virgin Mary. Although no miracle plays survive from the period, it is known that they contained allegorical or symbolic characters such as Envy, Pride, Good Deeds, and Charity. After they were banned from the church, miracle plays were performed at street fairs or on portable stages or pageant wagons.

miscellany [MIHS•suh•lay•nee] a medley or chapbook of diverse writings on a broad range of subjects by various authors collected in an anthology, for example, the Chinese chapbook *I Ching* (ninth century B.C.), a collection of folklore, poetry, and prose, Vyasa's Sanskrit genealogies, theogony, tales, songs, and fables in *Puranas* (first century A.D.), and Aulus Gellius's twenty-volume *Attic Nights* (ca. 180 A.D.), a valuable secondary source of lost Greek and Roman literature. In the late Middle Ages, crusaders returning from the eastern Mediterranean supplied tales and oddments for *Gesta Romanorum* [Deeds of the Romans]. Another vivid collection, *Carmina Burana* (thirteenth century), is a miscellany of profane and religious songs, scenarios, and satire. The Renaissance spawned a valuable trove of short pieces—Richard Tottel's miscellany, *Songs and Sonnets* (1557), Richard Edwards's *Paradise of Dainty Devices* (1576), and a ballad compendium, *Handful of Pleasant Delights* (1584). Influential in Shakespeare's day were *The Phoenix Nest* (1593) and *England's Helicon* (1600).

mock epic witty, heroicomical satire or burlesque about a trivial subject but composed in elevated style ruled by classic epic convention. Following the pattern set by Homer's *Iliad* and *Odyssey* (ca. 850 B.C.), Virgil's *Aeneid* (19 B.C.), and other serious works, the mock epic selects a ludicrous hero—usually male—and places him in reduced circumstances, where he attempts to settle a serious argument or counter menace or danger. Additional elements from heroic verse—invocation to a muse, division into cantos, strutting, prophecies, epic simile, a catalog of warriors, or the intervention of the supernatural—enhance the humor when applied to a lowly protagonist, such as *The*

Battle of the Frogs and Mice (eighth century B.C.), the harum-scarum fox and wolf escapades of the anonymous Flemish-French *Ysengrimus* (ca. 1160), and Geoffrey Chaucer's Chaunticleer, the main character and victim of a stalking fox in "The Nun's Priest's Tale" (ca. 1385).

A famous tongue-in-cheek struggle between a wounded beauty and a caddish beau energizes Alexander Pope's *The Rape of the Lock* (1714). The epic struggle takes place over a game of cards, during which the beau snips off a lock of the girl's hair. Pope ennobles the curl with supernatural significance:

> This Lock, the Muse shall consecrate to fame.
> And midst the stars inscribe Belinda's name.

mock-heroic an elevated style that imitates mock epic by creating a serious battle featuring lowly, ludicrous, undignified, or fantastic subjects, as in Thomas Gray's "Ode on the Death of a Favourite Cat" (1748), Lewis Carroll's poem "Jabberwocky" (1872), and Mark Twain's jousting match between Hank Morgan and Sir Sag in *A Connecticut Yankee in King Arthur's Court* (1886), in which Hank describes his use of a Western lariat against medieval weapons:

> *Bzz!* Here he came, like a house afire; I dodged; he passed like a flash, with my horsehair coils settling around his neck; a second or so later, *fst!* his saddle was empty.

A twentieth-century application is Gwendolyn Brooks's "The Anniad," a sendup of the *Iliad*, in *Annie Allen* (1950).

monograph a scholarly treatise or serious report, essay, or article on a limited subject, often economic or scientific, for example, William Owens's "Folklore of Southern Negroes" in *Lippincott's Magazine* (December 1877), an inaccurate article that impelled Joel Chandler Harris to pen a rebuttal, "Negro Folklore: The Story of Mr. Rabbit and Mr. Fox as Told by Uncle Remus" (July 20, 1879), the forerunner of *Uncle Remus: His Songs and His Sayings* (1880). Monographs take a variety of forms and subjects—a journal article on light pollution, a definitive essay on the Gullah dialect, a report on the educational uses of storytelling, or a discussion of hiring practices in a government report. *See also* treatise.

monologue   the extended dramatic speech, prayer, lament, or soliloquy of a single person, with or without an audience, which is the mode of Eudora Welty's *The Ponder Heart* (1954) and Ntozake Shange's postmodern roadway play, *for colored girls who have considered suicide/when the rainbow is enuf* (1976). *See also* dramatic monologue, internal monologue, soliloquy.

montage [mahn•TAHJ]   a narrative collage formed of a series of brief descriptions, glimpses, pictures, impressions, or interior thoughts or memories rushed past the reader in rapid order, usually to establish atmosphere or to create an effect or a sense of the passage of time; for example, John Dos Passos's "Newsreels" in *U. S. A.* (1938), the flurry of actions and images in the mind of a dying woman in Tillie Olsen's *Tell Me a Riddle* (1961), snippets from the media in Don De Lillo's postmodern novel, *White Noise* (1990), and the flight from ghosts in "Jumbie Picnic," a tall tale told by Guyanese storyteller Marc Matthews.

mood   the prevailing atmosphere of a literary work, which may be foreboding, solemn, languorous, joyous, relaxed, expectant, brooding, or intense, or a blend of several moods, as in the sensuous reveries of Sappho (ca. 610–580 B.C.), which

quickly turn to realism, or Elie Wiesel's religious ecstasy, which gives place to terror in his autobiography, *Night* (1960). The author may manipulate mood or ambience to stress humor or irony, as in a mock-serious combat in Lewis Carroll's poem "Jabberwocky" (1872) or a parody of a forbidding gothic mystery in Shirley Jackson's *We Have Always Lived in the Castle* (1948).

moral   a didactic teaching, point, or example or a practical lesson on appropriate conduct, often stated in an abstract aphorism or pragmatic maxim reflecting the value of right over wrong, as found in the concluding line of each of Aesop's fables (ca. 600 B.C.), the conclusion of Pindar's odes (fifth century B.C.), and the Indian classic *Panchatantra* (ca. second century A.D.).

morality play   a dramatic allegory that depicts the struggle between good and evil for the soul of an individual human being. The medieval morality play derived from homilies and other didactic sermon material to reflect everyman's temptation, fall from grace, quest for salvation, and death. Allegorical figures playing alluring vices and temptations often provide comic relief, as in a confrontation between an angel and a demon or the alluring spiel of Satan, as reflected in Christopher Marlowe's *Dr. Faustus* (ca. 1588).

motif [moh•TEEF]   a pattern or predictable arrangement of elements to express an abstract theme in a story, dance, painting, or other artistic work, for instance, flow, currents, eddies, and drifting boats in George Eliot's *The Mill on the Floss* (1860), the search motif in Mark Twain's *The Adventures of Huckleberry Finn* (1884) and in Yoko Kawashima Watkins's autobiographical *So Far from the Bamboo Grove*

(1986), cowboy lore in Zane Grey's *Riders of the Purple Sage* (1912), civil war in Tu Peng-cheng's novel *Defend Yenan* (1954), the journey in Trinidadian playwright Errol John's drama *Moon on a Rainbow Shawl* (1957) and N. Scott Momaday's *House Made of Dawn* (1968), or the pilgrimage motif in John Hersey's revised version of *Hiroshima* (1973), in which the author returns to the people he described in his first study of the bombing of the Japanese city and accounts for the changes in their lives or the causes of their deaths.

A motif orders events and defines characters' behaviors and expectations, such as the struggle for power in George Orwell's personal essay "Shooting an Elephant" (1950) and William Gibson's *The Miracle Worker* (1959), the abrupt appearances and disappearances of the ghost in Toni Morrison's novel *Beloved* (1987), the seer's prediction of the future in Isabel Allende's historical novel, *House of the Spirits* (1982), and the writing and receiving of letters from parted sisters in Alice Walker's novel *The Color Purple* (1982).

A recurrent motif from American literature is captivity, which dominates Mary White Rowlandson's *The Narrative of the Captivity and Restoration of Mrs. Mary White Rowlandson* (1682), R. B. Stratton's *Captivity of the Oatman Girls: Being an Interesting Narrative of Life Among the Apache and Mohave Indians* (1859), Ruthanne Lum McCunn's *Thousand Pieces of Gold* (1981) and *The Indian Captivity of O. M. Spencer* (1995), and in fictional accounts: Caroline Gordon's "The Captive" (1945), Conrad Richter in *The Light in the Forest* (1953), Janice Holt Giles's *Hannah Fowler* (1956), and Scott O'Dell's *Streams to the River, River to the Sea* (1986) and *Sing Down the Moon* (1970).

motivation justification or explanation of character behavior and attitudes or the reasons for choices in a dilemma, for example, the castigation of a wayward son in William Gilmore Simms's *The Yemassee* (1835) and empathy with ritually mutilated women in Alice Walker's *Possessing the Secret of Joy* (1992).

mystery play a medieval drama based on Bible stories from the Old or New Testament, such as the Christmas trope and passion play found in the *Carmina Burana* (thirteenth century), a miscellany of profane and religious songs, scenarios, macaronic verse, and satire. Begun in Europe, mystery plays were originally part of Christian worship, for example, Arnoul Gréban and Simon Gréban's play about the acts of Christ's apostles, performed in Anjou, France, in the mid-fifteenth century. Because English-speaking Church members were alienated from worship and ritual conducted in Latin, they performed tableaus or pantomimes of biblical stories to express important concepts of Bible lore and religious faith, usually in cycles or connected events from a book of the Bible, for instance, the Wakefield "Noah" and the Brome "Abraham and Isaac." Twentieth-century composer Benjamin Britten reprised the medieval genre in *Noye's Fludde* (1958), a musical drama.

mysticism figurative literature that chronicles the individual's search for an understanding of God, absolute truth, or secrets of nature through sense perception, religious ecstasy, transcendent experience, or intuition, as found in the writings of the Arab poet Ibn'l Farid (early thirteenth century A.D.), the Turkish poet Jalal al-Din Rumi's *Divani Shamsi Tabriz* (thirteenth century), the Sufi poet Hafiz's *Divan* (fourteenth century), and Spanish playwright Pedro Calderón de la Barca's poem "Life Is a Dream" (seventeenth century).

The American school of transcendentalists searched for meaning through experience with nature, as described in the essays of Elizabeth Peabody and in Henry David Thoreau's *Walden* (1854). Late-twentieth-century poet James Dickey appealed to ineffable mysteries in his verse, particularly "The Heaven of Animals" (1962) and "May Day Sermon" (1967), in which a father caught up in religious ecstasy prays for God to "pull down the walls of the barn like Dagon's temple/ set the Ark of the Lord in its place/change all things for good, by pain."

myth a form of folklore that accounts for creation of all things, the origin of good and evil, and the salvation of the soul, for example, the traditional Norse myth of Ragnarok from Iceland, the Zapotec story "The Bat," and the urban industrial myth "Joe Magarac, Man of Steel." Style and subject matter vary, as in the nature lore anthologized in King David Kalakaua's *The Legends and Myths of Hawaii* (1888), the frontier myth in James Fenimore Cooper's *The Last of the Mohicans* (1826), Sterling Brown's paean to black heroes in *Southern Road* (1932), Ras the Destroyer in Ralph Ellison's *Invisible Man* (1947), Nicaraguan poet Pablo Antonio Cuadra's poem "The Jaguar Myth" (1961), native American survival lore in N. Scott Momaday's *The Way to Rainy Mountain* (1969), a confrontation with the devil in Derek Walcott's folk play, *Ti-Jean and His Brothers* (1972), and the trickster El-ahrairah and his pal Rabscuttle in Richard Adams's *Watership Down* (1974) and *Tales from Watership Down* (1997).

N

narrative a style that expresses a long, involved plot or story or a series of related events, either true (episode, vignette, travelogue, memoir, autobiography, biography) or fictional (fairy tale, fable, story, epic, legend, novel). The narrative is typically told in chronological order, as Jayadeva's lyric narrative of the gods, *Gitagovinda* (twelfth century A.D.), Farid ud-Din 'Attar's *The Conference of the Birds* (1177), Elyas ebn Yusuf Nezami's *Quintet* (ca. 1200), Nur al-Din 'Abd al-Rahman Jami's *The Seven Thrones* (ca. 1490), William Gilmore Simms's "The Swamp Fox" (1832), Henry Wordsworth Longfellow's verse romance, *Evangeline, a Tale of Arcadie* (1847), John Greenleaf Whittier's two-person verse drama, "Barbara Frietchie" (1864), and Wole Soyinka's drama *A Play of Giants* (1984).

narrator the voice that relates a story; for instance, the title character in Mark Twain's *The Adventures of Huckleberry Finn* (1884), a semi-literate youngster who salts the narrative with fact mingled with tall tales as he repeats river lore:

> They talked about how Ohio water didn't like to mix with Mississippi water. Ed said if you take the Mississippi on a rise when the Ohio is low, you'll find a wide band of clear water all the way down the east side of the Mississippi for a hundred miles or more, and the minute you get out a quarter of a mile from shore and pass the line, it is all thick and yaller the rest of the way across.

See also point of view.

naturalism a philosophy of scientific or biological inquiry that views humankind as members of the animal kingdom influenced by heredity and environment but not by supernatural forces or deities. Fiction's evolution from realism moves the naturalistic author closer to mechanistic or socioeconomic determinism, a detached picture of life as though it were viewed through a microscope. This amoral study of human behavior stresses the absence of free will in human choices, a theme found in Stephen Crane's *Maggie, a Girl of the Streets* (1893), Thomas Hardy's *Jude the Obscure* (1895), Frank Norris's *McTeague* (1899), Jack London's *The Call of the Wild* (1902), James T. Farrell's *Studs Lonigan* (1934), and Richard Wright's *Native Son* (1940).

neologism [nee•AH•luh•jihzm] a newly coined word or term that has recently joined the language, for example, noble savage from the seventeenth century; namby-pamby from the eighteenth century, milquetoast, melting pot, humbug, and mugwump from the mid-nineteenth century, G. I., roger, babbitt, and A-OK from the mid-twentieth century, and website, yuppie, condo, hatchback sedan, gen-x, and in-line skates from the late twentieth century.

Resulting from population growth, social or economic development, or recent technology or weaponry, the neologism expresses new needs or names a current process or product. Unlike slang, neologisms become a part of standard English, for instance, the addition of cell phone, e-mail, on-line, and fax to acceptable business and communications terminology. Critic H. L. Mencken created "Homo boobiensis" and "booboisie" as a comic put-down of fools.

Authors of science fiction or futuristic literature often coin terms, for example, sexaphone, Podsnap's Technique, Orgy-Porgy, feelies, soma, violent passion surrogate, and Super-Vox-Wurlitzeriana from Aldous Huxley's *Brave New World* (1939).

new criticism literary analysis, often referred to as formalism. New criticism developed in Britain, France, and the United States after World War I. The focus of this new method of analysis was the work of literature itself, without con-sideration of historical milieu or biographical elements of the author's life. New criticism emphasizes words, emotions, and ideas within the text. In the United States, noted proponents of the movement include Allen Tate, Cleanth Brooks, Robert Penn Warren, and John Crowe Ransom, author of *The New Criticism* (1941). In England, the most notable figure was critic I. A. Richards, author of *The Principles of Literary Criticism* (1924). The French parallel to new criticism is known as *explication de texte*, an explanation of the text itself. *See also* criticism.

no or noh a spare form of Japanese drama that adheres to strict dramatic convention, blending costumes and masks, singing, music, dance, and poetic dialogue. No, which dates to the fourteenth century and derives from mime and dance, reflects the influence of Buddhist and Shinto philosophy. The characters, played by troupes of male actors and a chorus, reflect an allegorical focus or universal emotion, such as yearning or revenge, which is revealed through subtle gesture, dance, chant, or dialogue.

The high point of Japan's enduring no theater came in the early fifteenth century with the publication of technical manuals and 200 plays of Seami Motokiyo, author of *The Deserted Crone, The Damask Drum, The Dwarf Trees,* and *Atsumori,* a plot adapted from the thirteenth-century Japanese epic *The Tale of the Heike.* Modern adaptations continue to probe psychological meanings and apply them to current quandaries, for example, Yukio Mishima's updated version of *The Damask Drum* (1953).

nom de plume [NOHN•duh PLOOM] a pen name, pseudonym, or assumed identity, for example, Hilda Doolittle's choice of H. D., Mary Ann Evans's pseudonym George Eliot, William Sydney Porter's prison designation of O. Henry, Leroy Jones's choice of Amiri Baraka, and Hector Hugh Munro's professional use of Saki, the Japanese god of wine. Some assumed identities are temporary, for example, Joel Chandler Harris's Tellmenow Isitsoornot, which he used during the early years of his career in journalism, and Samuel Clemens's choices of Epaminondas Adrastus Perkins, Josh, and Thomas Jefferson Snodgrass before his permanent selection of Mark Twain, a term indicating a safe depth for shallow-draft sternwheelers on the Mississippi River. Science fiction author Ray Bradbury has also written under the family names Douglas Spaulding and Leonard Spaulding; essayist Isak Dinesen concealed her real name, Karen Blixen. Historical fiction writer Norah Lofts has changed names with Juliet Astley and name and gender with Peter Curtis.

nonfiction   a body of literature comprised of factual writing, including apologia, biography, autobiography, memoir, article, treatise, monograph, essay, pamphlet, tract, diary and journal, and journalistic reportage, for example:
• personal poem: the lyrics to John Newton's "Amazing Grace," one of his *Olney Hymns* (1779), which expresses his reclamation from slaver to devout evangelist
• almanac and dictionary: Samuel Johnsons's *Dictionary of the English Language* (1755) and Martha Daniell Logan's *The Gardners Kalender* (1772)
• anecdote: Bruce Chatwin's "Butch Cassidy" in *In Patagonia* (1977)
• autobiography: *The Book of Margery Kempe* (1433), Gustavus Vassa's *The Interesting Narrative of the Life of Olaudah Equiano, or Gustavus Vassa, the African* (1790), and Rigoberto Menchu's *I, Rigoberto* (1985)

• character study: Harry Mark Petrakis's *Stelmark* (1970)
• definitive essay: Joan Didion's essay on hippie culture in *Slouching Toward Bethlehem* (1968) and her character analysis of Georgia O'Keeffe in *The White Album* (1979)
• expository essay: Mari Sandoz's "The Sioux Woman" (1961)
• family history: Le Ly Hayslip's "When Heaven and Earth Changed Places," a reflective piece on her family's sufferings during the Vietnam War
• history: Venerable Bede's *Ecclesiastical History of the English People* (seventh century) and Elizabeth Cady Stanton and Susan B. Anthony's *A History of Women's Suffrage* (1900)
• investigative research: Margaret Mead's *Coming of Age in Samoa* (1928) and Rachel Carson's *Silent Spring* (1961)
• letters: Pierre Abélard's "Letters of Héloise and Abélard" (1616) and the exchange between Abigail Adams and John Adams in the spring of 1776
• oratory: Powhatan's "Algonquian Confederacy Speech" (1609), political speechwriter Peggy Noonan's "The *Challenger* Disaster" (1986), and Elie Wiesel's Nobel acceptance speech (1986)
• personal essay: Pliny the Younger's "The Eruption of Vesuvius" (114 A.D.) and Bette Bao Lord's *Eighth Moon* (1964)
• polemics: Thomas Paine's tract *The Crisis* (1776) and Gloria Steinem's articles and editorials for *Ms.* magazine
• prison memoir: Corrie ten Boom's *The Hiding Place* (1971) and Nelson Mandela's *The Long Walk to Freedom* (1995)
• protest: Sarah Grimké's *Letters on the Equality of the Sexes and the Condition of Women* (1838) and Ida Bell Wells-Barnett's protest article *Southern Horrors: Lynch Law in All Its Phases* (1892). James Baldwin's "Everybody's Protest Novel" (1949) is a serious rejection of the white-authored

Uncle Tom's Cabin. In contrast, he cites Richard Wright's *Native Son* as an authentic, sharp-edged protest against white America's denigration of blacks

• tabloid: the journalistic articles in Dorothy Day's *The Catholic Worker*, a liberal religious journal that has remained in publication since May 1, 1933

• treatise or learned discourse on a single subject: Ibn Khaldun's *Muqaddimah* (1377), an introduction to history, and Nicolo Machiavelli's *The Prince* (1517), a Renaissance overview of the enlightened art of ruling

• vignette: Anne Newport Royall's *Sketches of History: Life and Manners in the United States* (1826) and Varina Davis's magazine article "Christmas in the Confederate White House" (1896).

The six essentials of nonfiction include who, what, where, when, why, and how. In contrast to the imaginative elements of fiction, nonfiction stresses these clear, accurate details in describing an era, event, individual life, or situation, as demonstrated by Esther Hautzig's *The Endless Steppe* (1968), Dee Brown's *Bury My Heart at Wounded Knee* (1970), Yoko Kawashima Watkins's *So Far from the Bamboo Grove* (1986), John G. Neihardt's *Black Elk Speaks* (1932), and Zlata Filipovic's *Zlata's Diary* (1994). Truman Capote extended the application of nonfiction details to a journalistic novel, *In Cold Blood* (1966), an intense study of the murder of a Kansas farm family. Thomas Keneally applied the same method of fictional development of facts in *Schindler's List* (1982).

nonsense verse   light verse or occasional verse, such as extempo, jingle, macaronic verse, and doggerel. It sacrifices sense in its search for the right sound and rhythm, often from neologisms and made-up grammatical forms, a

favorite method of John Skelton, W. A. Spooner, Lewis Carroll, Edward Lear, G. K. Chesterton, W. S. Gilbert, Guillaume Apollinaire, Ogden Nash, e. e. cummings, and Paul Muldoon. Late twentieth-century developments in nonsense include Allan Kaprow's event poems or happenings, Roger McGough's concrete poems, John Ashbery's pantoums, and found poems.

novel   an extended work of prose fiction that is carefully controlled and features a varied cast of characters, clearly defined setting, an historical or social milieu, sustained action, a complicated plot, and usually one or more subplots, as found in Mori Ogai's ironic confessional novel *Vita Sexualis* (1909) and Ann Petry's historical fiction *Tituba of Salem Village* (1964), a reprise of the Salem witch trials. The novel is an offshoot of narrative verse such as *Sir Gawain and the Green Knight* (ca. 1350), tales like *The Thousand and One Nights* or *The Arabian Nights* (ca. 1000) and Giovanni Boccaccio's *Decameron* (ca. 1350), and the chivalric and prose romance, including Thomas Malory's *Le Morte d'Arthur* (1485), *Amadis of Gaul* (1508), and Philip Sidney's *Arcadia* (1590). The most flexible of long narrative works, the novel varies over a wide range of modes: comic, tragic, historic, lyric, romantic, episodic, melodramatic, sentimental, satiric, allegorical, fantasy, science fiction, utopian, dystopian.

The novel often parallels or echoes reality, as is the case with Robert Penn Warren's political novel, *All the King's Men* (1946), a study of the dynamic populism of Willie Stark, a fictional character resembling Huey P. "Kingfish" Long. Similar blurring of the separation between fiction and nonfiction occurs in Alex Haley's genealogical novels, *Roots: The Saga of an American Family* (1976) and

Queen (1993), and Truman Capote's *In Cold Blood* (1965), the first journalistic novel.

Subsets of the category include numerous applications, adaptations, and extensions of the basic concept of novel:

• the adventure novel, notably Daniel Defoe's *Robinson Crusoe* (1719), Alexandre Dumas Père's *The Count of Monte Cristo* (1845), and Robert Louis Stevenson's *Kidnapped* (1886)

• the anti-novel or new wave novel, also called the *nouveau vague* or *nouveau roman*, a studied, avant-garde art novel that deliberately violates traditional structure, as found in Nathalie Sarraute's *Tropismes* (1939), Maurice Blanchot's *Aminadab* (1942), Alain Robbe-Grillet's *La jalousie* (1957), and Julio Cortázar's *Hopscotch* (1963)

• the autobiographical novel, a thin facade over personal experience, as in George Sand's *Un hiver à Majorique* (1841), James Joyce's *A Portrait of the Artist as a Young Man* (1915), and F. Scott Fitzgerald's *Tender Is the Night* (1934)

• the *bildungsroman*, also called the apprenticeship or formative novel, often heavily autobiographical fiction that details the development of character, career, or education, including Charlotte Smith's *The Old Manor House* (1793), Samuel Butler's *The Way of All Flesh* (1903), Somerset Maugham's *Of Human Bondage* (1915), Thomas Mann's *Buddenbrooks* (1901), and Thomas Wolfe's *Look Homeward, Angel* (1929)

• the coming-of-age motif, for example, John Steinbeck's novella, *The Red Pony* (1938), and J. D. Salinger's *The Catcher in the Rye* (1951), a psychological study of a depressed teenager

• the character novel, exemplified by Daniel Defoe's *Moll Flanders* (1722), Samuel Richardson's *Clarissa Harlowe* (1748), Leo Tolstoy's *Anna Karenina*

(1876), Andre Gide's *La Symphonie pastorale* (1919), F. Scott Fitzgerald's *The Great Gatsby* (1925), Willa Cather's *Death Comes for the Archbishop* (1927), Nikos Kazantzakis's *Zorba, the Greek* (1946), Kawabata Yasunari's *Snow Country* (1948), and Colleen McCullough's *Caesar* (1997)

• detective fiction and spy thrillers, for example, Umberto Eco's *The Name of the Rose* (1981); also, the writings of Wilkie Collins, Patricia Cornwell, John Le Carré, Raymond Chandler, Agatha Christie, and Dashiell Hammett

• the domestic or family-centered novel, for instance, William Gilmore Simms's *The Yemassee: A Romance of Carolina* (1835), the first American work to treat native Americans as real characters, William Saroyan's *The Human Comedy* (1943), and Jessamyn West's *The Friendly Persuasion* (1945)

• the exposé or propaganda novel, a more pointed form of protest novel featuring some elements of the *roman à clef,* for example, Robert Graves's *I, Claudius* (1934), John Steinbeck's *The Grapes of Wrath* (1939), Alan Paton's *Cry, the Beloved Country* (1948), Pat Conroy's *The Water Is Wide* (1972), a novel revealing the substandard education foisted on outer islanders in South Carolina, and Barbara Kingsolver's anti-pollution *Animal Dreams* (1990)

• the gothic novel—Horace Walpole's *Castle of Otranto* (1765), Clara Reeve's *The Old English Baron* (1778), Anne Radcliffe's *Mysteries of Udolpho* (1794), Charles Brockden Brown's *Wieland* (1798), and Joyce Carol Oates's *A Garden of Earthly Delights* (1967)

• the grotesque novel, particularly Flannery O'Connor's *Wise Blood* (1952) and *The Violent Bear It Away* (1960)

• the historical or chronicle novel, an immersion in historical events, for example, the Chinese colloquial novels,

Shuihu Zhuan (fourteenth century) and *Sanguo zhi yanyi* (ca. 1375), Aphra Behn's *Oroonoko* (1688), Charles Dickens's *A Tale of Two Cities* (1859), Kamala Markandaya's *The Honeycomb* (1977), Michael Ondaatje's *The English Patient* (1992), and Diana Norman's *The Vizard Mask* (1995)

• the *kunstlerroman* or maturing artist narrative, particularly Marcel Proust's *Remembrance of Things Past* (1931) and Sylvia Plath's tormented self-evaluation, *The Bell Jar* (1963)

• the magic realism, a blend of reality with myth, ritual, and the supernatural, as found in Gabriel García Márquez's *One Hundred Years of Solitude* (1967), Salman Rushdie's *Midnight's Children* (1981), and Isabel Allende's *House of the Spirits* (1982) and *The Infinite Plan* (1991)

• metafiction, which includes digressive novels that philosophize about novelists, style, and fiction-writing; e.g. Laurence Sterne's *Tristram Shandy* (1767), Doris Lessing's *The Golden Notebook* (1962), and John Fowles's *The French Lieutenant's Woman* (1969)

• the mock epic, a rollicking parody of heroic lore, which is the defining mode of François Rabelais's *Pantagruel* (1532) and Henry Fielding's episodic *Tom Jones* (1749)

• the modern or experimental novel, an innovative departure from nineteenth-century style, particularly James Joyce's *Finnegans Wake* (1939), Virginia Woolf's *Orlando* (1928), and William Faulkner's *As I Lay Dying* (1930)

• the moral novel, related to novels of character, which aim to improve or uplift the human spirit, notably John Bunyan's *Pilgrim's Progress* (1684), Alexandre Dumas Père's *The Count of Monte Cristo* (1845), Pole Sienkiewicz's religious classic, *Quo Vadis* (1896), E. M. Forster's *Howard's End* (1910), Thornton Wilder's *The Bridge of San Luis Rey* (1927), Gra-

ham Greene's *The Power and the Glory* (1940), Albert Camus's *The Plague* (1947), and Kazuo Ishiguro's *The Remains of the Day* (1989)

• the novel of character, which stresses the development of human qualities, particularly Murasaki Shikibu's *Genji* (ca. 1000), Samuel Richardson's epistolary *Pamela: or, Virtue Rewarded* (1740), Chinua Achebe's *Things Fall Apart* (1958), Ruth Prawer Jhabvala's *Heat and Dust* (1975), and the works of Jane Austen, Gustave Flaubert, and Albert Camus

• the novel of manners, a fictional work that typifies the lifestyle, customs, and values of a social class, as in Fanny Burney's *Evelina* (1778), Jane Austen's *Pride and Prejudice* (1813), Henry James's *The Bostonians* (1886), Edith Wharton's *Age of Innocence* (1920), V. S. Naipaul's *The Mystic Masseur* (1957), and Gabriel García Márquez's *Love in the Time of Cholera* (1985)

• the novel of sensibility or sentimental novel, a study of character emotions, which is the focus of Samuel Goldsmith's *The Vicar of Wakefield* (1766) and Virginia Woolf's *To the Lighthouse* (1927)

• the philosophical novel, a work of fiction that draws themes from systems of thought or wisdom derived from a thinker, theologian, or historical movement. Hermann Hesse's *Siddhartha* (1922), which derives action and charaction from Buddhism in India in the sixth century B.C., expresses the earthly need for salvation, which Buddha supplies. The characters speak aphorisms akin to scripture

• the protest novel, an exposé of social or governmental impropriety, as in E. D. E. N. Southworth's *India* (1853) and George Washington Cable's protest of racism, *The Grandissimes* (1880)

• the psychological novel, an extreme form of the character novel that focuses on the mental landscape, as in Fyodor Dostoevsky's *Crime and Punishment* (1866), Joseph Conrad's *Heart of Darkness* (1902), Theodore Dreiser's *An American Tragedy* (1925), D. H. Lawrence's *The Plumed Serpent* (1926), Tanizaki Jun'ichiro's *Some Prefer Nettles* (1929), Erich Maria Remarque's *All Quiet on the Western Front* (1929), and Mishima Yukio's *The Temple of the Golden Pavilion* (1956)

• the realistic novel, an examination of real-life or problem situations, often urban in setting and origin, as displayed by Jack London's *The Iron Heel* (1907), Katherine Anne Porter's *Flowering Judas* (1930), Sholem Asch's *Three Cities* (1933), Herman Wouk's *The Caine Mutiny* (1951), Henry Roth's *Call It Sleep* (1934), and Wole Soyinka's *The Interpreters* (1965)

• the regional novel, for example, Maria Edgeworth's *Castle Rackrent* (1800), Elizabeth Gaskell's *Mary Barton* (1848), George Eliot's *Middlemarch* (1872), Thomas Hardy's *The Return of the Native* (1878), Sarah Orne Jewett's *The Country of the Pointed Firs* (1896), Ellen Glasgow's perusal of rural Virginia in *Vein of Iron* (1935), R. K. Narayan's *Swami and Friends* (1935), William Faulkner's reflection on frontier Mississippi, *Absalom, Absalom* (1936), Naguib Mahfuz's images of Cairo in *Bayn al Qasrayn* (1956), and Anita Desai's study of twentieth-century India, *Fire on the Mountain* (1977)

• the romance novel, for example, the Japanese classic, *Sumiyoshi Monogatari* (ca. 1200), Walter Scott's *The Heart of Midlothian* (1818), and Nathaniel Hawthorne's *The House of the Seven Gables* (1851)

• the rural novel, agrarian fiction depicting the struggle to earn a living from the land, the focus of Willa Cather's *O Pioneers!* (1913) and Pearl Buck's *The Good Earth* (1931)

• the saga, an extended study of a genealogy or dynasty sometimes expanding with epic sweep to a study of an entire generation or era, as found in Nikolai Tolstoy's *War and Peace* (1869), O. E. Rölvaag's fatalistic trilogy, *Giants in the Earth* (1927), *Peder Victorious* (1929), and *Their Fathers' God* (1931), and Boris Pasternak's *Dr. Zhivago* (1957)

• the satirical novel; for example Henry Fielding's *Joseph Andrews* (1742), Wu Ching-tzu's *The Scholars* (ca. 1750), Pierre Laclos's *Dangerous Liaisons* (1782), Max Beerbohm's *Zuleika Dobson* (1911), Evelyn Waugh's *The Loved One* (1948), Günter Grass's *The Tin Drum* (1959), and John Gardner's witty beast tale, *Grendel* (1971)

• science fiction or futuristic novel, which often questions the mechanization of society, particularly the works of Aldous Huxley, Ayn Rand, Ray Bradbury, Margaret Atwood, H. G. Wells, George Orwell, and Marge Piercy

• sociological novel or *roman à thèse*, reform literature that has much in common with the protest novel. The genre uses character and action to delineate a social problem, such as oppression, economic exploitation, racial discrimination, patriarchy, or unemployment. Notable examples include Harriet Beecher Stowe's *Uncle Tom's Cabin* (1852), Charles Dickens's *Hard Times* (1854), John Esten Cooke's *The Virginia Comedians* (1859), Mark Twain's *A Connecticut Yankee in King Arthur's Court* (1886), Upton Sinclair's *The Jungle* (1906), John Steinbeck's *The Grapes of Wrath* (1939), Sylvia Lopez-Medina's *Cantora* (1992), and N. Scott Momaday's *The Way to Rainy Mountain* (1969)

• the Western novel, exemplified by Jack Schaefer's *Shane* (1949), Louis L'Amour's *Hondo* (1953), and Larry McMurtry's *The Streets of Laredo* (1993). Note that some works fit under multiple headings: *Shane* is both Western and coming-of-age; *The Catcher in the Rye* contains elements of coming-of-age and psychological novel along with picaresque narration.

See also bildungsroman, epistolary novel, gothic novel, historical fiction, *kunstlerroman,* magical realism, novella, picaresque, psychological novel, *roman à clef,* saga, science fiction.

novella (or short novel) a shortened form of fictional development lying between novel and short story, ranging from 30,000 to 50,000 words, as demonstrated by Mark Twain's didactic morality novella, *The Mysterious Stranger* (1916), James Hilton's *Good-bye Mr. Chips* (1934), and Ernest Hemingway's *The Old Man and the Sea* (1952). The novella covers a single event, for example, a failed romance in Edith Wharton's *Ethan Frome* (1911) and the thwarted ambitions of two drifters in John Steinbeck's *Of Mice and Men* (1937).

occasional verse poetry written to celebrate and commemorate any important event, often written by a poet laureate, such as Alfred, Lord Tennyson's "The Charge of the Light Brigade" (1854), which honors a fierce battle of the colonial wars in India. The African-American writer Maya Angelou composed and read "On the Pulse of Morning" to commemorate the first inauguration of President Bill Clinton on January 21, 1993. A famous occasional poem by Dorothy Parker illustrates the forced patterning of end rhymes to link two witty couplets parodying a child's rhyme:

> Higgledy Piggledy, my white hen,
> She lays eggs for gentlemen.

> You cannot persuade her with gun or lar-
> iat
> To come across for the proletariat.

The unlikely pairing of gun or lariat/proletariat is the trademark of Parker's flamboyant verse style.

octave a poem, stanza, or set of eight lines of verse, also called an octet, a prominent form in Thomas Hood's nostalgic four-octave poem "I Remember, I Remember." A favorite with young readers, the second octave recalls:

> I remember, I remember,
>   The roses, red and white;
> The violets and the lily-cups,
>   Those flowers made of light!
> The lilacs where the robin built,
>   And where my brother set
> The laburnum on his birthday,—
>   The tree is living yet!

Adaptable to varied moods and purposes, the octave dominates the eighth-century Chinese poet Han-Shan's *Cold Mountain* and the triolets of W. E. Henley, Arthur Rimbaud, and Stéphane Mallarmé, and Dorothy Parker's satiric poem "Ultimatum."

The octave was popular with European troubadours and became the standard form of the thirteenth-century *ottava rima*, popular with Italian poets of the chivalric or epic mode. The term names the first half of a Petrarchan sonnet, which usually rhymes abbaabba. The sonnet's octave introduces a problem or situation in the span of the first eight lines and concludes in the final six lines or sestet. *See also* ballade.

ode a complex, grandly ceremonial verse form of considerable length once limited to intense, elegant lyric poems and paeans focusing on a single subject and grave or stately theme, the style of Persian poet Hafiz's *The Divan* (fourteenth century) and Korea's master odist, Yun Sondo, author of *The Angler's Calendar* (1651).

In its long history, the ode has adapted to more subjects and modes of expression. For example, Edgar Allan Poe uses ode form for "To Helen" (1831), a paean to ideal womanhood in which he elevates his subject with lofty images:

> Lo! in yon brilliant window-niche
> How statue-like I see thee stand,
> The agate lamp within thy hand!
> Ah, Psyche, from the regions which
> Are Holy Land!

Derived in the Western tradition from the choral songs of drama, the ode was advanced by the Greek poets Sappho, Alcaeus, Anacreon, Bacchylides, Alcman, and Pindar and followed the pattern of introduction, invocation, event or story, and moral envoi or conclusion. Odes remained a favorite of the Roman poet Horace (first century B.C.), who altered the direction from public ritual to personal events. Likewise, the ode was the preferred style of Arab poet Imr-ul-kais, author of *Moallakat* (545 A.D.), and Catullus for his marriage hymn, as well as Dante Alighieri, Edmund Spenser, Michael Drayton, Abraham Cowley, Andrew Marvell, Lady Anne Finch Winchilsea, Alexander Pope, John Dryden, Pierre Ronsard, Paul Valéry, Paul Verlaine, Victor Hugo, and Friedrich Schiller, whose "Ode to Joy," sung to Beethoven's music, buoys the spirits of women prisoners in Isabel Allende's *House of the Spirits*.

In the romantic era, the ode returned to popularity with forerunners William Cowper, William Collins, Walter Savage Landor, and Thomas Gray. The stylish verse serves Samuel Taylor Coleridge's "Dejection, an Ode" (1802), William Wordsworth's "Intimations of Immortality" (1804), John Keats's "Ode on a Grecian Urn" (1819) and "Ode to a Nightingale" (1819), and Percy Bysshe Shelley's

"Ode to the West Wind" (1819) and "To a Skylark" (1820), all of which comprise some of English poetry's most anthologized works. The tradition continued with Alfred, Lord Tennyson's "Ode on the Death of the Duke of Wellington" (1854) and Francis Thompson's "Ode to the Setting Sun" (1897); Walt Whitman adapted the ode for "Song of Myself" (1855), a free-form lyric celebrating self.

In the twentieth century, the ode surfaced in Allen Tate's "Ode to the Confederate Dead" (1977), W. H. Auden's elegaic odes, "In Memory of W. B. Yeats" (1939) and "In Memory of Sigmund Freud" (1939), Wallace Stevens's "The Idea of Order at Key West" (1954), Allen Ginsberg's "Kaddish" (1961), Frank O'Hara's *Odes* (1960), and John Berryman's *Dream Songs* (1964).

The ode form departs from dignified tone and subject in Pablo Neruda's "Ode to My Socks" and "Ode to a Watermelon," a witty mock-serious application of sedate poetry to mundane objects.

See also paean, qasida.

onomatopoeia or **echoism** [ah•noh•mah•toh•PEE•yuh] a mimetic word or word cluster that imitates the sound it represents, as with the verbs moan, pop, whisper, slash, growl, slither, dong, whirr, sizzle, gurgle, swish, splutter, hiss, crack, thump, hum, snort, plunk, and ping pong. Some adjectives imply by the physical act of pronouncing them some quality or inference about the noun modified, as ghoulish, sly, egregious, cocky, floundering, and dastardly. An example from Elizabeth Barrett Browning's *Aurora Leigh* (1857) demonstrates onomatopoetic language:

> I felt a mother-want about the world,
> And still went seeking, like a bleating
> lamb.

Often an obvious adjunct to vigorous children's rhyme or comic verse, onomatopoeia is also an evocative addition to the imagery and sense impressions of love poems, hymns, drama, and prose, as in the tense moment in the final battle scene from Orson Scott Card's science fiction classic *Ender's Game* (1977), when the hero asks himself, "What will I do then, shout Bang, you're dead?"

See also assonance, consonance.

oral history   storytelling or reflection, a frequent vehicle of oppressed people, especially women, children, and noncombatants, who express loss of freedom as a result of war, capture, or patriarchal enslavement. Oral history takes two forms:

• personal narrative, articles, letters, or journals that preserve and transmit meaningful experience

• oral recitation of eye-witness accounts of historical events that clarify gaps, dispel misconceptions, and correct false information.

An example from American fiction is the voice of Winnie, the protagonist of Amy Tan's *The Kitchen God's Wife* (1991), the controlling vision that fills in historical detail of China during World War II from numerous points of view: pilots battling a superior enemy air force, wives left to fend for themselves, refugees relying on shreds of rumor as a guide, and noncombatants who must choose an allegiance in chancy times.

In fiction and nonfiction, oral history is often a therapeutic act that exonerates or frees the speaker from despair, guilt, regret, mourning, or sorrow connected with a sweeping historical change, especially those alterations that occur during civil upheaval, for example, Elie Wiesel's childhood memory of the Holocaust in *Night* (1960), interviews with the forthright Miss Jane, a participant in the Louisiana civil rights movement and title character in Ernest Gaines's fictional *The Autobiography of Miss Jane Pittman* (1971), the dry humor of Jack Crabb, the binational child-turned-picaro, who tells of participating in the Battle of Little Big Horn in Thomas Berger's *Little Big Man* (1964), scenes of flight, hunger, and living by wits in Yoko Kawashima Watkins's *So Far from the Bamboo Grove* (1984), an autobiographical odyssey over war-torn Korea and Japan during World War II, and recounted personal experience in Donna Cross's fictional *Pope Joan* (1996), an historical novel detailing the strife of the Dark Ages and depredations of the Catholic church on superstitious believers.

oral tradition (or oral transmission)   the heritage of storytelling that encompasses folklore, fairy tale, myth, legend, ghost lore, war story, ballad, and fable. In general, oral stock is derived from preliterate societies and is often accompanied by strums of a lute, guitar, or sitar, rhythms of maracas or drums, and clapping or snapping fingers. It may be chanted or performed solo and stresses formulaic epithets, refrains, acoustic echo, or call-and-response mode, for example, native American coyote stories and war chants, African beast fable and genealogy, slave era High John the Conqueror legends and spirituals, and Caribbean Anansi the Spider lore.

Most oral lore is anonymous and generations or even centuries old by the time it is polished, formalized on paper, and its music recorded on staffs, as is the case with Homer's *Iliad* (eighth century B.C.), the Anglo-Saxon heroic poem *Beowulf*, the Spanish *Song of El Cid*, Scottish ballads, pre-Islamic verse, the Zulu epic, *Shaka* (late eighteenth century), and Latvian *dainas*.

Twentieth-century updates of oral transmission include numerous forms of the Appalachian ballad, "Barbara Allen," Albert B. Lord's collection, *Serbocroatian Heroic Songs* (1954), and Toni Cade Bambara's circular narrative, *The Salt Eaters* (1970). The African-American writer Zora Neale Houston was an enthusiastic collector of oral black folklore, as was the nineteenth-century journalist Joel Chandler Harris. *See also* griot.

oratory　　an original speech delivered formally and seriously to honor an occasion, celebrate a holiday or mark a religious ritual, persuade, refute false notions, or inform an audience, for example, William Faulkner's Nobel Prize acceptance speech delivered in Stockholm on December 10, 1950, honoring "the poet's voice."

One of America's noted nineteenth-century orators, Frederick Douglass, challenged audiences with "What the Black Man Wants" (1864), in which he encourages Americans to award full citizenship to former slaves:

> Slavery is not abolished until the black man has the ballot. While the Legislatures of the South retain the right to pass laws making any discrimination between black and white, slavery still lives there…. While a black man can be turned out of a car in Massachusetts, Massachusetts is a slave state. While a slave can be taken from old Massachusetts, Massachusetts is a slave state.

The following year, Robert E. Lee delivered his brief oration known as "Lee's Farewell Address to His Soldiers" (1865), which stressed to defeated Confederate troops "the satisfaction that proceeds from the consciousness of duty faithfully performed." Near the conclusion of the Indian Wars, Chief Joseph of the Nez Perce delivered extemporaneously a speech now anthologized as "I Will Fight No More Forever," marking his tribe's capitulation to U.S. troops in 1877.

Oratory may be a functioning part of the plot in fiction or drama, for example, Mark Antony's funeral oration in William Shakespeare's *Julius Caesar* (ca. 1599). Polished oration is frequently incorporated with nonfiction, as with Onondagan chief Hiawatha's speech to the Iroquois League, reported in ethnologist Henry Rowe Schoolcraft's *Historical and Statistical Information Respecting the History, Condition and Prospects of the Indian Tribes of the United States* (1857). Other noteworthy oratory can be found in the works of North American explorers and military and religious leaders, the histories of Francis Parkman, and a speech by Geronimo in *The Life of Tom Horn* (1904).

Female crusaders have added to the male-dominated genre, particularly Sarah Winnemucca, Elizabeth Cady Stanton, Carry Nation, Sojourner Truth, Emma Goldman, Susan B. Anthony, Wilma Mankiller, Shirley Chisholm, and Gloria Steinem. One of the memorable voices of the late twentieth century, Congresswoman Barbara Jordan expressed patriotic fervor with "Who Then Will Speak for the Common Good?" (1976).

ottava rima　[oh•TAH•vuh REE•muh]　an octave or octet formed of iambic meter rhyming abababcc. The value of the form to long, dramatic narrative is the rhythm of six and two: a surge of energy in the first six lines and the steadying rhymed couplet at the end, which provides a momentary summary or pause before pressing on to another episode. A humorous example comes from Lord Byron's *Don Juan* (1824), Canto 144:

> Under the bed they searched, and there they found—
> No matter what—it was not that they sought;

They opened windows, gazing if the
    ground
        Had signs of footmarks, but the earth
            said nought;
    And then they stared each other's faces
        round:
        'T is odd, not one of all these seekers
            thought,
    And seems to me almost a sort of blun-
        der,
    Of looking *in* the bed as well as under.

Popular in the Middle Ages and
Renaissance for Italian and Portuguese
epics, *ottava rima* was the stanza preferred
by Giovanni Boccaccio, Ludovico Ariosto,
Luis Camoëns, and Torquato Tasso, who
composed his epic, *Jerusalem Delivered*
(1575), in eight-line sequences. English
poets who adapted the Italian epic octave
include Sir Thomas Wyatt, Sir Edmund
Spenser, Thomas Drayton, Lord Byron,
and John Keats.

In the twentieth century, Irish poet
William Butler Yeats used the tight inter-
locking lines for fifteen poems, including
"Sailing to Byzantium" (1928) and
"Among School Children" (1928); Amer-
ican poet Kenneth Koch turned the form
to comic purpose for his Byronic poem,
Ko, or a Season on Earth (1960).

outdoor drama   a pageant or
spectacle play featuring song, dance, procession, folklore, legends, and historical
events on a local theme, for example, *The
Trail of Tears* in Tahlequah, Oklahoma,
The City of Joseph in Nauvoo, Illinois,
Honey in the Rock in Beckley, West Virginia, *Young Abe Lincoln* in Evansville,
Tennessee, and *From This Day Forward*,
the story of Waldensian settlers in
Valdese, North Carolina.

Outdoor drama stresses frontier values, customs, and notables, for example,
the hero, campfire, wigwams, medicine
man, flute player, breech-clouts, beads,
wampum, war-bonnets, and a compelling
tom-tom beat of dactylic tetrameter in

Constance D'Arcy Mackay's verse tableau,
The Passing of Hiawatha (1915), adapted
from the writings of Henry Rowe Schoolcraft and Henry Wadsworth Longfellow's
epic *The Song of Hiawatha* (1855) and performed to Coleridge Taylor's music in
Schenectady, New York.

On the North Carolina coast at
Manteo, Paul Green set *The Lost Colony*
(1937), the story of the doomed English
colony, which launched a national movement toward local spectacle and pageantry.
Green's colleague, Kermit Hunter, developed a series of outdoor dramas across the
southeastern United States, featuring
Horn in the West (1952), a tribute to Daniel
Boone, and *The Liberty Tree* (1970), the
story of the Southern role in the American Revolution. Hunter's long-lived
Cherokee pageant, *Unto These Hills: The
Tragic and Triumphant Story of the Cherokee* (1950), carries the chronicle from the
arrival of Hernando de Soto's *conquista-
dores* to the removal of Indians west to
Oklahoma over the 1,200-mile "Trail of
Tears." The drama recreates the wisdom of
Sequoyah, Junaluska's leadership, and the
martyrdom of Tsali, who dies to save the
few Cherokee who remain hidden in their
Appalachian homeland.

oxymoron [ak•sih•MOH•rahn]
a form of paradox that allies two extreme
opposites, for example, the contradictory
terms "bittersweet," "seriocomic," "tragicomedy," "chiaroscuro," "deafening silence,"
"wise fool," "rebel conservatives," "sweet
and sour," "honor among thieves," "falsely
true," and "pianoforte." Poets intensify situations through self-negating words and
phrases, for example, the mutually exclu-
sive combination in Catullus's tortured
love plaint "Odi et Amo" [I hate and I
love] (ca. 55 B.C.) and Geoffrey Chaucer's
statement in *The Canterbury Tales*:

The more she yaf [gave] awey
The more, y-wis, she hadde alwey.
(1380)

Other examples: Romeo's cry, "O brawling love! O loving hate!" in William Shakespeare's *Romeo and Juliet* (ca. 1593–1595); the witch's incantation "fair is foul and foul is fair" and the protagonist's exclamation "So foul and fair a day I have not seen" in *Macbeth* (ca. 1603–1606); the prophecy, "That when we live no more, we may live ever" in Anne Bradstreet's "To My Dear and Loving Husband" (1650); John Milton's description of hell as "darkness visible" in *Paradise Lost* (1667); T. S. Eliot's claim, "We are the hollow men/ We are the stuffed men" from *The Hollow Men* (1925); and Eleanor Ross Taylor's "timeless shadow" in *Welcome Eumenides* (1972).

See also antithesis, paradox.

paean [PEE•uhn]   a tribute song, praise anthem, or joyful hymn. One of the earliest paeans is Akhenaten's "Hymn to the Sun" (ca. 1350 B.C.), a landmark in world theology for its insistence on monotheism. In classical Greek literature, the paean was a triumphal cry, taking its name from an epithet for Apollo, the "striker" or deliverer. A paean introduced and closed a symposium, preceded a war cry, or followed a military prayer. In more recent times, the term applies to varied kinds of rejoicing, for example, the exultation in the final stanza of Lord Byron's "The Destruction of Sennacherib" (1815), which declares:

The widows of Ashur are loud in their wail,
And the idols are broke in the temple of Baal;

And the might of the Gentile, unsmote by the sword,
Hath melted like snow in the glance of the Lord!

Likewise sturdy of tone and subject is Edna St. Vincent Millay's "To Inez Milholland" (1928), which lauds three champions of women's rights with a Shakespearean sonnet. The concluding line challenges the reader (and the speaker) to "Take up the song; forget the epitaph."

palindrome   words or messages read backwards or forwards, as found in the title of Vladimir Nabokov's novel *Ada*. The amassing of palindromes is an amusing gimmick in Barbara Kingsolver's *The Poisonwood Bible* (1998). The term derives from the Greek for "run back again" and refers to these examples:
• words: aha, refer, gig, wow, bab, bib, bub, did, noon, pup, peep, tat, tot, toot, mom, dad, pop, sis, level, rotor, radar, minim, civic
• proper nouns: Aga, Alla, Nan, Asa, Bob, Anna, Oro, Oto, and Lillian and Vivian's nicknames, Lil and Viv
• words that become palindromes when ended in s: sees, stets, shahs, soos, salas, Saras, Sabas, and Sohos
• terms that involve punctuation marks and ampersands, as with ma'am, M&M, R&R
• Arabic and Roman numbers: 747, 727, 1881, XIX, CXC
• abbreviations in all-capital letters: CDC, AAA, AA, SS, RR, and SDS
• sentences, as in "Sums are not set as a test on Erasmus," "A man, a plan, a canal—Panama!," Napoleon's complaint, "Able was I ere I saw Elba," and the world's first introduction, "Madam, I'm Adam," which begins with a palindromic noun.

pamphlet   a short article or

timely essay on a single topic that is published on cheap stock paper. It is usually unbound as a single unit with or without a paper cover, for example, a scientific monograph, religious or polemical tract, or propaganda distributed free to sway allegiance or introduce an innovative thought about a controversial subject, such as birth control, civil rights, Apartheid, AIDS, or ecology. Akin to the broadside, chapbook, and corrido, the pamphlet is often an inexpensive vehicle for a common cause, as is the case with Thomas Paine's *Common Sense* (1776) and *The American Crisis* (1783). An example from the troubled period preceding the American Civil War is Mary Ann Shadd Cary's abolitionist pamphlet, *A Plea for Emigration or Notes on Canada West* (1852). Other famous authors and disseminators of pamphlets include Sir Thomas More, John Milton, Daniel Defoe, Jonathan Swift, John Knox, Martin Luther, Percy Bysshe Shelley, Frederick Douglass, Sarah Grimké, Angelina Grimké, Margaret Sanger, Dorothy Day, Dr. Marie Stopes, and Emma Goldman.

panegyric [pa•nuh•JIH•rihk or pa•nuh•JY•rihk] a formal encomium, eulogy, florid paean or oration, or poem lauding a person, gathering, event, or institution, for example, a plaque on a university administration building or courthouse or a proclamation honoring the founder of a city. Originally a festival presentation or funeral speech in classical Greek and Roman literature, the term expanded to include celebration of military victory and elaborate praise introductions to patrons.

A noteworthy encomium is John Fitzgerald Kennedy's salute to William Faulkner:

A Mississippian by birth, an American by virtue of those forces and loyalties which guided his work, a guiding citizen of our civilization by virtue of his art, William Faulkner now rests, the search done, his place secure among the great creators of this age.

See also encomium, epitaph, paean.

pantomime a stage presentation or performance without words, depending on gesture, facial expression, posture, masking, and body contortions, for example, outdoor Christmas crèches featuring live actors playing the holy family, shepherds, and wise men, and the traditional Anansi stories pantomimed at Christmas in Jamaica and Barbados. In the Kwakiutl potlatch described in Margaret Craven's *I Heard the Owl Call My Name* (1973), the author says of the Grouse Dance:

[It] lasted three hours, and there were twenty-six characters, each with his masks, his songs, and his dances. In came the old stump looking for its trunk, a little green spruce growing from its top. In came the mossy log, the fish swimming upstream, the long face, the laughing face, the giant and the skull of the man lost in the woods. Through it all the Indians sat without sound or movement, utterly attentive.

An element of circus acts, comedy, and drama, mimed or silent motions figure in the revelation of murder in "The Mousetrap," the play-within-a-play in William Shakespeare's *Hamlet* (ca. 1599–1600) and in the courtship scenes of *Love's Labour's Lost* (ca. 1593–1595). In the early years of American drama, the use of wordless drama, comedy, and shadow tableau performed behind scrim expanded the outreach of French language playhouses in Charleston and New Orleans. During the eighteenth century, Asian and European stage pantomime stressed elaborate makeup, wigs, and costumes; frequent shifts of scenery involved intricate lighting techniques and stage machinery.

In straight comedy, pantomime is also the metier of Marcel Marceau, Jacques Tati, Lorene Yarnell, Charlie Chaplin, and the California-based Japanese storytelling troupe Eth-Noh-Tec. It has been an adjunct of the *commedia dell'arte*, vaudeville acts, ballet, Indonesian puppetry, parades, spectacle, Pueblo clown societies, Hopi kachinas, Cherokee boogers, exaggerated gestures of Sioux heyokas or plains tribes' contraries, Japanese kabuki, Peking Opera, the elaborate dance tableaux originated by *Les Folies Bergère*, womanless weddings and other forms of camp art, and the comedy of the Marx Brothers, Jackie Gleason, Lucille Ball, Buster Keaton, Red Skelton, Bill Cosby, and Carol Burnett.

See also camp, kabuki, masque.

pantoum or **pantun** [pan•TOOM or pan•TOON] a Malaysian chain verse composed in catenated quatrains rhyming abab, the style of poems in John Ashbery's *Some Trees* (1956), a melodious, surrealistic verse sequence rich in personal experience through evocative sense impressions. The gimmick that unifies the style is the repetition of the second and fourth lines in the first and third lines of the succeeding stanza. The completed work resembles this model:

> First stanza: Line 1
> Line 2
> Line 3
> Line 4
>
> Second stanza: Line 2 repeated
> Line 5
> Line 4 repeated
> Line 6
>
> Last stanza: Line 5 repeated
> Line 7
> Line 6 repeated
> Line 8

The unusual genre formed of echoing lines intrigued poets Ernest Fouinet, Victor Hugo, Louisa Siefert, Leconte de Lisle, Théophile Gautier, Charles Baudelaire, James Brander Matthews, Robert Morgan, and Austin Dobson.

parable a verbal lesson or brief allegorical story focusing on one or two characters in a single incident from ordinary situations, as found in the Torah in Ezekiel 24:2–5, 17:2–10, and 24:2–5, Isaiah 5:1–7 and 14:3–4, and Second Samuel 12:1–4; the teachings of Jewish sages in the Talmud; the cave myth in Plato's *Republic* (fourth century B.C.); and the writings of the early Christian fathers. Secular parables include Charles Kingsley's *Water Babies* (1863), George Macdonald's *The Princess and the Goblin* (1872), Franz Kafka's "Before the Law" and "An Imperial Message," Danish philosopher Søren Kierkegaard's *Fear and Trembling* (1843), Frances Harper's short story "The Two Offers" (1859), and Edgar Allan Poe's "Shadow: A Parable" (1835).

The parable is a graphic illustration intended to demonstrate an abstract concept, to teach a moral about life, and to inculcate values or positive attitudes, for example, the illustrative stories that Zen masters use to teach young Buddhist monks, Nathaniel Hawthorne's "Rappaccini's Daughter" and "The Minister's Black Veil" (1842), Leo Tolstoy's morality tale "How Much Land Does a Man Need?" (1886), tales by Jorge Luis Borges, and poems by Edwin Muir. Longer examples of parable are found in Samuel Beckett's *Waiting for Godot* (1955), William Golding's *Pincher Martin* (1956), and Harold Pinter's *The Caretaker* (1960).

The most famous parables in Western tradition are reported in three of the four Gospels, some in lengthy versions, and some in a few verses:

• "The Good Samaritan" (Luke 10:30–35)

• "The Lost Sheep" (Matthew 18:12–14, Luke 15:3–7)

• "The Mustard Seed" (Matthew 13:31–32, Mark 4:30–32, Luke 13:18–19)
• "The Pearl of Great Price" (Matthew 13:45–46)
• "The Sower" (Matthew 13:24–30, 36–43)
• "The Talents" (Matthew 25:14–30, Luke 19:12–27).

Jesus told these didactic stories to a first-century Jewish audience for an evangelistic purpose: to illustrate errors in behavior through three levels of correspondence—literal, moral, and spiritual. In "The Prodigal Son" (Luke 15:11–32), perhaps the most influential of New Testament parables, the correspondence between character and symbolic meaning are simple and direct: the older son represents both obedience to the father and jealousy of the younger son, who equates with willful behavior and contrition. The worried father, who welcomes the wanderer home, symbolizes God's love and forgiveness.

Additional examples of parable style empower the morality tales and exempla of John Bunyan, John Milton, Thomas Carlyle, John Ruskin, James Joyce, Thomas Hardy, D. H. Lawrence, John Galsworthy, Martin Buber, Black Elk, and Elie Wiesel. One of the most anthologized is "The Metamorphosis" (1915), in which Franz Kafka utilizes parable style and tone as a means of drawing attention to the negative aspects of the Samsas' lives—devaluation, hopelessness, secrecy, and cruelty. John Steinbeck adapts parable form to longer prose in *The Pearl* (1948). Other parables from literature include Hermann Hesse's "The Poet" (1909), Wilfred Owen's "The Parable of the Old Man and the Young" (1920), James Thurber's "The Unicorn in the Garden" (1940), and Isak Dinesen's *Babette's Feast* (1953).

paradox   a surprising or intriguing statement of truth through contradiction, for example, the motif of increased vision through blindness, a concept that powers the myths of Teiresias and Wodin, the free but embodied self in the *Bhagavad Gita* (ca. 300 A.D.), the terror and joy of the Quaker hymn "How Can I Keep from Singing" (eighteenth century), and Haki Madhubuti's "African Poem," which states,

> We're an African people
> hard softness burning black
> the earth's magic color our veins.

Paradox serves most genres, as in the plots of absurdist drama, the thirteenth chapter of St. Paul's second letter to the Corinthians in which he states, "We see through a glass darkly, then face to face," Lao Tzu's complex epigrams in the *Tao Te Ching* (fourth century B.C.), Richard Lovelace's contrast of freedom and imprisonment in "To Althea" (1642), conflicting philosophies in Blaise Pascal's *Pensées* (1657), Muriel Rukeyser's image of "treaty before the war" in "Who in One Lifetime" (1944), Nguyen Thi Vinh's conflicting images in "Thoughts of Hanoi" (1953), Octavio Paz's "Poet's Epitaph," Wole Soyinka's "Season," and the title of Carson Mc-Cullers's *Sweet as a Pickle and Clean as a Pig: Poems* (1964).

As a vehicle for humor, Don Helder Camara's puzzle states a political paradox: "When I give food to the poor, they call me a saint. When I ask why the poor have no food, they call me a Communist."
See also oxymoron.

parallelism   the use of similar grammatical arrangement of words, phrases, or clauses, as in the biblical statement, "An eye for an eye, a tooth for a tooth" and Emiliano Zapata's declaration, "It is better to die on your feet than to live on your knees." Parallel phrasing is common to biblical Hebrew verse such as

Ecclesiastes 3:1–8, "To Everything There Is a Season," and to the modern poet Avrahim Ben-Itzhak's poem "Blessing" (1968). Stephen Crane uses parallelism in *The Red Badge of Courage* (1895) when he personifies combat: "war, the red animal— war, the blood-swollen god." Parallel construction utilizes the repetition of "your" to create an emotionally charged opener for Emma Lazarus's "The New Colossus" (ca. 1866):

> Give me your tired, your poor,
> Your huddled masses yearning to breath free,
> The wretched refuse of your teeming shore.

One of the classics of humorous parallelism comes from Mark Twain's introduction of Huck Finn in Chapter 6 of *The Adventures of Tom Sawyer* (1876):

> He slept on doorsteps in fine weather and in empty hogsheads in wet; he did not have to go to school or to church or call any being master or obey anybody; he could go fishing or swimming when and where he chose, and stay as long as it suited him; he was always the first boy that went barefoot in the spring and the last to resume leather in the fall; he never had to wash, nor put on clean clothes; he could swear wonderfully.

In a starker example, Donald Davidson's "Sanctuary" (1927) urges the victim of war in brief parallel commands, advising the fleeing survivor to run and not turn back. For safety's sake, he exhorts, "Go further on. Go high. Go deep."

paraphrase a short, succinct restatement or clarification of the sense of a piece of writing. As an aid to the lay reader or student, paraphrasing preserves the meaning of difficult passages by altering style and diction to straightforward denotative language. For densely figurative language, restatement in simple words is impossible without explaining subtleties

or inserting a personal interpretation. However, the method of paraphrasing is essential to the student who must learn the difference between restating text in simple terms and plagiarism, the theft of someone else's words. In most U.S. universities, plagiarism is sufficient grounds for expulsion.

parody a humorous or witty imitation of another work in a ridiculous or absurd style to demean the original piece or its author, for example, *The Battle of the Frogs and Mice* (eighth century B.C.), an anonymous ribbing of Homer's intense epic battles, and Aristophanes's *The Frogs* (405 B.C.), a send-up of Greek tragedy. Parody thrives as a retort to tyranny and became a standard feature of colonial oral tradition worldwide. A gibing Australian version of "Oh Dear, What Can the Matter Be" expresses a harmless outback irreverence for polite English folklore:

> Oh, dear, what can the matter be,
> Four old ladies stuck in the lavatory,
> Stuck there from Monday to Saturday,
> Nobody knew they were there.

These remnants of rebellion and derision appear in ballads, barrack and tavern refrains, erudite wit, rude jest, ribald love lyrics, and satire of the monarchy, judges, and high church clergy.

Parody is the intent of Miguel de Cervantes's *Don Quixote* (1615), which mocks heroic romance, James Kirke Paulding's play *The Lion of the West* (1831), ribbing the overstated exploits of Davy Crockett, C. H. Webb's *St. Twel'mo* (1867), a travesty of Augusta Jane Evans Wilson's best-selling romance, *St. Elmo* (1866), and an outpouring of anti-colonialism in cartoon, verse, and prose in consternation and outrage over the racist jingoism of Rudyard Kipling's poem "The White Man's Burden," published in *McClure's Magazine* in 1899 as a paean to England's civilizing mission among the darker races.

In the twentieth century, parody continues to express literary superiority and one-upmanship, as with Edward Paramore's parody of Robert Service in *The Ballad of Yukon Jake* (1921), James Thurber's versions of "Barbara Frietchie" and "Curfew Must Not Ring To-Night" in *Fables for Our Time* (1940), and John Gardner's *Grendel* (1971), a send-up of *Beowulf.*

Parody displays through style and tone the elements that it intends to ridicule, for example, Alexander Pope's *The Rape of the Lock* (1714) derides eloquent epic style and high-flown language by treating the theft of a girl's lock of hair in mock-serious style. As an expression of personal philosophy, Southwestern poet Mary Hunter Austin's verse "Ladybug, Ladybug" (1934) adapts a children's rhyme to twentieth-century feminism and warns that the scale bug is at large. As though calling out the militia, Austin urges, "Ladybug, ladybug, go and eat him!"

American humorist Florence King uses parody in the titles of several of her satires— *WASP, Where Is Thy Sting?* (1976), a humorous restatement of St. Paul's rhetorical question, "O death, where is thy sting?" in I Corinthians 15:55, and *Reflections in a Jaundiced Eye* (1989), a variation of Carson McCullers's title, *Reflections in a Golden Eye* (1941).

paso [PAH•zo] a comic interlude in idiomatic speech about common topics and presented between acts of longer plays. Spanish actor Lope de Rueda, a member of a company of strolling players in the mid-sixteenth century, created the genre, demonstrated by *The Olives.* These short, spicy skits prefaced the one-act plays that remained popular in Spain for centuries.

Passion play a theatrical production or procession based on a religious martyrdom. The Christian version displays the prophecy of a messiah, Christ's miracles, the Last Supper, Mary Magdalene's relationship with Christ, and the judgment, scourging, and mockery leading up to Christ's crucifixion. The cast features characters mentioned in the Gospels and includes Satan or Lucifer, the fallen angel, and enactments of the Last Judgment.

Medieval in origin, the genre began with readings from the Bible and evolved into the Celtic Passion cycles from Brittany and Cornwall and secular versions in the *Carmina Burana* (thirteenth century), a profane miscellany written by roving university students. After the genre degenerated into mugging and parody, prelates withdrew their support and left the plays to jokesters. During the Reformation, Protestants forbade the performance of Passion plays as papist idolatry.

Although sporadically protested by Jewish groups as anti–Semitic, contemporary Passion plays survive in countless open-air locales in Europe and the Americas. Usually performed on Good Friday, the production lasts most of the day and evening and tests the courage of the actor who plays Christ. The French *Mystère de la Passion* (1454), a 65,000-line play by Arnoul Gréban, was introduced in Anjou, France, and lasted six days. In the Netherlands, the Tegelen Passion play is performed during the warm months every few years. In Brussels, the Théâtre Toone presents a puppet version of the Passion play. In 1883, German actor Otto Devrient composed a Passion play at Jena to honor Martin Luther.

A famous example given every ten years is held at Oberammergau, Germany, in the southern Bavarian Alps. The play features local people as actors and chorus members. It was first performed in the town in 1634 as a thanksgiving to God for the citizens' survival during a plague and has continued except during the Franco-Prussian War and World War II.

Apart from Christian tradition, Passion plays occur in other religions. In Egypt, the Abydos Passion play began around 2686 B.C. and continued to 400 A.D. An annual resurrection or agricultural fertility ritual performed at temples, the play reenacts Seth's dismemberment of Osiris, whose wife Isis collects the pieces and son Horus restores them to living flesh. Herodotus's histories record his attendance at a performance in 450 B.C. Another spirited cycle is the body of Islamic Passion plays, or ta'ziyah, a mimetic tradition derived from the Shi'ite martyrdom and death of Husayn, son of 'Ali and grandson of Muhammad in 680 A.D. Performed in Turkey, Iraq, and parts of central Asia since the ninth century and printed in the seventeenth century, the subjects are predominantly religious with satiric overtones. During processions during the month of Muharram, villagers mutilate and whip themselves, shout, gesture, and bear blood-stained icons of martyrs as a form of ecstatic pageantry. Scenes stress symbolism and gimmickry with limbless victims brandishing swords held in the teeth and a bloodied skull of the martyr Husayn reciting scripture.

pastiche [pas•TEESH or pahs•TEESH]   a medley, hodge-podge, or patchwork of humorous or satiric phrases, sentences, or terms taken from other sources and pieced together for the sake of comedy, burlesque, or satire. A notable example from English literature is the literary hoax of Thomas Chatterton, who used found material from Geoffrey Chaucer and Sir Edmund Spenser for his medieval pastiche, "Œlle, a Tragycal Enterlude

Wrotenn bie Thomas Rowleie" (1777); in the twentieth century, John Fowles used snatches of Victorian convention for *The French Lieutenant's Woman* (1969) and John Gardner blended parodies of familiar styles for *Grendel* (1971). As an element of parody, pastiche imitates or adopts fragments of other writers' work to create satire or mockery.

The source of humor in "Hamlet's soliloquy" in Chapter 21 of Mark Twain's *The Adventures of Huckleberry Finn* (1884) is a blend of scraps of lines from Shakespeare's plays, which begins:

> To be, or not to be; that is the bare bodkin
> That makes calamity of so long life;
> For who would fardels bear, till Birnam Wood do came to Dunsinane,
> But that the fear of something after death
> Murders the innocent sleep,
> Great nature's second course,
> And makes us rather sling the arrows of outrageous fortune
> Than fly to others that we know not of.

The pastiche concludes, "Ope not thy ponderous and marble jaws,/But get thee to a nunnery—go!"

pastoral   a long-lived style that idealizes rural or country life by creating overly simple, sentimental characters—usually deities and nymphs and human figures, herders, and fishers, for example, the characters in Thomas Chatterton's *The African Eclogues* (1777) and Sir Philip Sidney's *The Arcadia* (1590), a common setting. Bearing stereotypical names such as Thyrsis, Michael, Phyllis, Daphnis, and Chloe, these innocents play the flute, dance, quibble, court, perform a singing match, and carry out other imaginative activities set in a golden age at an artificially serene pasture or glade marked by utopian bliss and passivity. The diction tends toward polite or overly mannered courtliness. The form varies from myth, idyll, elegy, love plaint, and *pastourelle*, to amoebœan verse, a patterned dialogue for two, and the more involved monologues and dialogues called eclogues, for example, the winsome exchange in Lady Anne Finch Winchelsea's "Friendship between Ephelia and Ardelia" (1685):

> Eph. What friendship is, Ardelia, show.
> Ard. 'Tis to love, as I love you.
> Eph. This account, so short (though kind)
> Suits not my inquiring mind.
> Therefore farther now repeat:
> What is friendship when complete?
> Ard. 'Tis to share all joy and grief;
> 'Tis to lend all due relief
> From the tongue, the heart, the hand;
> 'Tis to mortgage house and land;
> For a friend be sold a slave;
> 'Tis to die upon a grave,
> If a friend therein do lie.
> Eph. This indeed, though carried high,
> This, though more than e'er was done
> Underneath the rolling sun,
> This has all been said before.
> Can Ardelia say no more?
> Ard. Words indeed no more can show;
> But 'tis to love, as I love you.

The prototypes of the pastoral convention are Theocritus's "The Lament for Daphnis" from *Idylls* (third century B.C.), second-century imitations by Bion and Moschus, the Roman poet Virgil's ten eclogues (42–37 B.C.), and Longus's *Daphnis and Chloe* (ca. fourth century A.D.), which influenced pastoral verse in the Middle Ages, particularly May Day, Whitsuntide, and Michaelmas verses, Alcuin's dialogues (ca. 790), and an allegorical medieval Christian mystery play, *The Adoration of the Shepherds*.

Italian pastoral evolved into the *mescidato*, a secular drama borrowed from miracle plays. Renaissance and seventeenth-century models include Giovanni Boccaccio's pastoral novel *Ameto* (ca.

1335), Robert Henryson's *Robene and Makyne* (ca. 1500), Mantuan's Latin pastorals (ca. 1515), Edmund Spenser's twelve monthly poems that comprise *The Shepherd's Calendar* (1579), Michael Drayton's *Daffodil* (1593), Christopher Marlowe's "The Passionate Shepherd to His Love" (1599), William Shakespeare's pastoral romance *As You Like It* (ca. 1599), John Fletcher's *The Faithful Shepherdess* (1608), Sir Walter Raleigh's "The Nymph's Reply to the Shepherd" (ca. 1615), Phineas Fletcher's *Piscatorie Eclogs* (1633), John Milton's *Lycidas* (1637), Ben Johnson's *The Sad Shepherd* (1641), Izaak Walton's *The Complete Angler* (1653), Aphra Behn's "The Willing Mistress" (1673), and Anne Finch's "A Letter to Daphnis" (1685). Molière incorporates a parodied pastoral exchange between Angela and Cleanthes in *Le Malade imaginaire* [The Imaginary Invalid] (1673), in which the emotional maiden spurns love with the melodramatic line, "I'd rather, rather die than give consent,/Much rather, rather die."

In later times, pastoral style influenced Alexander Pope's *Pastorals* (1709), John Gay's *The Shepherd's Week* (1714), George Crabbe's *The Village* (1783), William Wordsworth's *Michael: A Pastoral Poem* (1800) and the philosophical *Intimations of Immortality* (1807), Percy Bysshe Shelley's somber *Adonais* (1821), and Matthew Arnold's *Thyrsis* (1867). American poets produced a more varied pastoral, as found in Walt Whitman's "When Lilacs Last in the Dooryard Bloom'd" (1866), W. E. Henley's experiments with the villanelle, Harold Bell Wright's *The Shepherd of the Hills* (1907), and Robert Frost's "The Telephone."

See also eclogue, idyll, *pastourelle*, pathetic fallacy.

pastourelle [pahs•too•REHL] or **pastorela** [pahs•toh•REH•lah]   a brief narrative poem depicting a meeting or light-hearted seduction scene between knight or scholar and a humble but virtuous shepherdess, gardener, pig herder, or goose girl. Their interaction takes the form of wooing, courtship game, and *querelle*, or debate, usually with the girl refusing the man's attentions. Popular with thirteenth-century French, German, and Italian poets, the *pastourelle* was a specialty of Marcabru, a Gascon troubadour. Other examples include five by Jehan Bodel of Arras, France (early thirteenth century), Adam de la Halle's "Jeu de Robin et de Marion" [The Game of Robin and Marion] (thirteenth century), two early examples by Theobald I of Troyes, France (mid-thirteenth century), and Scottish poet Robert Henryson's "Robene and Makyne" (late fifteenth century).

pathetic fallacy a common form of personification or conceit in which nature suspends its laws to reflect human emotion, whether joyful sunshine, dancing limbs, moaning wind, soothing zephyr, or the deep grief mimicked by clouds and rain, for example, Catherine Barkley's comment in Ernest Hemingway's *A Farewell to Arms* (1929) that the rain in Switzerland is more cheerful than the rain in Italy. A poetic convention of the pastoral elegy, the device marks Percy Bysshe Shelley's mournful *Adonais* (1821), Alfred, Lord Tennyson's *In Memoriam* (1850), Dante Gabriel Rossetti's "The Woodspurge" (1856), Katherine Mansfield's sketch, "Miss Brill" (1922), and Jean Toomer's "Song of the Sun" (1923). Lyricist Edna St. Vincent Millay demonstrates nature's regret over death in "The Buck in the Snow" (1928) with an image of the wild buck, "his wild blood scalding the snow."

Pepper's ghost a theatrical device that gives the illusion of a ghost onstage. Contrived by John Pepper (1821–1900), the trick requires a sheet of glass placed on an incline at the back of a stage. An actor walking in the pit is reflected in the glass like an apparition. Actors standing on either side of the glass can give the impression of passing their arms through the body of the ghost or of trying to grab it.

periodic sentence a dramatic or emphatic arrangement of words that saves the most important word or revelation to the end, a method that piques curiosity or builds suspense, for example, a pivotal line in Caitlin Thomas's *Leftover Life to Kill* (1957):

> What is more, the church, with all his ties, pulls, strings, and telephone services, had me just where he wanted me: useless for me to say what right he had over me; at his protective mercy.

The style is evident in Gandhi's statement, "There is no god higher than truth" and Sojourner Truth's declaration, "There's two things I've got a right to … death or liberty."

persona [puhr•SOH•nuh], pl. personae the role, voice, mask, tone, or traits of the author or a character. Persona varies from simple or formal to intimate, shy, opinionated, outraged, somber, overbearing, or teasing. Often identified as the implied author or spokesperson, which may vary or conflict with the author's point of view, persona expresses the controlling attitude, morality, and values in a literary work, for example, the disapproving granddaughter in Isabel Allende's *House of the Spirits* (1982) and the cynical, despairing wife in Allan Gurganus's *Oldest Living Confederate Widow Tells All* (1989).

personification a poetic device that assigns human intelligence and emotion to an abstract idea, animal, or inanimate object, for example, Mr. Death in August Wilson's play *Fences* (1986). A vivid portrayal of a cold winter day in Charles Dickens's *A Christmas Carol* describes the city of London:

> The ancient tower of a church, whose gruff old bell was always peeping slyly down at Scrooge out of a Gothic window in the wall, became invisible, and struck the hours and quarters in the clouds, with tremulous vibrations afterward, as if its teeth were chattering in its frozen head up there. (1843)

Personification exists in shorter statements and images, as in William Shakespeare's statement that "love is blind," as though the abstract concept of love could have eyes. The device colors the title of Chaim Nachman Bialik's "Summer Is Dying" (1934) and Oscar Peñaranda's depiction of white tongues of foam hissing from a green monster sea in "Sunday Morning" (1969).

Personified objects can project strong subjective or symbolic meaning, as found in the scorched trunk that becomes an accusing finger in Richard Wright's lynch scene poem "Between the World and Me" (1935).

See also allegory.

Petrarchan sonnet [pee•TRAHR •kuhn] a fourteen-line lyric poem in iambic pentameter that falls naturally into an octave and sestet, rhyming abbaab-bacdecde or some variable of the pattern. The octave presents a problem or describes a subject, which the poet resolves or concludes in the sestet. A popular melodious expression, the Petrarchan sonnet—also called the Italian sonnet—grew out of the love songs of troubadours. The Renaissance Italian poet Francesco Petrarch dedicated his sonnets to Laura, his idealized love, to whom he writes Sonnet 134. The poem owes much to the rhapsodies of Sappho and Catullus with its turbulent

emotions, beginning "There is no peace; I am too weak for war."

The genre is a vehicle for a variety of authors and topics: Sir Thomas Wyatt's "Whoso List to Hunt" (1557), Sir Philip Sidney's "With How Sad Steps" (1585), and Henry Wordsworth Longfellow's "The Sound of the Sea." A favorite of anthologists is John Milton's "On His Blindness" (1651), which illustrates the setting up of a problem and supplying the answer in the final six lines:

> When I consider how my light is spent
> Ere half my days in this dark world and wide,
> And that one talent which is death to hide
> Lodged with me useless, though my soul more bent
> To serve my Maker, and present
> My true account, lest He returning chide;
> "Doth God exact day-labor, light denied?"
> I fondly ask. But Patience, to prevent
> That murmur, soon replies, "God doth not need
> Either man's work or his own gifts. Who best
> Bear his mild yoke, they serve him best. His state
> Is kingly: thousands at his bidding speed,
> And post o'er land and ocean without rest;
> They also serve who only stand and wait."

picaresque narrative realistic adventure lore—also called the *roman à tiroirs* or "novel in the drawers"—that reveals the life and mishaps of the picaroon, a coarse, low-born menial, rascal, rogue, outlaw, or trickster. Development takes place through episodic adventures, scrapes with authorities, deception, and predicaments, as found in John Jones Hooper's *Some Adventures of Captain Simon Suggs* (1846), Cherokee author John Rollin Ridge's romantic biography, *The*

Life and Adventures of Joaquin Murieta, the Celebrated California Bandit (1854); Julia Mood Peterkin's low country plantation novel, *Scarlet Sister Mary* (1928), Jesús del Corral's short story "Cross Over, Sawyer" (1947), Guy Owen's ribald *The Ballad of the Flim-Flam Man* (1965), and Larry McMurtry's south-of-the-border imbroglios in *Lonesome Dove* (1985).

The hallmark picaros of literature are ancient forerunners of the novel—Petronius's *Satyricon* (A.D. 60) and Apuleius's *The Golden Ass* (ca. 160 A.D.)—and influenced the development of later picaroons, for instance, the Spanish romance *La Vida de Lazarillo de Tormes* (1554), François Rabelais's *Gargantua and Pantagruel* (1564), Miguel de Cervantes's *Don Quixote* (1605), Aphra Behn's *The City Heiress* (1682), Alain Le Sage's *Gil Blas* (1715), Henry Fielding's *Tom Jones* (1749), Lord Byron's *Don Juan* (1824), William Makepeace Thackeray's *Vanity Fair* (1852), Mark Twain's *A Connecticut Yankee in King Arthur's Court* (1889), Eudora Welty's *The Robber Bridegroom* (1942), J. P. Donleavy's *The Ginger Man* (1955), Erica Jong's sexual capers in *Fear of Flying* (1973), T. Coraghessan Boyle's *Water Music* (1982), *East Is East* (1990), and *The Road to Wellville* (1993), and the female scoundrel in Margaret Atwood's *The Robber Bride* (1993).

The controlling factor in picaresque fiction is the perpetuation of realistic escapades from which the picaro or rascal escapes by application of wit and daring, the salvation of Daniel Defoe's quick-witted survivor at the heart of *Moll Flanders* (1722) and Voltaire's title hero in *Candide* (1759). Character development varies little because the central figure learns nothing from a series of near-misses, as is the case with the title figures of Mark Twain's *The Adventures of Huckleberry Finn* (1884) and Saul Bellow's *The Adventures of Augie March* (1953).

plot a scheme, framework, or series of events or actions, their motivation, and their outcome. In drama, the progression from beginning to end follows a developmental paradigm: from exposition of character through crisis, complication, climax, and dénouement to the conclusion or catastrophe. In the novel, narrative verse, or short story, the pattern of events may create straightforward tension or suspense, as in the intrigues, crimes, or deceptions at the heart of Sir Arthur Conan Doyle's Sherlock Holmes detective stories, or may build on subplots or underplots. In the dual spheres of action in Marge Piercy's futuristic novel, *Woman on the Edge of Time* (1976), the author rescues Connie Ramos, the protagonist, from twentieth-century difficulties and places her among more daunting problems two hundred years later.

A dramatic subgenre, the well-made play, succeeds because of plot complexity and development. It features secret, slowly accelerating action marked by rises and falls, a reversal of fortune, credible falling action, and repeated structural motifs. Writers of well-made plays include Victorien Sardou, Augustin Scribe, Wilkie Collins, Émile Augier, Alexandre Dumas fils, Eugène Labiche, Georges Feydeau, and Arthur Pinero, author of *The Second Mrs. Tanqueray* (1893).

See also Freytag diagram.

poetry a body of highly compressed, unified literary works that appeal to emotion, rhythm, sense impressions, imagination, and theme as a means of giving pleasure or expressing a significant or esthetic truth, as found in *Shijung* [The Book of Songs], edited by Confucius around 475 B.C., Muhammad Iqbal's Persian devotional *Mysteries of Selflessness* (1918), and Korean poet Han Yong-un's love sequence, *Your Silence* (1926). The verbal art of poetry, whether humorous, whimsical, or serious, conveys subtle word pictures and a heightened sensibility that affects both the mind and emotions, as found in Percy Bysshe Shelley's "Love's Philosophy" (1819). The speaker assembles clichéd love plaints and the conventions of sentimental occasional verse for his own lament:

> See the mountains kiss high Heaven
>   And the waves clasp one another;
> No sister-flower would be forgiven
>   If it disdained its brother,
> And the sunlight clasps the earth
>   And the moonbeams kiss the sea:
> What is all this sweet work worth
>   If thou kiss not me?

Categories of poetry include didactic, doggerel, dramatic, elegaic, epic, lyric, macaronic, mock-epic, narrative, pastoral, satiric, and skeltonic.

point of view   the angle or perspective through which the author displays action and characters to the viewer. The most common points of view are these:
   • omniscient or all-knowing, through which the author can move freely among all the characters. A detached voice that often expresses the action from a panoramic point of view, the omniscient narrator is the most authoritative and reliable storyteller, as in Mariano Azuela's *The Underdogs* (1915), in which the speaker examines actions as though they were produced on a stage by known characters. Because the observer is not a character in the story, he anticipates the tragic end awaiting the protagonist.
   • first-person narrative, a limited viewpoint in which the narrator is a character in the text, as are the speakers of Catullus's love lyrics of late Republican Rome and T'ao Ch'ien's "Returning to Live in the Country" (ca. 425 A.D.), Ishmael in Herman Melville's *Moby-Dick* (1851), and Nick Caraway in F. Scott

Fitzgerald's *The Great Gatsby* (1925). Edgar Lee Masters allows deceased characters to speak in their own voices in *Spoon River Anthology* (1915), a series of graveyard portraits. Astronaut James B. Irwin carried aboard Apollo XV James Dillet Freeman's poem "I Am There," which he left on the moon for future space travelers. The work speaks from the limited point of view of an unidentified deity, who promises, "My faith in you never wavers, because I know you, because I love you."
   • stream of consciousness, a method of revealing action through the disconnected, erratic flow of thoughts, reveries and daydreams, and sense impressions derived from one character's mind. An extremely limited point of view, stream of consciousness produces ambiguity from disrupted chronology and distortions of time, as found in William Faulkner's *The Sound and the Fury* (1929), Katherine Anne Porter's story "The Jilting of Granny Weatherall" (1930), Dorothy Richardson's *March Moonlight* (1967), and N. Scott Momaday's *House Made of Dawn* (1968). In Daniel Keyes's *Flowers for Algernon* (1959), stream of consciousness reveals the mental state of a retarded adult and the chaos that occurs in his thinking processes after surgery enables him to develop into a genius. Margaret Atwood's *The Handmaid's Tale* (1986), a pun-rich anti-utopian fantasy, studies the thoughts of a captive breeder, Offred, whose thoughts stray over the misery of her daily life: "I want to go to bed, make love, right now. I think the word *relish*. I could eat a horse."
   • naive narrator, the use of a point of view that speaks meaningful details without realizing their significance. An ironic method, naive narration is a vehicle for Mark Twain's *The Adventures of Huckleberry Finn* (1884), Sherwood Anderson's short story "I'm a Fool" (1924), J. D. Salinger's *The Catcher in the Rye*

(1951), Ken Kesey's *One Flew Over the Cuckoo's Nest* (1962), and Kaye Gibbons's *Ellen Foster* (1987), in which an abused child expresses her fears, frustrations, and hopes without realizing the direction her life is taking.

• alternating first-person point of view, a group of first-person recitations, for example, Toni Morrison's *Jazz* (1992) and Barbara Kingsolver's *Animal Dreams* (1990), which extends first-person point of view by establishing a rhythm of chapters spoken by an ailing father and his adult daughter Codi, who returns to her childhood home to help him close his medical practice and begin to cope with Alzheimer's disease.

• third-person narrative, which applies the view of an observer who stands outside the scope of the story and knows what will happen and how actions will affect the characters. Victor Villaseñor's saga *Rain of Gold* (1991), a fictional work based on family history, examines actions, conversations, and thoughts as though they were known to the author. He presents attitudes, prejudices, animosities, and personal details of his parents' courtship as though he remembers them.

• intrusive narration, the use of omniscience as a vehicle for the author's personal opinions, for example, William Makepeace Thackeray's insertion of commentary and moralizing essays on the behaviors of characters in *Vanity Fair* (1847), a study of social conniving and manipulation.

• circular narrative, a composite picture of an action drawn from individual testimony of several characters. The most complicated mode of fiction, circular narrative produces conflicting stories, events out of chronological order, questionable data, and suspect opinions that tell more about the narrator than about the person or action being described, a method used by novelist Carson McCullers in *The Heart Is a Lonely Hunter* (1940). A major American work, William Faulkner's *As I Lay Dying* (1930), uses a variety of voices and points of view to express a family's loss of the mother figure. Toni Morrison employs a circular style of presentation for *Beloved* (1987), a ghost story that accounts for a mother's murder of her infant daughter to save her from the life of the slave breeder.

pornography a bawdy, immoral, obscene, or erotic literary work that appeals to or arouses lust, prurience, ribaldry, deviance, or voyeurism. Many works have been challenged by courts or postal systems and labeled pornography in lieu of discernible serious or esthetic intent, notably Aristophanes's *Lysistrata* (411 B.C.), Ovid's *Art of Love* (ca. 1 B.C.), *Carmina Burana* (ca. 1230), Aphra Behn's *The Rover* (1681), John Cleland's *Fanny Hill* (1749), Giacomo Casanova's *Memoirs* (1838), Richard Burton's translation of Vatsayana's *Kama Sutra* (1883), James Joyce's *Ulysses* (1922), D. H. Lawrence's *Lady Chatterley's Lover* (1928), Radclyffe Hall's *The Well of Loneliness* (1928), Lawrence Durrell's *Black Book* (1936), Vladimir Nabokov's *Lolita* (1955), H. D.'s *Bid Me to Live* (1960), Erica Jong's *Fear of Flying* (1973), Rita Mae Brown's *Rubyfruit Jungle* (1973), and Tony Kushmer's *Angels in America* (1993).

postmodernism avant-garde or non-traditional literary developments since the 1950s. Anticipated in the 1930s, some of the reactionary elements are evident in Nagai Kafu's *A Strange Tale from East of the River* (1937), a minimalist treatment of some of the novelist's earlier fiction, and the moody meditations of Shiga Naoya's *A Dark Night's Passing* (1937), a novel of disaffection and yearning. Postmodernism is a loose and inclusive term encompassing less structured fictional modes, particularly magical realism, theater happenings, anti-fiction, web E-zines, other electronic anthologies, elusive actions and motivations, and stream-of-consciousness or hallucinatory dreamscapes, the mode of Belgian short story writer François Mallet-Joris's "Air des Clochettes" (1970), Jesús Papoleto Meléndez's experimental bilingual poem "Oye Mundo/Sometimes," Jean Rhys's *Wide Sargasso Sea* (1966), and Maxine Hong Kingston's *The Woman Warrior: A Girlhood Among Ghosts* (1994), a stage adaptation of Kingston's novels.

Writers usually associated with postmodernism include Thomas Pynchon, Vladimir Nabokov, William S. Burroughs, Kurt Vonnegut, Tony Kushner, and Alejo Carpentier and influenced the fiction of Jorge Luis Borges, Günter Grass, and Italo Calvino. Other postmodernists are Mikhail Bulgakov, Alice Munro, Salman Rushdie, Milan Kundera, Bernard Malamud, Umberto Eco, Isabel Allende, Gabriel García Márquez, John Barth, Alain Robbe-Grillet, Donald Barthelme, Harold Pinter, John Fowles, John Gardner, Marge Piercy, Tom Stoppard, and Angela Carter.

pourquoi story [poo•KWAH] literally a "why" story, a component of narrative that blends fable and myth by explaining or accounting for a phenomenon in nature, for instance, the Toba Indian tale from Argentina, "How Man Learned to Make Fire," the Australian aboriginal explanation of "How the Dingo Came to Australia," the Jicarilla Apache story, "How the People Sang the Mountains Up," and the Algerian version of "How Mankind Learned to Make Bread."

The *pourquoi* story is a benign, uplifting cosmic narration that explains the interaction of deities, animals, and humans

and illustrates the necessary punishments of human weakness or rebellion against the gods. In the Old Norse *pourquoi* tale in Snorri Sturluson's *Edda* (ca. 1150–1250), Mani the Moon ends child abuse by rescuing Hjuki and Bil, two overworked children who parallel Jack and Jill in the English version. Still clinging to the bucket and pole they used to fetch water, the pair live in the sky. As is true of folk narrative, the various explanations reveal more about tribal values than about the cosmos, as demonstrated in Rudyard Kipling's *Just-So Stories* (1902), "Why Mr. Cricket Has Elbows on His Legs," in Joel Chandler Harris's *Told by Uncle Remus: New Stories of the Old Plantation* (1905), and the Hmong story "Why Monkey and Man Do Not Live Together."

précis [PRAY•see]   a short, concise summary or abstract of essential data in a literary work, stated in their original order and maintaining the intent and emphasis of themes and objectives. Longer than a paraphrase, the *précis* is shorter than a synopsis of a Shakespearean play or an abridgment of Leo Tolstoy's *War and Peace*.

preface [PREHF•ihs]   the introductory statement, essay, or explanation composed by the author or editor to precede a longer work, for example, Oscar Wilde's prefatory essay on art and the artist in *The Picture of Dorian Gray* (1891). Unlike a foreword, which may contain comments by another author or editor, the preface summarizes the intent and scope of a literary work. One of the most familiar prefaces from American fiction is Nathaniel Hawthorne's "The Custom House," the preface to *The Scarlet Letter* (1850), which accounts for the political and religious climate of colonial New England. In 1989, Maya Angelou provided an unusual preface for a photographic essay in *National Geographic* entitled "They Came to Stay." The introduction stands alone as tribute to black female settlers of the United States. *See also* prologue.

prequel [PREE•kwihl] a sequel written out of chronological order. The prequel typically describes a time previous to the work it follows, for example, Theodore Taylor's young adult novel *Timothy of the Cay* (1993), which establishes characters and explains events preceding the action of *The Cay* (1969).

prologue a prefatory comment, preface, or introductory scene that sets the tone of a narrative, particularly a novel, story-poem, or speech; also, the speaker who introduces a play, for example, the Chorus in William Shakespeare's *Henry V* (1599), who calls on the muse of fire to tell of warlike Henry. The Chorus also states that he regrets that stage actors cannot accurately recreate the spectacle of Henry's victory over France. In more recent writing, Sylvia López-Medina introduces her saga *Cantora* (1992) with reasons for linking events and people in a family story.

propaganda persuasive or didactic literature that disseminates an idea, belief, or political agenda, such as the polemics of Ida Bell Wells-Barnett, who fought violence against ex-slaves with *Southern Horrors: Lynch Law in All Its Phases* (1892), *The Reason Why the Colored American Is Not in the Columbian Exposition* (1893), and *A Red Record: Tabulated Statistics and Alleged Causes of Lynching in the United States, 1892–1893–1894* (1895). Notable examples from American literature are found in Thomas Jefferson's *A Summary View of the Rights of British America* (1774) and *Declaration of Causes and Necessity of Taking of Arms* (July 6,

1775); *The Interesting Narrative of the Life of Olaudah Equiano, or Gustavus Vassa, the African; by Himself* (1790), a two-volume exposé of slavery; Angelina Grimké's *Appeal to the Christian Women of the South* (1836) and *Letters to Catherine Beecher in Reply to an Essay on Slavery and Abolitionism Addressed to A. A. Grimké* (1837); and Mary Ann Shadd Cary's pamphlet, *Hints to the Colored People of North America* (1849) and *A Plea for Emigration, or Notes on Canada West, in Its Moral, Social and Political Aspect* (1852), a treatise that argues for self-reliance among newly freed blacks.

More literary examples include the abolitionism of Harriet Beecher Stowe's *Uncle Tom's Cabin* (1852), anti-technology of Karel Capek's *R. U. R.* (1920), Marxism in Bertolt Brecht's play *The Caucasian Chalk Circle* (1948), Paul Monette's public appeal in *Borrowed Time: An AIDS Memoir* (1988), the anti-pollution stance of Barbara Kingsolver's *Animal Dreams* (1990), and Alice Walker's speech delivered at the Auburn Theological Seminary on April 25, 1995, "The Only Reason You Want to Go to Heaven," a challenge to the male absolutism that mars orthodox Christianity.

See also corrido, pamphlet.

prose unmetered and unrhymed language, the usual vehicle for the straightforward discourse, as found in the sermon, article, oration, pamphlet, essay, novel, and short story, for example, Raja Rammohum Roy's prose exposition, *The Precepts of Jesus, a Guide to Peace and Happiness* (1820), John James Audubon's descriptive compendium, *The Birds of America* (1838), and Marjory Stoneman Douglass's treatise, *The Everglades: River of Grass* (1947).

prose poem a literary work that appears to follow the style and dictates of prose yet incorporates poetic rhythms, alliteration, assonance, internal rhyme, and imagery, as found in John Donne's sermon "Devotions upon Emergent Occasions" (1624), which was originally written in paragraph form and later set on the page like lines of poetry and entitled "No Man Is an Island." James Agee's lyrical *Let Us Now Praise Famous Men* (1941) is an example of an ambiguous piece of poetic prose—a purported treatise on Southern sharecroppers that deviates from prose to paean, prayer, encomium, and hymn. Other examples include Margaret Atwood's "Bread," from *Murder in the Dark* (1994), Ana Castillo's epistolary narrative *The Mixquiahuala Letters* (1986), and Jamaica Kincaid's "Holidays" (1995).

prosody [PROH•suh•dee] metrics or versification; also, the study or analysis of patterned accents to produce rhyme, rhythm, meter, and stanza form, for example, a marking of normal cadences in an English translation of the first line of Genesis in the Bible:

In the beginning, God created the heaven and the earth.

protagonist the focal or principal character, usually the enemy of the antagonist, in drama, story, or longer fiction, for example, the title characters in Ella Deloria's novel *Waterlily* (1944), Randall Jarrell's poem "Lady Bates" (1945), Leslie Marmon Silko's story "Yellow Woman" (1981), and Gail Godwin's novel *The Good Husband* (1994).

prototype [PROH•tuh•typ] the original model or standard by which other examples are judged, for example, Owen Wister's *The Virginian: A Horseman of the Plains* (1902), the prototype of the literary Western.

proverb a short, pithy traditional saying of unknown authorship reflecting a self-evident truth, advice, or good sense, as found in these Chinese proverbs:

- If one plants melons, one gets melons.
- It is impossible to clap with only one hand.
- Paint a snake and add legs.
- Paper cannot wrap up fire.
- There are no waves if there is no wind.

See also aphorism, maxim.

psalm a sacred song, hymn, or lyrical paean, such as a liturgical canticle, chant, or anthem praising God; for example, an "Alleluia," "Hosanna," or "Te Deum." *See also* lauda, paean.

pseudonym [SOO•doh•nihm] a writer's alias or pen name. While working as a journalist, Joel Chandler Harris chose the lighthearted "Marlowe" and "Tellmenow Isitsoornot"; Ambrose Bierce used the name "Dod Grile" for three story collections—*Nuggets and Dust Panned Out in California* (1872), *The Fiend's Delight* (1872), and *Cobwebs from an Empty Skull* (1874). *See also* nom de plume.

psychological novel a study of the interior or emotional landscape with emphasis on motivation, private thoughts, internal dialogue, and circumstance, for example, William Wells Brown's *Clotelle: A Tale of Southern States* (1853), Kate Chopin's *The Awakening* (1899), Walter Van Tilburg Clark's *The Ox-Bow Incident* (1940), N. Scott Momaday's *House Made of Dawn* (1968), Pat Conroy's *The Prince of Tides* (1986), and *A Lesson Before Dying* (1993), Ernest Gaines's study of a black youth condemned to die.

An incisive psychological study of racism comes from Ralph Ellison, whose *Invisible Man* (1947) expresses the quandary of black Americans:

I am an invisible man. No, I am not a spook like those who haunted Edgar Allan Poe; nor am I one of your Hollywood-movie ectoplasms. I am a man of substance, of flesh and bone, fiber and liquids—and I might even be said to possess a mind.

Under the cloak of buffoonery and humor, Ken Kesey's *One Flew Over the Cuckoo's Nest* (1962) conveys a power struggle between a work-shirking prisoner and a former army nurse who tyrannizes a psychiatric ward. Kesey expresses his opinions on free will, behavior, medical ethics, and civil rights by examining the intensity of character conflict, for example, the doctor's explanation of democratic ward management.

Similarly, Alexander Solzhenitsyn's *One Day in the Life of Ivan Denisovich* (1963) justifies the habits and choices of the prisoner Shukhov, emphasizing the need to be warm and well fed, the use of tools and fuel, and the inner workings of the prison underground. Consequently, much of the strife takes place in his mind, where he relives military service, arrest, a term in a lumber camp, and incarceration in the Russian steppes.

pun   a witty play on similar meanings or sounds of words, for example, the play on the homonyms all/awl produced by a Roman soldier interrogating a working man in the opening act of William Shakespeare's *Julius Caesar* (ca. 1599). Flavius asks, "Thou art a cobbler, art thou?," to which the cobbler replies, "Truly sir, all that I live by is with the awl. I meddle with no tradesman's matters nor women's matters, but withal." A witty bit of wordplay lightens the somber scene between the ghost of Jacob Marley and Scrooge, who declares, "There's more of gravy than of grave about you, whatever you are!" A sly twist of words in Margaret Atwood's dystopian classic *The Hand-maid's Tale* (1986) produces "Underground Frailroad," a comparison of escape routes taken by fleeing slaves during the Civil War and by incarcerated female breeders in the fictional, futuristic Republic of Gilead.

Punch and Judy   leading characters in Europe's noisy puppet shows marked by extravagant overacting and violence, such as throwing the baby out the window or the wife beating the husband over the head. Punch and Judy glove puppet shows replaced the complex string-directed marionettes. Controlled by puppeteers known as Punchmen, they were a valued family trade, whose scripts and puppets were passed down like heirlooms. Opening the show with the familiar drum and panpipes overture, the Punchman enhanced the piercing high voices by speaking through a squeaker held between the lips. A cathartic form of fun, the shows traveled the countryside to summer festivals, seaside resorts, homes, crossroads gatherings, and autumn fairs.

The cowardly Punch owes his persona to Pulcinello or Punchinello, a stereotypically foolish flunky, country bumpkin, scofflaw, and dupe caricatured with a hook nose and humped back. Derived from the clown of Roman comedy, Punch is a grotesque figure who wages a running battle with authority. His wife, the shrewish Judy, detests Punch's indiscretions and bumbling misadventures. She delights in beating him with a cudgel. Usually, the errant Punch ends up being hanged or eaten by an alligator. Other standard characters in Punch and Judy shows are the couple's dog Toby, a baby, doctor, black servant, crocodile, devil, beadle, clown, ghost, Mr. Jones, police officer, Hector the horse, and a hangman. The French version, Polichinelle, and the Russian Petroushka or Petrouchka were similarly popular.

Polichinelle gave place to the French rage, the Grand Guignol.

The popular Punchman Signor Bologna appeared in London in the mid-seventeenth century and impressed diarist Samuel Pepys in May 1662. From 1711 to 1713, Martin Powell directed London's Punch Theatre at Covent Garden. The familiar puppet husband appears in *A Second Tale of a Tub* (1715), a polemical attack by Powell on a personal enemy, Robert Harley. In the nineteenth century, novelist Charles Dickens developed *The Old Curiosity Shop* (1841) on Punch. A contemporary, Payne Collier, published the first Punch and Judy scriptbook, which was illustrated by George Cruikshank. The American dramatist Philip Barry composed the play *A Punch for Judy* (1920), drawing on the conventions of the puppet pair. In 1992, dramatists David Gordon and son Ain Gordon produced the play *Punch and Judy Get Divorced*, an updated cartoon view of the marital battlefield that evolved from the Mikhail Baryshnikov White Oak Dance Project and appeared on PBS-TV.

pyrrhic foot   an unaccented metrical unit composed of two short syllables (˘ ˘).

qasida [kah•SEE•dah]   in early Arab-Islamic literature, a long, richly imaged ode or rhapsody ranging from 40 to 120 lines, featuring intricate meter and bound by a single end assonance. The qasida, which spread to Africa and Malaysia and remained popular from 500 to 1950 A.D., centers on themes of lost love, quests, hunting, religious rapture, and lyrical praise of a monarch or caliph. An example by Mowlana Rumi exclaims:

> A Sufi, I am
> Pure of heart
> In rapture, my very being cries out: Ali Ali.

The classic model and forerunner of the ghazal, *Mu'allaqat* or *The Seven Golden Odes* (ca. 650 A.D.), was composed by a group of seventh-century pre-Islamic poets, including 'Antara, author of a stirring work on warfare. The late ninth-century poet Abu Tammam produced an influential courtly qasida that links the emergence of spring to the leadership of his caliph.

See also ghazal.

qita [KEE•tah]   in Arabic literature, a thematic grouping of verses or poems.

quatrain [KWAH•trayn]   a common stanza form in world poetry containing four lines, either rhymed or unrhymed, which forms the working unit of the ballad, hymn, and Petrarchan or Elizabethan sonnet. In a corrido from the Mexican Revolution era cited in John Reed's *Insurgent Mexico* (1914), a four-line refrain urges:

> Fly, fly away, little dove,
> Fly over the prairies,
> And say that Villa has come
> To drive them all over forever.

rake   the angle of a canted stage, which is inclined upward from front to back to improve audience sightlines. Initiated by Sebastiano Serlio in his book *Architettura* (1545), the sloping of the stage increases the illusion of forced perspective, an asset of the Duke's Theatre in Dorset Garden, the Drury Lane theater in London, and L'Opéra in Paris. The practice continued into the Restoration and can be found on contemporary stages, for example, the American Shakespeare Festival Theatre in Stratford, Connecticut. Performing on a raked stage is difficult, but the construction increases audience comprehension of the interplay of actors at the back of the stage.

rap a shallow, loosely phrased dialect rhyme derived from the fast talk of radio disc jockeys, griot rhymers, scat and blues singers, sales spiels, political speeches, road gangs and prison inmates, and call-and-response gospel litany. Rap dialogue is a form of insult exchange and has been known as playing the dozens, toasting, sounding, dissing or dishing, signifying, and capping. The verbal meter and staccato beat permeate novels, poetry, drama, and screenplays and reflect the oral ancestry of Africa and the Caribbean. Rap relieves racial, social, religious, and personal tensions by taunting or replying to an enemy, unfair law, or social stigma, particularly racism.

Derived from the urban scene, rap's monotonous verse gives the impression of impromptu composition. Rap encases nonsensical, sing-song sentiments about joblessness, drugs, explicit sexual practice, police brutality, and school and workplace discrimination in a strong political statement, complaint, or protest. For example, the dope dealer struts and boasts:

> No troubles for me, all reet and cool;
> At home in the street, don't need no school.
> Tending to business all by myself,
> Selling my stuff from off the shelf.

See also doggerel, jingle.

realism a recreation of life in theme, plot, setting, mood, and characterization, as displayed by the starkness of rural life in "Under the Lion's Paw," a story from Hamlin Garland's *Main-Travelled Roads* (1891):

Something deep and resonant vibrated within my brain as I looked out upon this monotonous and commonplace landscape. I realized for the first time that the east had surfeited me with picturesqueness. It appeared that I had been living for six years amid painted, neatly arranged pasteboard scenery. Now I dropped to the level of nature unadorned down to the ugly unkempt lanes I knew so well, back to the pungent realities of the streamless plain.

Understated realism is the aim of two Western stories from Dorothy Johnson's *Indian Country* (1949): "The Man Who Shot Liberty Valance" and "A Man Called Horse." Similarly, displacement from the Appalachians to a city slum colors Harriette Arnow's novel *The Dollmaker* (1954).

An element of realistic drama, verismo, is a style of acting, writing, and operatic performance that gained international popularity when it was introduced in Italy and France in the late nineteenth century. Influenced by Baudelaire, Edgar Allan Poe, and German romanticism, verismo dramas and acting styles stress utmost realism and naturalism, particularly impassioned speeches. In terms of themes and ideas, verismo dramas parallel works by Émile Zola and Honoré de Balzac. Its chief ingredients were social themes and working class characters.

Outstanding examples of veristic literature—also known as *scapiagliatura* or Milanese bohemianism—include Giuseppe Rovani's saga *The Hundred Years* (1865), Luigi Capuana's short stories in *Studies of Women* (1877), Pietro Mascagni's opera *Cavelleria Rusticana* (1890), derived from the play by Sicilian novelist Giovanni Verga, Ruggero Leoncavallo's opera *Pagliacci* (1892), Federico de Roberto's novel *The Viceroys* (1894), Giacomo Puccini's opera *Tosca* (1900), Federigo Tozzi's *With Closed Eyes* (1919), and Nobelist Grazia Deledda's novel *The Mother* (1920).

The rise of Mussolini's fascists during World War II suppressed the movement, but it revived in the late 1940s as neorealism, displayed in the screen work of Roberto Rossellini and Anna Magnani and in the English translation of Verga's *The House by the Medlar Tree* (1953).

refrain   a repeated word, line, chant, or stanza at regular intervals that echoes an emotion or rounds out a series of verses in a narrative poem, ballad, or song, as in the nonsense tag, "Hey nonny, nonny" in William Shakespeare's *Much Ado About Nothing* (ca. 1598), the line "Follow the drinking gourd" in the spiritual by the same name, the call "You'll come a-waltzing, Matilda with me!" in A. B. Paterson's "Waltzing Matilda" (1895), the vendors' cries in Indian poet Sarojini Naidu's poem "Street Cries," and the chorus, "Never free, never free, never free" in Grenadian poet Abdul DeCoteau Malik's poem "Revo." Refrains are also a conspicuous element in speech, short story, and novel, as found in the echoing cry "O lost" in Thomas Wolfe's novel *Look Homeward, Angel* (1929). Variations on the recurrent refrain, called incremental repetition, may emphasize some new aspect in a stanza by a slight shift in diction, tense, or rhythm, or may provide closure.

regionalism   concentration on a particular geographic area and its inhabitants, lore, history, customs, speech, and beliefs, for example, the local settings of Sean O'Faolain's Irish short stories and Tayeb Salih's stories of Sudan. From American literature, significant contributions to regionalism are found in Sidney Lanier's coastal poem "The Marshes of Glynn" (1878), Lafcadio Hearn's *Chita: A Memory of Last Island* (1889), Robert Frost's immersion in the spare New England landscape in "Home Burial" (1914), "The Death of the Hired Man" (1914),

"Birches" (1916), and "Stopping by Woods on a Snowy Evening" (1923), Julia Peterkin's plantation lore in the novel, *Scarlet Sister Mary* (1928), Earl Hamner, Jr.'s sentimental family scenes in *The Homecoming* (1970), and Freddie Rhone's Trinidadian radio play, *Calabash Alley* (1973). A popular Southern compendium, Eliot Wigginton's *The Foxfire Book* (1969) contains photos, essays, tales, songs, ritual, and descriptions, for example, an interview with "Aunt Arie," who says of her life in the Appalachian mountains, "We made a good life here, but we put in lots'a'time. Many an' many a night I've been workin' when two o'clock come in th'mornin'-cardin'n'spinnin'n'sewin'."

renga   [REHN•gah]   a lengthy series of complex, interlocking tanka or lyric verses written by a group of Japanese poets, who extended the finished show piece to hundreds or even a thousand units. Artificial in style and tone and similar to a round robin, the renga developed as entertaining exercises in impromptu versification during the thirteenth century, when court poets collaborated on interconnecting stanzas written in a few hours in competition for a prize. Matsuo Basho, a seventeenth-century poetry master, preferred a limit of thirty-six stanzas. His and other renga were often destroyed after the contest. Others survive in anthologies and chapbooks.

Like tanka poets of the royal Japanese court, current renga participants of many nationalities use the opening stanzas as an opportunity to introduce themselves and to show off their expertise, for example, in an internet exercise in group verse. The integrated subject matter tends toward imagism, such as evanescence in nature or the seasons. Each segment relates to the preceding poem, either in subject matter, as a contrast to a previous mood, or through pun, repetition, alliteration, or rhythm. The closing verses focus on a positive, restful image, such as peace, serenity, or the arrival of spring.

repartee   a fast-paced exchange of words or series of witty comebacks during a verbal duel, as found in comic scenes involving Falstaff in William Shakespeare's *The Merry Wives of Windsor* (ca. 1597). The tone and subject matter of repartee ranges from the sniping dealings between horse-seller and buyer in Charles Portis's *True Grit* (1968) to the darkly comic exchange that is the substance of Marsha Norman's suicide play, *'night Mother* (1982).

In vaudeville and musical comedy, repartee spices up dialogue by emphasizing a volley of humorous give and take. In Gilbert and Sullivan's popular *H. M. S. Pinafore* (1878), the ship's captain claims that he never uses bad language:

> Captain: I never use a big, big D—
> All: What, never?
> Captain: No, never!
> All: What, never?
> Captain: Hardly ever!
> All: Hardly ever swears a big big D—.

In the discussion of the smoking habits of apostles and saints in Leonore Fleischer's *Agnes of God* (1985), Mother Miriam Ruth chortles, "Saint Ignatius, I think, would smoke cigars and then stub them out on the soles of his feet." In reply, Dr. Martha Livingston mimics Mary Magdalene, saying, "You've come a long way, baby."

repetition   a sound device that emphasizes an idea through multiple uses of a syllable, word, phrase, or sentence, for example, Uncas's plaintive invocation to the Algonquin god Manitou in James Fenimore Cooper's *The Last of the Mohicans* (1826):

> Manitou! Manitou! Manitou!
> Thou art great, thou art good, thou art
>   wise:
> Manitou! Manitou!
> Thou art just.

Repetition spans world literature, invigorating the title of Guyanan playwrights David Caudeiron and Alwin Bully's *Speak Brother Speak* (1972), the insistent anaphora or repeated paragraph openings in John Kennedy's inaugural address (1960), and the dramatic cry in Randall Jarrell's poem "The Woman at the Washington Zoo" (1960), which concludes,

> You know what I was.
> You see what I am: change me, change
>   me!

Repetition is the soul of an anonymous verse dialogue between divinities recorded in the Japanese anthology, *Nihonshoki* (720 A.D.):

> How happy I am! I have met a handsome maid.
> How happy I am! I have met a lovely maid.

Repetition is also an element of abstract writing, for example, Allen Ginsberg's multiple use of "holy" in *Howl* (1956), which results in a litany of sacredness: "The typewriter is holy the poem is holy the voice is holy the hearers are holy the ecstasy is holy." Echoed thoughts form a sober undercurrent in James Dickey's "Angina" (1970), which speaks the sufferer's mantra, "I must be still and not worry, not worry, not worry, to hold my peace, my poor place, my own."

Repetition is common to wise sayings, sports chants, advertising, nursery rhymes, children's literature, folk songs, hymns, and popular music and in titles of varied genres, as in Walt Whitman's poem "Pioneers, O Pioneers!" (1855), William Faulkner's complex dynasty novel *Absalom,*

Absalom! (1936), and Maya Angelou's screenplay *Georgia, Georgia* (1971). In *Walden* (1854), philosopher Henry David Thoreau summarizes his disdain for a hurried, complicated lifestyle with his famous admonition, "Our lives are frittered away by detail…. Simplify, simplify." As a model of profusion, Mark Twain heightens his humorous travelogue on Honolulu, Hawaii in *Roughing It* (1872) with a recounting of

> cats—tomcats, Mary Ann cats, long-tailed cats, bobtailed cats, blind cats, one-eyed cats, walleyed cats, cross-eyed cats, gray cats, black cats, white cats, yellow cats, striped cats, spotted cats, tame cats, wild cats, singed cats, individual cats, groups of cats, platoons of cats, companies of cats, regiments of cats, armies of cats, multitudes of cats, millions of cats, and all of them sleek, fat, lazy, and sound asleep.

See also parallelism, refrain.

resolution   the settling of differences, adapting to change, or solving of a problem or dilemma in the falling action of a play, for example, in August Wilson's *Fences* (1986), a tense, confrontational domestic drama about Troy Maxson, a willful, wayward husband and father whose dreams and plans conclude with his funeral. At his death, his wife Rose struggles to requite feelings and resentments that derive from the dead man's failures. *See also* drama, Freytag diagram, plot.

rhapsody   a literary or musical work resulting from a profuse outpouring of feeling, as contained in the rhapsodic line from the medieval Persian narrative romance *Layla and Majnun* that pleads, "Let me not be cured of love, but let my passion grow!" Usually unstructured, incoherent, and ranging out of control, the rhapsody demonstrates obsessive ecstasy.

Derived from the recitation of impromptu verses or fragments by the Greek rhapsodist or minstrel, rhapsody has become a blanket term for wild, rushing emotion or extravagant outbursts, as found in the love lyrics of Sappho and Catullus, the Chinese compendium *Wen Xuan* (ca. 530 A.D.), and Sufist poet Rumi's *Divan-e Shams* [The Collected Verse of Shams] (ca. 1260). The genre is implied by the title of T. S. Eliot's somewhat subdued "Rhapsody on a Windy Night" (1917).

Other works contain rhapsodic passages, for example, the ravings of the lover besotted with passion in Emily Brontë's *Wuthering Heights* (1846), the rapturous wooing in the balcony scene and love letter in Edmond Rostand's *Cyrano de Bergerac* (1897), the frenzied pacing and mental torment of the female speaker fearing for the safety of her love in Amy Lowell's poem "Patterns," from *Men, Women and Ghosts* (1916), the Virgin Mary's euphoric epiphany in Lucille Clifton's "Holy Night" (1980), and the mythic yearnings and physical cravings of a pueblo dwellers in Leslie Marmon Silko's "Yellow Woman" (1993).

rhetoric [REH•toh•rihk]   the art of persuasive expression. Composing clearly and effectively is the rhetorician's purpose, whether in written or spoken form. In ancient times, rhetoric formed the core of advanced education for young Greek and Roman men seeking careers in law and public life. The rules of rhetoric were a major concern of such effective speakers and writers in ancient Greece and Rome as Tisias and Corax of Syracuse, who first established the discipline of rhetoric, and Julius Caesar, noted for oratory as well as for military acumen. Model works include Lysias's *Olympicus* (388 B.C.), Demosthenes's *Philippics* (351 B.C.), Plato's *Phaedrus* (ca. 349 B.C.), Aristotle's *Rhetoric* (ca. 335 B.C.), Cicero's *De Oratione* (ca. 45 B.C.), Quintilian's *Institutio*

Oratorio (97 A.D.), Tacitus's *Dialogues of the Orators* (ca. 105 A.D.), and Longinus's *On the Sublime* (ca. first century A.D.). Essays and handbooks on the subject remained in vogue among scholars, rising to a new height in the Middle Ages. Rhetoric deviates from poetry by avoiding the emotions to stress logical development of straightforward ideas in declamation, debate, and ceremonial address.

In modern times, the term "rhetoric" has deviated from a reference to public speaking or persuasive composition to the equivalent of hype. Rhetoric is currently a pejorative maligning the insincerity, adornment, or manipulation of political harangue or a contrived sales spiel. Examples of studied artifice appear in the protagonist's sermons in Sinclair Lewis's *Elmer Gantry* (1927) and a huckster's effusive pitch in Meredith Willson's *The Music Man* (1957), which promises: "River City's gonna have her Boys Band! As sure as the Lord made little green apples, and that band's gonna be in uniform!"

rhetorical question   a statement phrased in the form of a question merely for effect; also, a question that does not anticipate or require an answer, as in François Villon's question, "Where are the snows of yesteryear?" which Tennessee Williams repeats in the staging of *The Glass Menagerie* (1945). Joel Chandler Harris's griot persona uses the rhetorical question to propose a dialect aphorism: "Youk'n hide de fier, but w'at you gwine do wid de smoke?" Dramatist Bertolt Brecht compounds the rhetorical question in *The Good Woman of Setzuan* (1940) by expanding on his question with possible answers given as questions: "How could a better ending be arranged? Could one change people? Can the world be changed? Would new gods do the trick? Will atheism? Moral Rearmament? Materialism?"

A more lyric approach in Isak Dinesen's *Out of Africa* (1937) follows a similar method of expanding possibilities through a series of questions:

> If I know a song of Africa,—I thought, —of the Giraffe, and the African new moon lying on her back, of the ploughs in the fields, and the sweaty faces of the coffee-pickers, does Africa know a song of me? Would the air over the plain quiver with a colour that I had had on, or the children invent a game in which my name was, or the full moon throw a shadow over the gravel of the drive that was like me, or would the eagles of Ngong look out for me?

rhyme   a pattern of words that contains identical or similar sounds, for instance the echo words hurly burly, helter-skelter, and pell mell. Rhyme enriches structure by linking words and sounds that echo the sense or theme of poetic lines. Aside from true rhyme—also called complete, perfect, or full rhyme, as in said/white, head/right in Lewis Carroll's "Father William" in *Alice in Wonderland* (1865)— variances include:

• approximate rhyme—also called slant, oblique, half, near, partial, or imperfect rhyme—which is a less exacting patterning of words, for example, woods/intrudes in lines 1 and 3 in Lord Byron's *Childe Harold's Pilgrimage* (1812):

> There is a pleasure in the pathless woods,
> There is a rapture on the lonely shore,
> There is a society where none intrudes,
> By the deep sea, and music in its roar:
> I love no man the less, but nature more.

• assonance, which rhymes only vowels, for example, the *oo* sound in loose/spoon, the long *a* sound in quail/play, and the *yu* sound in you/spume
• consonance, which rhymes several consonant sounds, as in the *f* and *t* in fight/fate, the *p* and *s* sounds in pass/press, and the *tr* and *n* sounds in train/string

- false rhyme, the alternation of perfect and approximate or imperfect rhyme, as in Sam/am, seek/sake, call/tall, as/was

- internal or leonine rhyme, which links words with duplicate sound patterns within a line of verse, as in Randall Jarrell's "The Death of the Ball Turret Gunner" (1955), where the speaker refers to "black flak"

- ironic, strained, or misplaced rhyme, which links an accented and an unaccented syllable, for example, labor/no more, hoe-down/reknown, and timeless/my guess

- mosaic rhyme, which matches one rhyming word with a cluster of words, as found in cuccu/wude nu in an Anglo-Saxon rondel dating to 1240:

> Sumer is icumen in
>   Lhude sing cuccu!
> Groweth sed, and bloweth med,
>   And springth the wude nu:
>   Sing cuccu!

Mosaic rhyme is an element in Eleanor Fargeon's "Morning Has Broken" (1931), which allies sunlight/one light and new fall/dewfall. Ogden Nash turns mosaic rhyme into a comic pattern in "The Emmet" (1931), in which "The modern ant, when trod upon,/Exclaims 'I'll be a son-of-a-gun!'" Sylvia Plath creates an unexpected linkage in "Daddy" (1962) with not do/black shoe/achoo.

- pararhyme, a type of consonance that duplicates a spelling pattern of consonant letters, as in clan/clone and fire/fare

- random rhyme, which wanders in and out of formal rhyming patterns with occasional passages in tight full rhyme and the rest unrhymed, alliterated, or scarcely rhyming, for example, said/wed, wont, lay/play, called, loved/ moved

- *rime riche,* or identical rhyme, a French pattern of rhyming that pairs homophones or homophonic syllables, as in sees/seize and repair/compare

- sight rhyme or eye rhyme, a style of ending lines with words that give the appearance of rhyme through similar spelling patterns, as in soot/boot and love/prove

- surprise rhyme, the witty or ridiculous pairing of unexpected end rhymes, as found in W. S. Gilbert's *Ferdinando and Elvira* (ca. 1875):

> Tell me whither I may hie me, tell me, dear one that I *may* know—
> Is it up the highest Andes? down a horrible volcano?"
> But she said, "It isn't polar bears, or hot volcano grottoes,
> Only find out who it is that writes those lovely cracker mottoes!"

- synthetic rhyme, the alteration of sounds and spellings to fit words into a cadence and pattern of rhymes, as in the ballad lines "He rode through the leafy willow/Across the frozen ground-o/To see his lady fair"

- tail rhyme, a short tag line or lines echoing or murmuring after each stanza of a poem, for example, concluding alleluias in St. Francis of Assisi's "All Creatures of Our God and King" (thirteenth century) and the lone foot "Come soon" at the end of a stanza in Percy Bysshe Shelley's "To Night" (1824). A variant of tail rhyme is the short prefatory line, "Even now," before each stanza of twelfth-century Brahmin poet Chauras's "Black Marigolds," and the title that precedes each stanza of Lebanese Islamic poet Mikha'il Nu'ayama's poem "O Brother" (1963).

- triple rhyme, a feminine rhyme ending with two unstressed syllables, as found in tenderness/slenderness, bantering/cantering, and cheerfully/fearfully

Another differentiation in rhyme involves the placement of accent. If the final syllable of a pair of rhymed words is unstressed, as in hearken/darken or gracing/placing, the line demonstrates feminine or double rhyme, a flowing pattern often found in humorous or lyric verse. If the final syllable is stressed, as in correct/select and intone/condone, the line demonstrates terminal or masculine rhyme, the standard linkage of hymns.

rhyme scheme the pattern of rhymed words at the ends of lines. Each rhyme is given a letter of the alphabet, as in the ends of lines from Robert Frost's "Stopping by Woods on a Snowy Evening" (1923):

- stanza 1 ends in know/though/here/snow or aaba
- stanza 2 ends in queer/near/lake/year or bbcb
- stanza 3 ends in shake/mistake/sweep/flake or ccdc
- the final stanza rounds out the poem with deep/keep/sleep/sleep or dddd. The interlocking rhyme scheme, which begins a new stanza with the rhyme of line 3 in the previous stanza, bonds the poem into a unified whole. To end the sequence, Frost departs from the pattern with four lines rhymed alike

Significant rhyme schemes include these:

- Elizabethan or Shakespearean sonnet, rhyming ababcdcdefefgg
- Petrarchan sonnet, which rhymes abbaabbacdecde
- rhyme royal, a rhyme scheme allying seven-line stanzas, ends in the pattern ababbcc. This tight connecting pattern of end rhyme appears in Geoffrey Chaucer's *Troilus and Criseyde* (ca. 1380) and *The Parlement of Foules* (ca. 1380), William Shakespeare's *The Rape of Lucrece* (1594), William Wordsworth's "Resolution and Independence" (1802), and John Masefield's *The Widow in the Bye Street* (1912)

- Spenserian stanza, which rhymes ababbcbcc, as found in Edmund Spenser's *The Faerie Queene* (1596)
- terza rima [TEHRT zuh REE muh], the linking of triplet lines in a chain, rhyming aba, bcb, cdc, ded, etc., a flexible pattern that was Dante Alighieri's choice for the *Divine Commedia* (ca. 1320)
- villanelle, the nineteen-line French verse stanza composed in iambic pentameter and rhyming aba aba aba aba abaa, the pattern of Dylan Thomas's famed death poem, "Do Not Go Gentle into That Good Night" (1952).

See also couplet, sonnet, Spenserian stanza.

rhythm a cadence arising from a natural progression of stresses within long and short syllables, for example, the ecstatic pulsing of Rumi's *Masnavi-ye Ma'navi* [Spiritual Couplets] (thirteenth century) and the quantitative acoustical music of four measures or beats in the opening stanza of Mary Elizabeth Coleridge's "Regina" (1908):

> My Queen her scepter did lay down,
> She took from her head the golden crown
> Worn by right of her royal birth.
> Her purple robe she cast aside,
> And the scarlet vestures of her pride,
> That was the pride of the earth.
> In her nakedness was she
> Queen of the world, herself and me.

Variant patterns of rhythm include these:

- common running rhythm, a normal English cadence containing feet marked by two or three syllables. When the line opens with stress, the rhythm is called falling rhythm; if the line ends with stress, the rhythm is called rising rhythm
- falling rhythm, in which a stressed syllable begins each line of verse, as found in a segment of pessimistic doggerel from the *Carmina Burana* (thirteenth century):

Ordo languet
Pudicitia sordescit
Pietas refugit
Doctrina rarescit
Sophia habescit.

• rising rhythm, the most natural to English speech, which ends each line with a stress, for example, a stanza from Elizabeth Barrett Browning's *The Runaway Slave at Pilgrim's Point* (1850):

> O pilgrim-souls, I speak to you!
>   I see you come proud and slow
> From the land of the spirits pale as dew
>   And round me and round me ye go.
> O pilgrims, I have gasped and run
> All night long from the whips of one
>   Who in your names works sin and
> woe!

• rocking rhythm, a form of running rhythm that involves the sandwiching of a stressed syllable between two unstressed syllables, for example, "for Susan in May-time"

• sprung rhythm, the energetic cadence of ordinary speech and written language, which counts only the stressed beats, often multiple stressed syllables occurring together. Sprung rhythm disregards the number of unaccented beats that accompany them, as in Emily Dickinson's conversational verse, "I'm Nobody" (1891):

> I'm Nobody! Who are you?
> Are you—Nobody—Too?
> Then there's a pair of us?
> Don't tell! they'd advertise—you know!

See also meter.

riddle   a child's question-and-answer game, puzzling definition, or teasing comparison; also, conundra and enigma concerning religious, ethical, and moral truths, for example, Jain non-canonical literature such as Bhavadeva Somadeva's *Katharatnakara* (ca. 1082), a Sanskrit story collection, and the pre-Columbian Lenape riddle that predicted seven years in advance the European sailing vessels that would bring white adventurers to North America. The prophet pictures the strange European ship as a swimmer lying on his back while smoking and extending a knife. The graphic image foresees the cannon smoke billowing above the sharp prow that slices its way through the Atlantic waters.

Various levels of riddling are indigenous to folk literature and song from Persia, Bible settings in the Middle East, Africa, Greece and Rome, and Celtic England. From classical Eastern lore, the *Vetalapancavimsati* contains this ethical puzzle:

> A man, about to have his meal, feels that the paddy from which his rice was prepared grew in a land near a crematory. Another man cannot sleep on a fine upholstered bed, because, under several layers of cushions, there is a strand of hair. Of these two, who is the greater epicure?

Prominent among folk collections from India are collections of riddle stories and the riddle-questions of Rajasekhara's *Antarakatha-samgraha* (early tenth century). Among world classics, the riddle is an identifiable form in the writings of the epic *Rigveda* (ca. 1000 B.C.), Sophocles's tragedy, *Oedipus Rex* (409 B.C.), Petronius Arbiter's *Satyricon* (60 A.D.), Aldhelm's *Enigmata* (ca. 708), Cynewulf's poems (eighth century), Firdausi's *Shahnamen* (1000), *Exeter Book* (tenth century), and works by Spain's Dunash ben Labrat (tenth century) and Arabia's Al-Hariri (ca. 1120). Riddling enhances verse inquiry, as found in Emily Dickinson's "A Narrow Fellow" (ca. 1880) and in twelve sign-by-sign quatrains forming Joseph Addison's mild satire of zodiac stereotypes, for example:

> Who criticizes all she sees:
> Yes, e'en would analyze a sneeze?

Who hugs and loves her own disease?
Humpf, Virgo.

A 28-line geographical puzzler from the world of ocean steamers comes from the tenth fable of Rudyard Kipling's *Just-So Stories* (1902), a children's compendium written to please the author's daughter Josephine.

Reprised in modern literature, the riddle may employ pun or wordplay or may reflect a motif or theme. Playwright George Bernard Shaw employs a teasing conundrum to illustrate the concept of mixed identity in his riddling rhyme from *Pygmalion* (1912), a math stumper based on three nicknames for Elizabeth:

Eliza, Elizabeth, Betsy and Bess,
They went to the woods to get a bird's nes':
They found a nest with four eggs in it:
They took one apiece, and left three in it.

Later examples include questions about animals and plants of the desert in Mary Hunter Austin's *Children Sing in the Far West* (1928), a shift in point of view in Craig Raine's poem "A Martian Sends a Postcard Home" (1979), and wish fulfillment in "The Riddle Tale of Freedom," a slave-era story in Virginia Hamilton's *The People Could Fly* (1985).

rising action the revelation of differences, crises, or problems following the exposition of setting and characters in the first half of a play.

See also drama, Freytag diagram, plot.

Ritterdrama a prose knight drama, popular during the *Sturm und Drang* in eighteenth-century Germany. A manifestation of romanticism, Ritterdrama contains a grab-bag of medieval elements—from costuming, scenery, jousting, and armor to vows of chastity and mad monks. Themes tend toward patriotism, idealism, and passion. The most suc-cessful producers of Ritterdrama are Josef August von Törring and Joseph Marius Babo. The genre faltered when reactionaries banned Ritterdrama in Munich, yet it continued to thrive in Austria. Because of the stress on medieval pageantry at the expense of the dramatic storyline, the genre waned by the end of the nineteenth century.

roman à clef [roh•MAHN•ah•CLAY] a "novel with key" or work of fiction that thinly conceals actual characters and events, for instance, revelations in William Wells Brown's *Clotelle* (1853), a slave-era romance reflecting the love relationship between Thomas Jefferson and his slave, Sally Hemings; Robert Penn Warren's social novel, *All the King's Men* (1946), a study of the dynamic populism of Willie Stark, a fictional character resembling Huey P. "Kingfish" Long; *Answered Prayers: The Partial Manuscript* (1986), Truman Capote's subdued memoir of notables and hangers-on to New York's esthetic set; and Carrie Fisher's revelations about her mother, actress Debbie Reynolds, in *Postcards from the Edge* (1990).

romance a broad term for an action story or narrative poem based on elements of fantasy, idealism, adventure, pursuit, mystery, escapism, and love, for instance, Kalidasa's heroic romance *Shakuntala* (ca. 460 A.D.), medieval stories of Parsifal and the ill-fated loves of Tristram and Iseult, the French *Aucassin and Nicolette* (ca. 1220), the mountain lovers Tom Dooley and Laura Foster of Appalachian ballads, Bankim Chandra Chatterjee's *Anandamath* (1882), and Arab-American novelist Afifa Karam's *Badiyah and Fuad* (1906).

Romance is a common theme in platform storytelling, as reflected by the multiple versions of "Sir Gawain and the

Green Knight," a poem of enchantment from Arthurian lore, as performed and recorded by platform storytellers Ed Stivender, Heather Forest, Chuck Larkin, and Robert Wilhelm.

Notable romances from American literature include John Pendleton Kennedy's plantation idyll *Horse-Shoe Robinson* (1835), E. D. E. N. Southworth's tale of foundered love in *The Planter's Northern Bride* (1851), Herman Melville's themes of obsession and retribution in *Moby-Dick* (1851), Helen Hunt Jackson's story of racial identity in *Ramona* (1894), Edna Ferber's frontier sagas *Saratoga Trunk* (1941) and *Giant* (1952), Robert Penn Warren's American Civil War motifs of miscegenation and loss in *Band of Angels* (1955), Margaret Walker's *Jubilee* (1966), and Diane Wolkstein and Samuel Noah Kramer's recreation of a Sumerian love saga, *Inanna: Queen of Heaven and Earth, Her Stories and Hymns from Sumer* (1983).

romantic comedy   a drama that reveals how love overcomes obstacles, such as disapproving parents, harsh laws, or discrimination based on social class, race, religion, or background. Common elements include mix-ups in identity, disguises, cross-dressing, flight from authority figures, and happy endings, as found in William Shakespeare's *As You Like It* (ca. 1599), George Washington Parke Custis's *Pocahontas, or The Settlers of Virginia* (1830), Anita Loos's *Gentlemen Prefer Blondes* (1925), and Jerome Lawrence and Robert Edwin Lee's *Auntie Mame* (1957).

romanticism   a tendency in prose or poetry to rebel against the strictures of classicism and to exult in imagination, grotesquerie, untamed nature, gothic details, coincidence, symbolism, individualism, love of liberty, faraway places, and melancholy, as demonstrated by Johann Goethe's *Werther* (1773),

Johann Schiller's *Raüber* (1782), William Wordsworth's *Lyrical Ballads* (1798), Mary Shelley's *Frankenstein* (1818), and Victor Hugo's *Hernani* (1830).

Charlotte Brontë's *Jane Eyre* (1847) is a romantic novel that embroiders a love story with such romantic touches as the heroine's flight to the moors, a chance meeting with her three cousins, and receipt of an unexpected inheritance from an uncle in Madeira. Jane represents the romantic ideal in her prayers and telepathic communion with her true love and in a climactic reunion with Rochester, whose loss of vision and a hand from a fall during a fire symbolize his penance for attempted bigamy, which he expiates by trying to rescue his insane wife Bertha. A key factor in the novel's romanticism is Jane's individuality and her insistence on self-expression through art and natural conversation rather than the stilted drawing-room behaviors favored by her rival, Blanche Ingram.

See also Ritterdrama.

rondeau [RAHN•doh]   a strict poetic style popular in France in the sixteenth century for sprightly poems consisting of thirteen-fifteen lines divided into three stanzas and based on two rhymes. The opening phrases return in the second and third stanzas as a refrain, or *rentrement*, producing a rhyme scheme aabba, aab and refrain, aabba and refrain. W. E. Henley's reclaimed rondeau, "O, Falmouth Is a Fine Town" (1878), demonstrates a reclaimed medieval refrain rhyming aaaa:

> For it's home, dearie, home—it's home I
>   want to be.
> Our topsails are hoists, and we'll away
>   to sea.
> O, the oak and the ash and the bonnie
>   birken tree
> They're all growing green in the old
>   countrie.

Other adapted versions appear in nine-teenth-century English verse: Henry Austin Dobson's "The Paradox of Time" (1875), Robert Bridges's "Awake, My Heart" (1890), and Ernest Dowson's "A Last Word" (1899). Marilyn Hacker produced a more recent imitation with "Rondeau after a Transatlantic Telephone Call" (1980).

More complicated versions of the rondeau include these restrictive verse styles:

• *rondeau redoublé* [ruh•doo•BLAY], a rarer, more intricate form that maintains two rhymes in a 24-line text divided into six stanzas. The rhyme scheme varies abab, baba, abab, baba, abab, baba; the refrain repeats lines from stanza 1, a style found in poems by Jean de la Fontaine and Antoinette Deshoulières

• rondel [RAHN•d'l], a straight-forward song of thirteen lines and two rhymes. Like the rondeau, the rondel repeats its opening lines as a refrain

• rondelet [rahn•duh•LAY] a seven-line stanza rhyming abaabba, with the third and last lines retaining the gist of line 1

• roundel, the English style of ron-deau featuring eleven lines and two rhymes, the form Algernon Swinburne uses for "Triads" (1878), a series of three questions about nature which begin with

> The word of the sun to the sky,
> The word of the wind to the sea,
>   The word of the moon to the night,
>   What may it be?

The two controlling rhymes continue in stanza 2 with fly/tree/light/me

• roundelay, any jocular rondeau or rondel set to music, featuring short stan-zas ending with a refrain

• roundlet, an abbreviated roundel.

rubai [roo•bah•AY], pl. rubaiyat [ROO•bay•aht] a four-line imagist verse. The ancient quatrain, which rhymes in the first, second, and fourth lines, was favored by the Persian poet Omar Khay-yám, author of *The Rubá'iyát* (ca. 1130 A.D.), which Edward Fitzgerald translated in 1868. A memorable passage about death notes:

> Strange, is it not? that of the myriads who
> Before us pass'd the door of Darkness through,
>   Not one returns to tell us of the Road,
> Which to discover we must travel too.

rune   an ancient symbolic charac-ter conveying secret or mystical meaning. The rune, which is also called a *futhark* from the first six letters—*f, u, th, a, r, k*—of a ritual Teutonic alphabet, is found on coins, drinking horns, weapons, amulets, and stone lintels and steles and in inscrip-tions, recipes for healing herbs, poems by Cynewulf, and the *Kalevala* (1100 B.C.), the Finnish epic. Scandinavian, Ger-manic, and Anglo-Saxon writers used runic letters as magic charms, which Argentine poet Jorge Luis Borges men-tions in his ode, "Hengest Cyuning" (1968). J. R. R. Tolkien, an Anglo-Saxon scholar who assisted in the compilation of the *Oxford English Dictionary*, revived the mystique of runes for his fantasy classics, *The Hobbit* (1937) and *The Lord of the Rings* (1955).

saga   a framework story of both noble and unworthy deeds that interlace the history of a family, clan, tribe, or nation, as found in the Icelandic *Saga of Gunnlaug Serpent-Tongue* (ca. 1250). North American sagas include James Fen-imore Cooper's Leatherstocking series, which begins with *The Pioneers or, The*

Sources of the Susquehanna (1823); also, Edna Ferber's *Cimarron* (1929), Louis L'Amour's *Sitka* (1957), an adventure saga of frontier Alaska; Ariyoshi Sawako's *The River Ki* (1959), Colleen McCullough's Australian saga, *The Thorn Birds* (1977); and Sylvia López-Medina's *Cantora* (1992), which returns to ancestors in Mexico through interview, documents, and visits to the former residences of family members.

Victor Villaseñor's *Rain of Gold* (1991) exemplifies the compounded shortcomings and strengths of the speaker's family and reflects individual and native Mexican elements, for example, tolerance of bootleg liquor, compassion toward deprived Indians, flight from legal authorities, devotion to the church and the Virgin Mary, and gambling as methods of securing a better life in the United States. Overall, the saga expresses the good and bad points of the Gomez-Villaseñor family story. The author gleans material from interviews, family oral history, and research into the Mexican Revolution and Prohibition.

A similar pattern of evils and strengths of the Buendía family emerges in Gabriel García Márquez's *One Hundred Years of Solitude,* in which faulty morals corrupt each generation until the family produces a freak—a boy born with a pig's tail, which the midwife intends to cut off "when the child got his second teeth." A symbolic warning from the family's past, the pigtail presages the saga's violent end, when a lethal wind destroys the dynasty—an end that is inevitable because family members have learned nothing from their past.

sarcasm   wry or spiteful commentary that says the opposite of what is meant, for example, in *I Know Why the Caged Bird Sings* (1970), Maya Angelou's

commentary on the term "quarters" as "a lingering term used wistfully by whites." In William J. Lederer and Eugene Burdick's *The Ugly American* (1958), a Burmese journalist, U Maung Swe, delivers a jolting speech to American diplomats at a dinner party in Rangoon, where he sneers, "Poor America. It took the British a hundred years to lose their prestige in Asia. America has managed to lose hers in ten years."

satire   a vigorous, sharply pointed, and, at times, embarrassingly or cruelly effective mockery that may employ wit and derision to reveal weaknesses in human character. This is the subject of Harry Golden's essay "The Vertical Negro Plan" (1944), a political satire that ridicules pre-integration racism, which focused on the refusal of whites to sit beside non-whites on buses and in schools, churches, and restaurants.

Literary history is dotted with triumphs of truth in laughter in varied genres: the satire of stage comedies— Aristophanes's *The Birds* (414 B.C.), Li Ho's "Joys of the Honorable Princess" (ca. 810 A.D.), William Shakespeare's *The Taming of the Shrew* (ca. 1589), and Aphra Behn's *The Rover* (1677)—as well as Jonathan Swift's acerbic essay "A Modest Proposal" (1729), Robert Browning's dramatic monologue, "Soliloquy of the Spanish Cloister" (1842), Lewis Carroll's children's dystopia, *Alice in Wonderland* (1865), Ambrose Bierce's witty lectionary, *The Devil's Dictionary* (1906), Robert Frost's beast fable, "Departmental: The End of My Ant Jerry" (1930), Claire Boothe Luce's play *The Women* (1935), Shirley Jackson's short story "The Lottery" (1949), Kazuo Ishiguro's social novel *Remains of the Day* (1989), Theodor Geisel's "Dr. Seuss" classic *How the Grinch Stole Christmas* (1957), Gary Larson's ongoing cartoon, *The Far Side*, and Marge

Piercy's poem "The Grey Flannel Sexual Harassment Suit" (1995).

A wickedly funny bit of antiromanticism is John Gay's *The Beggar's Opera* (1728), which applies vigorous political satire, melodrama, and low comedy to the life of folk hero Macheath, a bandit leader and roué whose jilted loves conspire to set him free from jail. Another popular satire of that era, Alexander Pope's *The Dunciad* (1728) uses droll comedic imagery and mock epic seriousness to skewer Colley Cibber, a second-rate author and model of mediocrity. Pope explains the purpose of satire: "Deformity becomes an object of ridicule when a man sets up for being handsome; and so must dullness when he sets up for a wit." In a more jovial vein, Jane Austen employs social satire in *Pride and Prejudice* (1813) to mock the dissension among class levels, misalignment of potential mates, and incongruity in community social behaviors.

A high point in American satire, Sinclair Lewis's *Babbitt* (1922) ridicules the snobbery, insincerity, and soullessness of a dull, egocentric social climber, George Babbitt. The term babbittry serves the English language as an indication of shallow boosterism, complacency, and senseless conformity.

Molly Ivins's compendium, *Molly Ivins Can't Say That, Can She?* (1992), lampoons and ridicules President George Bush. Her derision of late twentieth-century political figures parallels the caricatures and foibles of *Doonesbury*, Garry Trudeau's comic strip, which has satirized President Ronald Reagan as a demented flake and President Bill Clinton as a waffle.

satiric comedy biting humor that scrutinizes such human faults and vices as pride, ambition, avarice, or personal quirks, a favorite target in three popular twentieth-century anti-war novels, Joseph Heller's *Catch-22* (1961), Kurt Vonnegut's *Cat's Cradle* (1963), and Richard Hooker's *MASH* (1968), and in Margaret Atwood's dark romantic comedy, *The Robber Bride* (1993). In family satire, Amy Tan alternates hilarity and family misunderstandings in *The Kitchen God's Wife* (1992), which stresses the customs of Chinese New Year, a holiday that requires celebrants to mend broken relationships and settle debts and quarrels. The comic mishaps at a Buddhist funeral for a departed aunt precede a wrenching war story that explains to a young woman the difficult choices her mother made before fleeing China for a new life in California.

satyr play a short, absurdly comic scene or an interlude that contrasts the intensity of tragedy with vulgar jest, lewd antics, gags, pratfalls, clowning and mumming, and posturing in animal costumes. The source of stage and television skits, blackouts, and send-ups, Greek satyr plays such as Sophocle's *Trackers* (ca. 495 B.C.), Pratinas's fifty examples, and Aeschylus's *The Net-Drawers* (450 B.C.) have vanished over time. The only exception is Euripides's *Cyclops* (438 B.C.).

scansion [SKAN•shuhn] a method of marking lines of verse to determine the rhythmic patterns that dominate a literary work and to highlight variances in rhythm. Each syllable receives either a long or short mark indicating which are stressed and which unemphasized. A single unit of rhythm, called a foot, is set off by a pair of vertical lines, as in this example from "Barbara Frietchie," a poem from John Greenleaf Whittier's *In War Time and Other Poems* (1864):

"Who tou|ches a hair | on this old | gray head

Dies | like a dog, | march on," | he said.

As is common in poetry, the model is a blend of rhythms, in this case, primarily iambic and anapestic feet. The meter is labeled tetrameter because there are four strong beats per line.

scatology   a form of comedy or satire that focuses on bawdy or obscene language, ribaldry, or other questionable or improper jest related to sex and genitalia, excrement and other human effluvia, and normal anatomical functions usually kept private, as found in the German folk classic *Till Eulenspiegel* (1515). A Middle English classic fool tale replete with scurrilous jest and folk humor, Geoffrey Chaucer's "The Miller's Tale" (1385) turns trickery and adultery into a ludicrous comeuppance after a trickster sticks his buttocks out a window and receives a jab with a poker from a fop who had vied with the joker for the attentions of a married woman. Other examples include teethpicking and belchings in François Rabelais's *Gargantua and Pantagruel* (1562), snide references to copulation with Egypt's queen in William Shakespeare's *Antony and Cleopatra* (ca. 1605), intestinal gas and urination in Jonathan Swift's *A Tale of a Tub* (1704) and *Gulliver's Travels* (1727), pimples, bad breath, and dirty teeth in J. D. Salinger's *Catcher in the Rye* (1951), birthing methods in Florence King's *When Sisterhood Was in Flower* (1982), homosexual practices in Umberto Eco's *The Name of the Rose* (1980), dinosaur spoor in Michael Crichton's *Jurassic Park* (1990), vomiting in Laura Esquivel's *Like Water for Chocolate* (1992), purges in Alan Bennett's *The Madness of George III* (1993), and excrement in T. Coraghessan Boyle's *Water Music* (1982) and *The Road to Wellville* (1993), in which a promoter of health foods and regimens maintains a large collection of human stool samples.

scene   a subsection of an act presenting a unified event that takes place in a single setting and is dominated by the confrontation or dialogue among a set of characters, for example, the grave digging scene in William Shakespeare's *Hamlet* (ca. 1599–1600), the accident in Moss Hart and George S. Kaufman's *The Man Who Came to Dinner* (1939), the courtship in Burt Shevelove, Larry Gelbart, and Stephen Sondheim's *A Funny Thing Happened on the Way to the Forum* (1963), the meeting of son and father in Hugh Leonard's *Da* (1973), and the reunion of three sisters in Beth Henley's *Crimes of the Heart* (1979).

science fiction   any fantasy, utopia, jeremiad, or romance that probes the influence of scientific technology, invention, or manipulation on the human form or condition. Sci-fi may denounce experimentation on human life, the focus of Mary Shelley's *Frankenstein* (1818); warn of challenges in the future, as in H. G. Wells's *The Time Machine* (1895) and Ray Bradbury's "There Will Come Soft Rains" (1950) and *Fahrenheit 451* (1953); or predict a vast change in lifestyle, such as interplanetary travel in Arthur C. Clarke's *2001: A Space Odyssey* (1968). Significant works of the ample sci-fi genre include Yevgeny Zamyatin's *We* (1921), Robert A. Heinlein's *Starship Troopers* (1959), Daniel Keyes's *Flowers for Algernon* (1966), Egyptian playwright Tawfiq al-Hakim's *The Fate of a Cockroach* (1966), Ursula K. Le Guin's *The Left Hand of Darkness* (1969), Robert Silverberg's *Good News from the Vatican* (1971), Joanna Russ's "When It Happened" (1972), Marge Piercy's *Woman on the Edge of Time* (1976), P. D. James's *The Children of Men* (1993), and Lois Lowry's *The Giver* (1993).

scripture   any literary text that holds religious or moral implications for a cult or denomination, for example, the

Torah and the Holy Bible, which exists in numerous translations. The meditations of Syrian poet Abul-'Ala al-Ma'arri reflect Koranic style, as found in Canto XVII:

> Whene'er we ask what end
> Our Maker did intend,
> Some answering voice is heard
> That utters no plain word.

World classics include the Indian *Rigveda* (1000 B.C.), Persian *Gathas*, a collection of religious lyrics (seventh century B.C.), Confucius's *Analects* (mid-sixth century B.C.), Lao-tzu's *Tao Te Ching* (300 B.C.), the Hindu *Bhagavad Gita* (first century B.C.), the Buddhist *Dhammapada* (first century B.C.), the Chinese *Li-chi* (ca. 222 A.D.), the *Koran* (seventh century A.D.), Jayadeva's sensuous religious poem *Gita Govinda* (twelfth century A.D.), Rumi's *Mathnawi* (late thirteenth century A.D.), a compendium of Sufi scripture, Joseph Smith's *Book of Mormon* (1830), and *Black Elk Speaks* (1932), which John Neihardt transcribed from interviews with the Sioux holy man.

sedoka [say•DOH•kah] a Japanese verse form consisting of two katautas or stanzas of nineteen syllables varying 5, 7, 7, 5, 7, 7 and composed by a single author. The six lines vary in rhythm and resemble the katauta, which is the work of a pair of poets. *See* katauta.

semantics [sih•MAN•tihks] the study of how words express meaning and how word meanings have varied over time, for example, the denotative and connotative implications of "hussy" and "gay," which have altered from their original meaning of "housewife" and "gladsome" to altogether different meanings in current parlance. Expert opinions on semantic evolution appear in the writings of critic and newspaper columnist H. L. Mencken and in the updated fables of James Thurber.

senryu [SIHN•roo] brief light-hearted, comic, or ironic Japanese verse about everyday situations composed in three lines of five, seven, and five syllables for a total of seventeen syllables, for example,

> My dog is faithful,
> Especially when hungry.
> Then I am master.

The most famous writer of senryu was Karai Hachiemon, an eighteenth-century Japanese poet who wrote, collected, and anthologized the best of comic verse.

sense impressions mental pictures or images that appeal to touch, taste, smell, sight, and sound, as found in the Zuñi prayer that begins "Cover my earth mother four times with many flowers" and the Iglulik Eskimo song that praises the morning by proclaiming, "My face is turned from the dark of night." The Hebrew psalmist describes a limitless physical relationship with God in Psalm 139:7–12:

> Whither shall I go from thy spirit? or whither shall I flee from thy presence?
> If I ascend up into heaven, thou art there: if I make my bed in hell, behold, thou art there.
> If I take the wings of the morning, and dwell in the uttermost parts of the sea,
> Even there shall thy hand lead me, and thy right hand shall hold me.
> If I say, Surely the darkness shall cover me; even the night shall be light about me.
> Yea, the darkness hideth not from thee: but the night shineth as the day: the darkness and the light are both alike to thee.

Sense impressions are the elements that flesh out, dramatize, and enrich the best in nature lore, love poetry, and adventure and war stories, for example, the nature poems of Gerard Manley Hopkins, frontier fiction of Jack London, hikes and observations of Scottish-American naturalist John Muir, the romantic verse of Sappho, Catullus, John Keats, Christina Rossetti, and Amy Lowell, and the combat impressions of Mariano Azuela, John Reed, Erich Maria Remarque, Stephen Crane, Dalton Trumbo, Walter Dean Myers, and Michael Ondaatje.

sentimental comedy a predictable play composed of a superficial plot and shallow characterization that tends to the extremes of vice and virtue. The sentimental comedy overindulges in benevolence, tender reunions, forgiveness, and reconciliation.

Sentimentality is the focus of Mary Chase's *Harvey* (1944), a humorous, lightly satirical comedy that pits the bumbling, harmless alcoholic Elwood P. Dowd against his witless sister, Veta Louise. She blames his obsession with an invisible six-foot rabbit for scaring off potential beaux for her spinster daughter, Myrtle Mae. As is common in sentimental comedy, all ends well for the family: Although Veta schemes to have Elwood committed to an asylum, she relents and returns with her forgiving brother, who leads home his beloved phantasm.

sequel a literary work that parallels or extends the setting, characters, and themes of a previous work by taking the original action beyond the scope of the prototype, for example, George L. Aiken's *Uncle Tom's Cabin* (1852) and its sequel, *The Death of Uncle Tom, or The Religion of the Lowly* (1852), both derived from Harriet Beecher Stowe's best-selling novel, and Guinean novelist Camara Laye's *A Dream of Africa*, a sequel to *The Radiance of the King* (1956). In 1967, French novelist Michael Tournier produced *Vendredi*, a fable that reprises the characters and situations of Daniel Defoe's *Robinson Crusoe* (1719), this time set on a desert isle off Chile and with tables turned—the native Friday teaches Crusoe how to free himself of eighteenth-century technology. Alex Haley reprised the setting and characters of *Roots* (1976) with *Roots, the Next Generation* (1979). Roger Lea MacBride produced *Little House on Rocky Ridge* (1993), *Little Farm in the Ozarks* (1994), and *In the Land of the Big Red Apple* (1995), three sequels to Laura Ingalls Wilder's *Little House* series. A much touted sequel from American fiction is Alexandra Ripley's *Scarlett* (1991), the long-anticipated extenuation of Margaret Mitchell's *Gone with the Wind* (1936).

serial a method of publishing common to the nineteenth century, when literary works were produced piecemeal, usually ending abruptly at an intriguing moment, surprise, or cliffhanger to entice the public to continue reading, for example, many of the novels of Charles Dickens, which appeared in installments in journals and became so popular that they were standard home reading in Victorian households. Notable American serials include Washington Irving's *The Sketch Book of Geoffrey Crayon, Gent.* (1818) and Harriet Beecher Stowe's *Uncle Tom's Cabin* (1852). In 1881, Robert Louis Stevenson published *Treasure Island* in installments in *Young Folks* magazine under the title of "The Sea Cook or Treasure Island." Rudyard Kipling serialized *The Light That Failed* (1890) in *Lippincott's Magazine* and his sea adventure, *Captains Courageous* (1897), in *McClure's Magazine*.

Twentieth-century serials tend to be television series parceled out over several nights or weeks, the presentation used for the television version of Robert Graves's popular exposé *I, Claudius* (1934) and Larry McMurtry's *Lonesome Dove* (1985).

sermon an illustrative or didactic oration, exemplum, parable, or exegesis that imparts religious beliefs, scriptural interpretation, or moral teachings, such as the works of Cotton Mather and Jonathan Edwards in Colonial American literature, abolitionist harangues by former slave Frederick Douglass, the sonorous lyrics of James Weldon Johnson's "The Creation," a dramatic monologue from *God's Trombones: Seven Negro Sermons in Verse* (1927), Martin Luther King, Jr.'s "I Have a Dream" speech (1963), and Ned's "The Sermon at the River" in Ernest Gaines's *The Autobiography of Miss Jane Pittman* (1971).

See also exemplum, exegesis, parable.

sestet   a stanza containing six lines, for instance, a tightly organized six-line poem rhyming ababcc or the second stave of the Italian or Petrarchan sonnet, which usually rhymes cdecde. Elizabeth Barrett Browning employs an interlocking rhyme scheme for the six-line stanzas of "The Romance of the Swan's Nest," which describes the swan's nesting place with lines that rhyme abcabc:

> Pushing through the elm-tree copse,
>   Winding up the stream light-hearted,
>   Where the osier pathway leads,
> Past the boughs she stoops—and stops.
> Lo, the wild swan had deserted,
>   And a rat had gnawed the reeds!

An intricate variation is the sestina, a show piece favored by medieval and Renaissance jongleurs who selected six rhymes for a stanza, then reshuffled the rhymes, placing the last rhyme of stanza one at the end of the first line of stanza two.

setting   the place of action at a particular time, whether past, present, or future, as demonstrated by "Miss Jane and I" (1978), in which novelist Ernest James Gaines establishes his oneness with the South in a salute to the state that is the center of his fiction:

> I wanted to smell that Louisiana earth, feel that Louisiana sun, sit under the shade of one of those Louisiana oaks, search for pecans in that Louisiana grass in one of those Louisiana yards next to one of those Louisiana bayous, not far from a Louisiana river.... And I wanted to hear that Louisiana dialect—that combination of English, creole, Cajun, Black. For me there's no more beautiful sound anywhere.

Setting is a controlling factor in Edgar Allan Poe's Gullah dialect story, "The Gold Bug" (1843), O. Henry's reflective tale, "A Municipal Report" (1910), Harriette Arnow's realistic novel of displacement, *The Dollmaker* (1954), and Theodore Taylor's young adult historical novel, *The Cay* (1969), which describes an isolated act of sabotage in the Caribbean during World War II.

Setting is linked with a specific time. For example, E. R. Braithwaite's *To Sir with Love* (1986) is set in East London in the late twentieth century; H. G. Wells's *The Time Machine* (1895) occurs in the same place over a series of scenarios ranging from the nineteenth century to a faraway future time.

Shakespearean sonnet   a lyric fourteen-line poem about love or strong emotion composed in iambic pentameter with a variable rhyme scheme that tends to the pattern abab, cdcd, efef, gg, the style of William Shakespeare's collected sonnets (1609) and of later imitations, including Rupert Brooke's "The Soldier" in *The War Sonnets* (1914). The Shakespearean form, which comes to a tight closure of theme in the concluding couplet, dominates Edna St. Vincent Millay's *Sonnets from an Ungrafted Tree* (1923), for example, Canto XIV:

> She had a horror he would die at night.
> And sometimes when the light began to
>   fade

She could not keep from noticing how
white
The birches looked—and then she
would be afraid,
Even with a lamp, to go about the house
And lock the windows; and as night
wore on
Toward morning, if a dog howled, or a
mouse
Squeaked in the floor, long after it was
gone
Her flesh would sit awry on her. By day
She would forget somewhat, and it
would seem
A silly thing to go with just this dream
And get a neighbor to come at night and
stay.
But it would strike her sometimes, mak-
ing the tea:
*She had kept that kettle boiling all night
long, for company.*

shih [shee]   a Chinese subgenre of
poetry that contains an even number of
syllables per line in a series of parallel couplets expressing simple, direct images and
ideas. Dating to the second–twelfth centuries A.D., shih verse rhymes abcb and
stresses the intricacies of Chinese characters, which convey several levels of meaning. A fifth-century master of the genre,
T'ao Ch'ien drew on both Confucianism
and Taoism for his themes and subjects.

short story   a short work of
fiction that compresses action and tension,
for example, Pu Songling's *Liaozhai Zhi*
(1675), a collection of 494 Chinese stories,
the historical tales of Akutagawa Ryunosuke, including "The Rasho Gate" (1915),
and the Sardinia-based stories of Grazia
Deledda. In a review of Nathaniel
Hawthorne's *Twice-Told Tales* for the
April-May 1842 issue of *Graham's* magazine, critic Edgar Allan Poe states his concept of short fiction:

> In the whole composition there should
> be no word written of which the ten-
> dency, direct or indirect, is not to the one
> pre-established design. And by such

means, with such care and skill, a picture is at length painted which leaves in
the mind of him who contemplates it
with a kindred art, a sense of the fullest
satisfaction. The idea of the tale, its thesis, has been presented unblemished.

Examples of classic American short
stories include Poe's "The Tell-Tale
Heart" (1843), Bret Harte's "The Luck of
Roaring Camp" (1868) and "The Outcasts
of Poker Flat" (1869), Charles Waddell
Chesnutt's ironic story of snobbery and
racism, "A Matter of Principle" (1899), and
Katherine Anne Porter's realistic revenge
story, "María Concepción" (1922).

The genre of short fiction—called
conte in French and *cuento* in Spanish—is
a flexible literary form that can take a variety of directions, tones, and styles:

• detective plot or tale of ratiocina-
tion, a form pioneered by Edgar Allan Poe
in "The Murders in the Rue Morgue"
(1841)

• horror fiction in Edgar Allan Poe's
"The Black Cat" (1843)

• humanistic themes in Indian
writer Rabindranath Tagore's collection
The Hungry Stones (1916)

• nature lore in William Faulkner's
"The Bear" (1942) and Ernest Hemingway's "Big Two-Hearted River"

• caricature in Ellen Gilchrist's
"Rhoda" (1995)

• revenge motif in Zora Neale
Hurston's "Sweat" (1926)

• existential theme in French philosopher Jean-Paul Sartre's "The Wall"
(1939)

• protest or social reform in Lu
Hsun's *Call to Arms* (1923) and Italian
author Anna Maria Ortese's "A Pair of
Glasses" (1953).

One favorite ploy of the short story
writer is the surprise ending, as in "Dési-
rée's Baby," a story about miscegenation
in Kate Chopin's collection, *Bayou Folk*

(1894), and in "Athénaïse" from *A Night in Acadie* (1897), an account of wifely rebellion that concludes with an abrupt end of a romantic dilemma.

sibilance a specific instance of alliteration that stresses the repetition of *s*, *z*, or *sh* sounds, variably spelled in pace, sand, scenic, class, schism, glisten, circle, psyche; the *sh* sound in ocean, cache, official, fish, schnauzer, conscious, propulsion, issue, patience; and the *z* sound in pays, scissors, xylophone, crazy, and frizzy. Robert Frost emphasizes sibilance in "Birches" when he declares, "So I was once myself a swinger of birches." Similar uses occur in Carole Etzler's "We are Dancing Sarah's Circle" (1975), Hattie Gossett's "King Kong" (1988), Philip A. Porter's "When Darkness Nears" (1991), and Mark L. Belletini's jubilant Hebrew folk song, "Bring Out the Festal Bread" (1992).

simile a comparison using like, as, or than, for example, Persian poet Omar Khayyám's "I came like water, and like Wind I go," from *The Rubáiyát* (1130). Poet Ishikawa Takuboku uses simile as an element of imagism in his early twentieth-century verse:

> Like a kite
> Cut from a string,
> Lightly the soul of my youth
> Has taken flight.

Similes are often parallel statements, as in St. Thomas Aquinas's opinion, "Man is the beginning of woman and her end, just as God is the beginning and end of every creature." In Part 1 of Hermann Hesse's *Siddhartha* (1922), the protagonist withdraws from ascetic monks to study his inner feelings and sees himself in a bleak image—standing apart like a star in an empty firmament. A humorous comparison comes from Dolly Levi, the resilient character in Thornton Wilder's *The Matchmaker* (1954), in which she cau-

tiously observes, "Money, I've always felt, money—pardon my expression—is like manure; it's not worth a thing unless it's spread about encouraging young things to grow."

skeltonic verse [skehl•TAH•nihk] a rollicking, energetic verse that varies short lines of diameter and trimeter but maintains a single rhyme to excess for the sake of humor or satire. Named for John Skelton, an English poet of the early sixteenth century, the doggerel stanzas stress action verbs, as in a segment from Skelton's *Colin Clout* (1520):

> He wotteth never what
> Nor whereof he speaketh;
> He crieth and he creaketh,
> He prieth and he peeketh.

slang colorful, sometimes cynical street language such as "Okay" and "right on"; also swear words, racist and suggestive terms such as "honky" for white person and "wasp" for white Anglo-Saxon Protestant. Slang is comprised of code words for medicine, sports, the military, drugs, sex acts, and police, as in "goner" for a dying patient, "kayo" for knockout, "grass" for marijuana, "second louie" for second lieutenant, and "narc" for narcotics agent. Slang is the driving force of strongly contemporary works such as Alice Childress's *A Hero Ain't Nothin But a Sandwich* (1963) but quickly dates a work when the terms go out of style or are no longer intelligible to subsequent generations.

slapstick vigorous, roughhouse comedy or satiric skit, often a segment of parody, farce, satyr play, kabuki, puppetry, pantomime, or travesty. Named for a stick or paddle used by a victimizer, the performance of slapstick humor centers on the victim's exaggerated facial and body response to mock punishment, which may result in a look of dismay, cry of distress, lurch, or swoon, for example, the response of the victims of Arlecchino, a stock comic attacker in the *commedia dell'arte*; of the husband in a Punch and Judy; a curmudgeon in a Muppets puppet show; or of Charlie Chaplin in his silent films.

Slapstick colors the low comedy of William Shakespeare, particularly in the antics of Bottom in *A Midsummer Night's Dream* (ca. 1593–1595), Sir John Falstaff and his pals in *The Merry Wives of Windsor* (ca. 1597), Dogberry and his deputies in *Much Ado about Nothing* (ca. 1598), and the willful twin servants in *A Comedy of Errors* (ca. 1580s-1594).

Television comics Sid Caesar, Red Skelton, Lucille Ball, and Carol Burnett carry on the slapstick tradition.

soliloquy [soh•LIH•loh•kwee] a dramatic convention that presents a character's direct address to an audience, often in the form of extensive musings, verbal discussion with self about misgivings and dilemmas, or spoken thoughts and fears. Longer than the aside and spoken to no identifiable listener, the soliloquy was typically delivered from the apron of the stage. It survives in electronic methods on stage, television, or film, which may present taped voice-overs, a common ploy of soap operas. The most famous soliloquy from William Shakespeare's tragedies appears in *Hamlet* (ca. 1599), in which the protagonist weighs the possibilities of escape from duty through suicide against fear of the unknown that awaits him in the grave.

son et lumière [sohn ay loom•YAYR] or **sound and light** sumptuous productions enhanced by electronics. Spectacular *son et lumière* shows, pageants, outdoor dramas, and operas usually are based at castles, battlefields, or grand architectural sites, such as the Parthenon, Roman Baths of Caracalla, or pyramids of Egypt. They feature recorded monologue, dialogue, music, and lighting effects to focus on the grandeur of past times, local settlers or heroes, combat, or other historical aspects of a region.

sonnet a lyric poem composed in iambic pentameter in fourteen rhymed lines, for example, the Shakespearean sonnet sequence of George Eliot, *Brother and Sister* (1869), which concludes:

> School parted us; we never found again
> That childish world where our two spirits mingled
> Like scents from varying roses that remain
> One sweetness, nor can evermore be singled.
> Yet the twin habit of that early time
> Lingered for long about the heart and tongue:
> We had been natives of one happy clime,
> And its dear accents to our utterance clung.
> Till the dire years whose awful name is Change
> Had grasped our souls still yearning in divorce,
> And pitiless shaped them in two forms that range
> Two elements which sever their life's course.
> But were another childhood-world my share,
> I would be born a little sister there.

See also Petrarchan sonnet, Shakespearean sonnet.

Spenserian stanza a poem consisting of nine lines rhyming ababbcbcc. Eight of the lines follow iambic pentameter; the ninth an alexandrine. Named for Sir Edmund Spenser, who improvised the stanza for *The Faerie Queene* (1596), the Spenserian stanza thrived during the Romantic and Victorian eras in James Thomson's *Castle of Indolence* (1748), Robert Burns's *The Cotter's Saturday Night* (1785), Lord Byron's

Childe Harold's Pilgrimage (1816), John Keats's "The Eve of St. Agnes" (1820), and Percy Bysshe Shelley's *Adonais* (1821). A stanza of Alfred, Lord Tennyson's "The Lotos-Eaters" (1860) describes setting:

> The charmed sunset linger'd low adown
> In the red West: thro' mountain clefts the dale
> Was seen far inland, and the yellow down
> Border'd with palm, and many a winding vale
> And meadow, set with slender galingale;
> A land where all things always seem'd the same!
> And round about the keel with faces pale,
> Dark faces pale against that rosy flame,
> The mild-eyed melancholy Lotos-eaters came.

spondee an energized or emphatic metrical foot or unit that contains two syllables, both stressed, as found in the repeated line of Dylan Thomas's "Do Not Go Gentle into that Good Night" (1951), urging the reader to "Rage, rage against the dying of the light"; also in the opening line of Albert Schweitzer's prayer, "Hear our humble prayer, O God, for our friends the animals."

spoonerism a form of punning in which the initial sounds or syllables are reversed, producing silly or absurd phrases, as in low stones/slow tones or rightful faith/frightful wraith. The term derives from the wit of W. A. Spooner (1844–1930), a clergyman of New College, Oxford, who dotted his sermons with misstatements that produced humor or insight.

spy thriller an offshoot of the detective novel that reached a peak in novels and film during the tense standoffs of the Cold War between the United States and Russia in the 1960s. The spy thriller augments the usual motif of murder or theft to national or international intrigue, reconnaissance, and deception, as found in John Le Carré's *The Spy Who Came In from the Cold* (1963), Ken Follett's *The Key to Rebecca* (1981), and Ian Fleming's James Bond series.

stage the platform on which drama is performed. The early Greek theater is the prototype on which modern playhouses and outdoor stages are modeled. Evolved from open-air hillside arenas, the Mediterranean theater follows a standard plan: a semicircular *theatron* or "seeing place" for audience seating, with its front row reserved for local officials and priests, followed by rows of male citizens and *ephebi* or young military recruits. The last rows were reserved for aliens, women, children, and slaves. The *orchestra* or dancing place stood at ground level within the U-shaped theatron. At its center was the *thymele*, an altar to Dionysus, the god of wine, whose worship inspired the first plays. The chorus entered at the *parados*, either all marching in from one side or divided into antiphonal choirs and emerging on right and left simultaneously. Actors appeared on a raised *skene* or stage and used the platform, the *proscenium* or apron, and orchestra for their spheres of action. When the plot called for a temple or ship, actors often used the *thymele* as an imaginary setting. Single *pinakes* or scenery or three-sided *periaktoi* were set in slots in the proscenium columns or on the stage floor to display painted vistas. Behind the *skene*, noisemakers imitated thunder, marching feet, or the uproar of battle. A *mechane* or derrick raised and lowered scenery by ropes on pulleys. When deities appeared, they could be lowered from above by *deus ex machina*, literally "god from a machine."

stage left, stage right directional terms applying to the actors' right

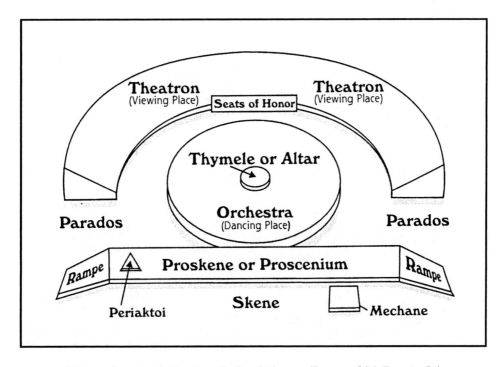

Stage and seating design in early Greek theater. (Raymond M. Barrett, Jr.)

and left sides rather than the audience's point of view. Richard Rodgers and Oscar Hammerstein's production of *Oklahoma!* startled its first audience by opening with a farmhouse on stage left, a backdrop of a cornfield, and no characters. A revolutionary beginning, it caused first-night critics to assume that actors hadn't received their cues or had suffered opening night anxiety. The action got underway as far on stage right, the hero Curly sang "Oh what a beautiful morning!" He remained unseen at stage right until his voice boomed to the upper balcony, when he finally appeared on stage. A risky opening, the innovation brought thunderous applause that made theater history.

stanza a strophe or unified group of lines, often of predetermined rhythm. A stanza is rhymed at the ends and conforms rigid standards, such as:

- monostich, a single line
- couplet, a pair of lines
- tercet or triplet, a three-line unit
- quatrain, a four-line unit
- cinquain, a five-line unit
- sestet or sixain, a six-line unit
- septet, a seven-line unit.
- octave or octet, an eight-line unit.

Stanzas from the chain verse of the Korean *Koryo Songs* (ca. fourteenth century) are written to stand alone, for example:

> Ring the gong, strike the chimes!
> In this age of calm and plenty,
> Let's live and enjoy.

stereotype a one-dimensional character given to clichéd or predictable behaviors, for example, violent fits of anger, taciturnity, or silly giggles. A contemporary example comes from Michael Crichton's *Jurassic Park* (1990), in which the computer specialist, Dennis Nedry, is a slovenly, sour-tempered, and venal pig whose surname suggests the behaviors, interests, and obsessions of a nerd.

See also character; symbolic names.

storytelling a form of oral transmission to a live audience. Storytelling values immediacy and inventiveness, as found in Jataka tales, Jamaican Anansi trickster tales, and episodes of High John the Conqueror, Daddy Mention, and Uncle Remus's Br'er Rabbit. Storytellers tailor material and delivery to their hearers by expanding or condensing, suiting the version to tastes, sensibilities, maturity, and needs. Modes of telling include the dilemma tale of Senegal, Togo, and Gambia, which presents a complicated plot requiring a blend of pragmatism, social ethos, and morality, but which leaves the resolution to the audience. Answering to the name of gleeman, harper, griot, minstrel, seanachie, kahuna, scop, or *rhapsodes*, the teller may select a *pourquoi* story, fable, or wisdom lore to entertain, instruct, or chasten.

Turkish tellers direct attention to themselves with the *tekerleme*, a nonsense jingle, such as "When the camel was a town crier and the cock was a barber, when the sieve was in the straw and I was rocking my mothers' cradle." The Caribbean teller may choose "Cric? Crac!," while the Ghayan teller ends, "*ray ras,* the story is over." Storytellers enhance performances with such instruments as bells, Hawaiian koa guitar, drums, reed zither, shaker gourd rattle, or the mbira, the African thumb piano.

Current tellings include aboriginal folklorist Eustan Williams's "Dirrangun at Tooloom" and "Dirrangun at Baryulgil," Cajun performer J. J. Reneaux's "Why Alligator Hates Dog," Pleasant De Spain's "Cardinal's Red Feathers," the griot tradition displayed in Rex Ellis's slave era stories, Australian fabulist Peter Dargin's Jack the Jolly Swagman stories, and Brother Blue's rambling visions.

strophe [STROH•fee] in Greek drama, a choral ode or stanza chanted by one segment of the chorus in unison, followed by the anti-strophe, or antiphonal reply, from the remaining half of the chorus. Movements were also regimented— one chorus dancing out and the other chorus mimicking the motion in reverse order. The verse pattern concluded with an epode, spoken while the chorus stood still. The playwright used the carefully delineated stanzas to debate opposite sides of a moral or ethical question, such as the nature of courage or patriotism in the actions of the protagonist in Sophocles's tragedy *Antigone* (441 B.C.). The play's dilemma presents pros and cons of the title character's violation of a vengeful local law prohibiting burial of her brother. Currently, strophe can apply to any stanza or unit of lines.

subjective personal, emotional, visionary, or biased. Subjectivity is a private, experience-centered style that counters such straightforward, explicit prose as journalism, definition, and explanatory essay. In *Insurgent Mexico* (1914), author John Reed's reportage of the heroism of Pancho Villa during the Mexican Revolution veers from objective reportage to inward ideals and transcendent response.

sublime the eloquent, noble, affective, or esthetic quality of literature that creates awe in an audience through the ineffable grandeur of style, tone, and presentation, which appeals to intellectual worth, spiritual excellence, and moral purity. A seminal essay on the term appears in *On the Sublime*, an informal letter written by the critic Longinus about the first century A.D., of which only parts survived to modern times. He writes:

Inevitably what inspires wonder casts a spell upon us and is always superior to what is merely convincing and pleasing. Our convictions are usually under our own control, while such passages exercise an irresistible power of mastery and get the upper hand with every member of the audience.

The essay lauds the sense impressions that power the imagery of the poet Sappho, of whom Longinus remarks,

Is it not wonderful how she summons at the same time, soul, body, hearing, tongue, sight, color, all as though they had wandered off apart from herself? She feels contradictory sensations, freezes, burns, raves, and reasons—for one that is at the point of death is clearly beside herself. She wants to display not a single emotion, but a whole congress of emotions. Lovers all show such symptoms as these, but what gives supreme merit to her art is, as I said, the skill with which she chooses the most striking and combines them into a single whole.

surah [SOOR•ah] a chapter or subdivision of the Koran. The opening surah, the "Al-fatih" [The Opening] (613 A.D.), called "The Essence of the Koran," contains a seven-verse prayer or invocation to "Allah, the beneficent, the merciful," declaring:

Thee alone we worship; Thee alone we ask for help.
Show us the straight path,
The path of those whom Thou hast favored;
Not the path of those who earn Thine anger nor of those who go astray.

Muslims utter this passage daily in formal worship and on special occasions calling for piety and personal commitment. Like the Jewish "Hear, O Israel" and the Lord's Prayer in Christian worship and liturgy, the Al'fatih precedes other surahs and serves as the summary and essence of Islamic doctrine.

surrealism [suhr•REE•uh•lizm] a literary style defined in the 1920s that encourages the free association of unexpressed thoughts and unrestrained feelings from the subconscious mind, for example, the illogical dreamscape in Rudolfo Anaya's *Bless Me, Ultima* (1973), in which Tony experiences the beginnings of his people's history:

In my dream I flew over the rolling hills of the llano. My soul wandered over the dark plain until it came to a cluster of adobe huts. I recognized the village of Las Pasturas and my heart grew happy. One mud hut had a lighted window, and the vision of my dream swept me towards it to be witness at the birth of a baby.

Toni Morrison's *Beloved* (1987) draws on a similar experience of primitive thought and racial experience in the ghost's return to the minds of slaves being transferred from Africa aboard slave ships. In fleeting, unpunctuated images, Beloved recalls:

the men without skin are making loud noises I am not dead the bread is sea-colored I am too hungry to eat it the sun closes my eyes those able to die are in a pile I cannot find my man

suspense the anticipation of the outcome of a plot or the solution to an uncertainty, puzzle, or mystery, for example, the cause of the strange smell and unexplained disappearance of a brother in George Washington Cable's story "Jean-ah Poquelin" (1875), the outcome of the switching of a black infant with a white infant in Mark Twain's *Pudd'nhead Wilson* (1895), and the court's decision at a murder trial in Ernest J. Gaines's *A Gathering of Old Men* (1983). An adjunct to suspense is foreshadowing, as found in hints of national crisis or revolution in Isabel Allende's *House of the Spirits* (1991).

symbol a concrete object that

stands for a complex or abstract idea or relationship and implies more than the literal meaning of the word or words, as with Caribbean poet St. John Perse's esoteric verse in *Anabasis* (1924). Symbolism powers the title images of Argentine writer Jorge Luis Borges's "Garden of Forking Paths" and James Hurst's story "The Scarlet Ibis" (1960), a title naming a spindly, dying bird that replicates the weakness of a frail but unusual child. The bird's bright blood and plumage prefigure the boy's manner of death. In William Gibson's *The Miracle Worker* (1956), references to a crocheted wool chain and door keys stress the role of language as the end of Helen's confinement and her entrée to communication. Likewise, the badly eroded marble angel in Ruth Prawer Jhabvala's *Heat and Dust* (1975) represents the loss of distinctive customs and lifestyle among the English colonialists in India.

symbolic names   a character or place name derived from an allusion or a concrete object that stands for a complex or abstract idea or relationship, for example, the town of Raveloe in George Eliot's *Silas Marner* (1861), where Godfrey's ill-begun family is raveled and rewoven and where the old weaver creates a family for himself and his foundling. Character names carry symbols: Bishop Latour and Father Joseph Vaillant, "John the Tower" and "Joseph the Valiant," in Willa Cather's *Death Comes for the Archbishop* (1927) and Esperanza, the Spanish word for hope, who narrates Sandra Cisneros's *The House on Mango Street* (1958).

Abstract naming of characters was the fashion in Restoration Comedy, which peopled its casts with Sir Martin Mar-All, Captain Bluffe, Mockmode, Mrs. Loveit, Sir Fopling Flutter, Sir Wilfull Witwoud, Dashwell, Fainall, and Lady Wishfort.

In Thornton Wilder's drama *Our Town* (1938), most names are common Anglo-Saxon surnames. Of major significance is the name Webb, which indicates the family linkage that draws a community into an interrelated whole, a fact replicated in the familiar Protestant hymn "Blessed Be the Tie That Binds."

synecdoche [sih•NEHK•doh•kee]   an image that substitutes part to represent the whole, for example, "the long arm of the law" referring to a network of law enforcement agencies, "private eye" for a detective, "hired hands" referring to employees, "all ears" meaning attentive, "tracking ivory" meaning to hunt elephants for profit, or "the heart overruling the head," an aphorism implying that emotions take precedence over reason. In Stephen Crane's *The Red Badge of Courage* (1895), the setting depicts a fictionalized segment of the Battle of Chancellorsville, but the author conceals the identity of the conflict except for references to blue and gray uniforms, symbolic of the Union and Confederate armies.

synesthesia [sy•nihs•THEE•zyuh]   the blending of sense impressions, for example, the description of an aroma as green or of a handclasp as thunderous. Edith Sitwell combines senses in her poem "En Famille" (1922), in which shutters clap together "like amber" and eyelids close "as soft as the breeze." William Faulkner mixes sense impressions for his description of the boy's quarry in "The Bear" (1942), which is "colored like a thunderclap."

T

tableau pl. tableaux, both pronounced [ta•BLOH]   a form of dumb show, an arrangement or grouping of silent characters and objects in a static scene or interlude, for example, the figures on a parade float or in a living crêche or founder's day ceremony, a scene from a procession, ballet, pantomime, or other moment frozen in time. "The Nine Worthies" is a traditional tableau in William Shakespeare's *Love's Labour's Lost* (ca. 1593–1595). Tableaux enact the race scene at Ascot in *My Fair Lady*, Alan Jay Lerner and Frederick Loewe's stage version of George Bernard Shaw's *Pygmalion* (1913). In Stephen Crane's *The Red Badge of Courage* (1895), the protagonist identifies a battlefield tableau:

> The men saw a ground vacant of fighters. It would have been an empty stage if it were not for a few corpses that lay thrown and twisted into fantastic shapes upon the sward.

tale   a short action-centered verse or prose narrative derived from the oral tradition, either written or spoken in form, focusing on a single, loosely plotted incident found in the folk tale, fool tale, personal anecdote, exemplum, yarn, tall tale, wonder tale, and the enigma tale or dilemma tale, for example, the Japanese court tales collected in *Ise monogatari* (tenth century) and open-ended African stories meant to draw listeners into the act by requiring them to furnish plausible conclusions.

Examples of tales flourish in all cultures: the traditional Canadian Indian trickster story, "How Raven Brought Fire to the Indians," the winsome marriage tale, "Savitri's Love" from the Indian *Mahabharata* (200 B.C.), Giovanni Boccaccio's "Patient Griselda" (1353), Welsh heroic tales of Macsen Wledig retold in Mary Stewart's *The Crystal Cave* (1970) and *The Hollow Hills* (1973), and the fourteenth-century Hawaiian folk tale of the supernatural, "The Story of Laieikawai."

Other models include Lady Murasaki Shikibu's *The Tale of Genji* (ca. 1030), *The Romance of Anbtar*, a collection of Persian tales (thirteenth century), *The Thousand and One Nights* (sixteenth century), the eighteenth-century Japanese compendium, *Hyaku Monogatari* [100 Tales], Washington Irving's *Tales of a Traveller* (1824), Edgar Allan Poe's *Tales of the Grotesque and Arabesque* (1839), Henry Wadsworth Longfellow's *Tales of the Wayside Inn* (1863), George Bird Grinnell's *Blackfoot Lodge Tales* (1892), J. Frank Dobie's *Apache Gold and Yaqui Silver* (1928) and *Tales of Old-Time Texas* (1955), ghostly or supernatural incidents in Maxine Hong Kingston's *The Woman Warrior* (1975), Heather Forest's *The Baker's Dozen ... A Colonial American Tale* (1989), Joseph Bruchac's Abenaki tale, "Gluscabi and the Wind Eagle" (1994), Gayle Ross's "How Turtle's Back Was Cracked" (1995), Linda Fang's *The Ch'i-lin Purse* (1995), J. J. Reneaux's beast tale, "Why Alligator Hates Dog" (1995), and Richard Adams's *Tales from Watership Down* (1996).

talk-story   a parable or story passed down from parent to child to illustrate a lesson or dramatize a warning or model of bad behavior or poor choice of action. In Maxine Hong Kingston's *The Woman Warrior* (1975), the author's mother relates a story about an aunt who became pregnant out of wedlock and was so severely punished for her community transgression that she killed herself and her infant. By telling the daughter this story, the mother hopes that she will guard her virginity. The mother warns, "the village is watching."

tall tale   a humorously outlandish or exaggerated tale of improbable or superhuman incidents, a genre comprised of the European rhozzum, shaggy dog story, frontier "stretchers," and the *fabliau*.

Examples include exploits contained in Rudolf Erich Raspe's *Narrative of Baron Munchausen's Marvellous Travels* (1785), Davy Crockett's rollicking *Crockett Almanacks* (1835–1838), Stephen Vincent Benét's "The Devil and Daniel Webster" (1939), and Heather Forest's "The Talking Skull" (1994). A classic example of overblown frontier lore, Mark Twain's "The Celebrated Jumping Frog of Calaveras County" (1866) gives an anthropomorphic description of the frog:

> Quicker'n you could wink he'd spring straight up and snake a fly off'n the counter there, and flop down on the floor ag'in as solid as a gob of mud, and fall to scratching the side of his head with his hind foot as indifferent as if he hadn't no idea he'd been doin' any more'n any frog might do.

tanka [TAHN•kah] a popular Japanese imagist verse form consisting of 31 syllables in five unrhymed lines alternating seven and five syllables, the vehicle of anonymous Japanese lyrics in the anthology *Kokinshu* (tenth century A.D.) and pensive verse by poets Akahito and Hitómaro in the eighth century. The latter muses:

> A strange old man
> Stops me,
> Looking out of my deep mirror.

The tanka contains a compressed essence of mood and image. It expresses intense feeling in a brief, evocative unit composed of striking word pictures in simple language, as demonstrated by poets Narihira, Jakuren, Princess Nukada, Ono Komachi, Ki no Tsurayuki, Kobayashi Issa, and Minamoto no Toshiuyori. Legend declares that the god Susanoo introduced tanka to the royal Japanese court in 712 A.D. by issuing *Kojiki*, Japan's earliest poetry anthology. The introductory verse is a wedding verse:

> yakumo tatsu
> Izumo yaegaki
> tsumagomi ni
> yaegaki tsukuru
> sono yaegaki wo

In the English translation, it requires more syllables:

> Eightfold rising clouds
> Build an eightfold fence
> An eightfold Izumo fence
> Wherein to keep my bride—
> Oh! splendid eightfold fence.

The seventeenth-century tanka master, Matsuo Basho, composed an intriguingly minimalist tanka word picture about masks:

> Year after year
> on the monkey's face
> a monkey face.

See also choka, renga.

tantra [TAHN•truh] one of a populist class of late medieval Hindu or Buddhist scriptures intended for the masses. The tantra outlines ritual and technique for meditation and sexual practice or comments on dreams, omens, and superstitions. The *Kama Sutra*, one of the least understood handbooks outside Asia, contains advice on infatuation, romance, sensual pleasures, intercourse, and a mutually pleasing male-female relationship. Translated by Sir Richard Burton in the late nineteenth century, the manual was ranked among Victorian England's erotica and pornographia.

theme the main idea of a work, as summed up in such abstract terms as patriotism, grace, isolation, motherhood, forgiveness, or wartime loss, found in Chinese lyricist Tu Fu's anti-war verse from the mid-eighth century A.D., the discourse on love in Abu Muhammad 'Ali ibn Ahmad ibn Hazm's *The Ring of the Dove* (ca. 1030), the *carpe diem* concept in Cavalier poet Robert Herrick's "To the Virgins, to Make Much of Time" (1648), imminent danger in Mary Boykin Chesnut's *Diary from Dixie* (1886), native persistence in Norwegian writer Åsta Holth's story "Salt," the concept of slave breeder in Toni Morrison's *Beloved* (1989), emphasis on the finality of death in John Crowe Ransom's "Bells for John Whiteside's Daughter" (1924), and an aura of community support in Harriette Arnow's *The Dollmaker* (1954).

thesis   a social issue, problem, or proposition at the heart of a treatise, *roman à thèse*, political novel, propaganda or sociological novel, *pièce à thèse,* or problem play. Issues cover human situations: slavery and the dissolution of the family in Harriet Beecher Stowe's *Uncle Tom's Cabin* (1852), dangers of industrialization in Charles Dickens's *Hard Times* (1854), the challenge to patriarchy in Henrik Ibsen's *A Doll's House* (1879), racism in Alan Paton's *Cry, the Beloved Country* (1948), and democracy in Barbara Jordan's speech "Who Then Will Speak for the Common Good?" (1993).

threnody   [THRIH•nuh•dee]   a dirge, elegy, encomium, or lamentation for the dead. Alfred, Lord Tennyson is best known for *In Memoriam* (1850), a mournful verse cycle honoring poet Arthur Hallam. Sara Teasdale combined respect with a musing tone for "Effigy of a Nun," which closes with a question about the nature of death:

> She who so loved herself and her own
>   warring thoughts,
> Watching their humorous, tragic
>   rebound,
> In her thick habit's fold, sleeping, sleeping,
> Is she amused at dreams she has found?
>
> Infinite tenderness, infinite irony
> Are hidden forever in her closed eyes,

> Who must have learnt too well in her
>   long loneliness
> How empty wisdom is, even to the wise.

tone   the author's attitude toward the subject and audience, which accrues directly, subtly, and sometimes ambiguously from hints, diction, stylistic touches, and texture, for example, Duke Ellington's tender invocation, "Come Sunday" (1966), which calls on God to "please look down and see my people through." Tone can range from accusational and grim to detached, intimate, casual, conciliatory, light-hearted, seriocomic, or mocking, as demonstrated by the poignance of Jesse Stuart's story of intergenerational misunderstanding in "Split Cherry Tree" (1939), imminent doom in Tennessee Williams's play, *A Streetcar Named Desire* (1947), brooding resentment of William Styron's historical novel, *The Confessions of Nat Turner* (1967), conciliation in Alfred Uhry's *Driving Miss Daisy* (1986), and pent emotion in Cynthia Rylant's young adult novel, *Missing May* (1992). In Mark Mathabane's autobiography, *Kaffir Boy* (1987), the forthright tone suggests that the author hides nothing from the reader in the stark portrait of his early life in a South African ghetto.

tone poem   a melodious style of verse that orchestrates sounds and rhythms as though they were notes and phrasing of a tune or aria, for example, Sidney Lanier's "The Marshes of Glynn" (1878) and Gerard Manley Hopkins's "Inversnaid" (1884), which glories in the arching trees and tumbling waters of a stream in the wild.

topic   the subject matter or field of interest of a literary work, for example, mature love in Zora Neale Hurston's feminist novel, *Their Eyes Were Watching God* (1937), greed and falsehood in Tennessee Williams's virulent inter-generational drama, *Cat on a Hot Tin Roof* (1955); and racism and class envy in Horton Foote's plays *Hurry Sundown* (1967) and *Barn Burning* (1980).

tragedy   a serious drama in which the main character, usually a prominent, noble, or royal person, falls or dies as a result of some human failing, which the Greeks called by the archery term *hamartia*, a missing of the mark. In the case of William Shakespeare's *Othello* (ca. 1603–1604), the tragic hero's inconstancy to a loyal, gentle wife and his susceptibility to a conniver result in multiple deaths and suicide. In Edmond Rostand's *Cyrano de Bergerac* (1897), the protagonist's unrequited love for Roxane and the misery of courting her for another man result from the protagonist's low self-esteem and pride, his tragic flaw. A modern tragedy, Tennessee Williams's *A Streetcar Named Desire* (1947), expresses the looming destruction of a vain woman fighting economic and moral ruin.

A subset of tragedy is the revenge tragedy or tragedy of blood, which is usually motivated by the obligatory requital of the murder of a family member. Unlike classical tragedy, in which mayhem occurs offstage, revenge tragedy simmers with virulent emotions and strews the stage with corpses. The mood is uniformly brooding and horrific. Plots are carefully articulated with secrets, betrayals, subplots, moody soliloquies, delays and errors in judgment, and apparitions. Still popular as an ingredient in movie and television westerns, the sensational genre survives from the Elizabethan and Jacobean eras, when the anonymous *Revenger's Tragedy* (1607) launched a British fad.

Revenge tragedy derives motivation and resolution from the Roman playwright Seneca, the prolific first-century author of *Octavia, Medea, Hercules Furens, Troades,*

and *Phaedra*. Elements include murder, vows of vengeance, bloodletting, spying, madness, and intrigue. William Shakespeare's *Hamlet* (ca. 1599–1600) is perhaps England's finest model; other masterpieces include Thomas Kyd's wildly popular *The Spanish Tragedy* (1586), Christopher Marlowe's *Tamburlaine* (1587), Shakespeare's *Titus Andronicus* (ca. 1594), John Marston's *Antonio's Revenge* (1599), Cyril Tourneur's *The Atheist's Tragedy* (ca. 1611), and John Webster's *The Duchess of Malfi* (1614). A contemporary example is Federico García Lorca's *Blood Wedding* (1933).

tragicomedy   a serious play or novel in which situations threaten to end in catastrophe but resolve into a happy conclusion through an improbable or unforeseen turn of events or intervention of a savior or rescuer. William Shakespeare wrote notable tragicomedies—*Cymbeline* (ca. 1608–1610) and *The Winter's Tale* (ca. 1610–1611). A popular favorite in Japan is Nagai Saikaku's tragicomic novel, *The Life of an Amorous Woman* (1686), which describes the decline of a court mistress to the seamy life of a common prostitute.

Three twentieth-century examples include Robert Harling's *Steel Magnolias* (1987), Fannie Flagg's darkly comic *Fried Green Tomatoes at the Whistle Stop Cafe* (1987), and Calder Willingham's satiric *Rambling Rose* (1972). This last relates the rise and fall of Rose, a lusty housekeeper and governess who indiscriminately seduces a policeman, a young teenage boy, and various townsmen of questionable morality. The story reaches a high point— the turn from tragedy to felicity—when Rose's employer, Mrs. Hillyer, defends the girl from a doctor who plots with Mr. Hillyer to remove the girl's reproductive organs to halt her permissive behavior.

transcendentalism [tran•sehn•

DEHN•tuh•lihzm] a philosophy linking idealism with romanticism. Transcendental topics include conscience-centered morality, love of nature, respect for experience, reverence for intuition and intellect, social reform, feminism, abolitionism, and an individual grasp of mysticism and the divine, which is the hallmark of Unitarianism.

In the mid-nineteenth century, American transcendentalists—Margaret Fuller, Bronson Alcott, Ellery Channing, Henry David Thoreau, and the driving force, Ralph Waldo Emerson—derived their doctrines from the writings of Thomas Carlyle, Samuel Taylor Coleridge, and Johann Goethe. Fuller expresses the transcendental attitude toward self-fulfillment for women in *Woman in the Nineteenth Century* (1845), which declares:

> Women must leave off asking [men] and being influenced by them, but retire into themselves, and explore the groundwork of life till they find their peculiar secret. Then, when they come forth again, renovated and baptized, they will know how to turn all dross to gold, and will be rich and free though they live in a hut, tranquil if in a crowd. Then their sweet singing shall not be from passionate impulse, but the lyrical overflow of a divine rapture, and a new music shall be evolved from this many-chorded world.

translation the presentation of a written work in a language other than the original, for example, George Chapman's *Iliad* (1611), the King James Bible (1613), Lady Charlotte Guest's translation of the Welsh *Mabinogion* (1849), Edward Fitzgerald's English edition of Persian poet Omar Khayyám's *The Rubáiyát* (1859), Sir Richard Burton's translations of the *Kama Sutra* and *The Arabian Nights* in the late nineteenth century, Ambrose Bierce's version of *The Monk and the Hangman's Daughter* (1892), Edith Hamil-

ton's recreation of Greek and Roman myths, Carolyn Kizer's translation of Asian verse in "Knock upon Silence" (1965), and Babette Deutsch's translations of Rainer Marie Rilke, Alexander Pushkin, and Boris Pasternak.

travelogue a guidebook or account of trips, exploration, and exploits, often compiled by sailors, mercenaries, diplomats, researchers, missionaries, and troubadours, for example, Ki no Tsurayuki's *Tosa Diary* (ca. 925 A.D.) and Korean memoirist Pak Chiwon's record of a trip to Peking, *Yorha ilgi* (1780). A perennial favorite among literary genres, the travelogue includes George Catlin's *Last Rambles Amongst the Indians of the Rocky Mountains and the Andes* (1868), Mark Twain's *Innocents Abroad* (1869), *The Gilded Age* (1873), and *A Tramp Abroad* (1880), John Muir's *A Thousand Mile Walk to the Gulf* (1916), Robin Lee Graham's around-the-globe sailing adventure, *Dove* (1977), and Jasper N. Wyman's Alaskan trek in *Journey to the Koyukuk* (1988).

treatise [TREE•tihs] a scholarly study of a topic, which may derive from science, politics, religion, ethics, or literature, for example, Aristotle's pivotal *The Poetics* (fourth century B.C.), Captain John Smith's *A Map of Virginia with a Description of the Country, the Commodities, People, Government, and Religion* (1612), John James Audubon's *The Birds of America* (1838), Mary Wollstonecraft's *A Vindication of the Rights of Woman* (1792), and George Catlin's *Letters and Notes on the Manners, Customs and Condition of the North American Indians During Eight Years' Travel Amongst the Wildest Tribes of Indians of North America* (1841).

Notable examinations of regions, customs, mindsets, and history include *The Mind of the South* (1941), an influential social history by W. J. Cash, and John

Ehle's *The Trail of Tears: The Rise and Fall of the Cherokee Nation* (1988). In Pat Conroy's introduction to Mary Edwards Wertsch's *Military Brats: Legacies of Childhood Inside the Fortress* (1991), he typifies the misery of a military childhood:

> I was born and raised on federal property. America itself paid all the costs for my birth and my mother's long stay at the hospital. I was a military brat—one of America's children in the profoundest sense.... The sound of gunfire on rifle ranges strikes an authentic chord of home in me even now.

trickster   a rascal, con artist, or picaro who dominates much of oral and written folklore, often in the form of a wily animal, such as the Shoshone Old Man Coyote, the Micmac Glooskap the Frog, the Tlingit raven, the Yoruba story of Eshu, and Anansi, the clever spider from West Africa, described in the mid-twentieth century by Jamaican storyteller Andrew Salkey. Popular children's fables feature such devious animals as Reynard the Fox in medieval stories, Joel Chandler Harris's Br'er Rabbit in *Night with Uncle Remus* (1883), Gayle Ross's tricky rabbit and turtle in *How Rabbit Tricked Otter* (1994) and *How Turtle's Back Was Cracked: A Traditional Cherokee Tale* (1995), and J. J. Reneaux's dog in *Why Alligator Hates Dog* (1995). Human tricksters invigorate world lore, notably Prometheus in Greek mythology, the fox in Aesop's fables (sixth century B.C.), Krishna in the *Bhagavata Purana* (tenth century), Hindustani storyteller Bhatta Somadeva's "The Confidence Man" (twelfth century), Christopher Marlowe's Mephistopheles in *Dr. Faustus* (1592), and in episodes of the *commedia dell'arte* (sixteenth century), Pulchinello and Arlecchino, the harlequin figure based on Momus, the Greek god of ridicule and the theatrical god of clowns, Johann Goethe's beast epic, *Reineke Fuchs* (1794),

the child-stealing dwarf in Jacob and Wilhelm Grimm's "Rumplestiltskin" (1815), Davy Crockett's frontier yarns, Appalachian Jack tales, Mark Twain's Tom Sawyer and Huck Finn, and a conniving spouse in Isaac Singer's *Gimpel the Fool* (1957).

trochee   a metrical foot or unit that contains two syllables, a stressed syllable followed by an unstressed syllable ('.), the opposite of the iamb, the dominate rhythm of English poesy. A popular nursery rhyme from Australia exemplifies the value of a strong first beat to children's songs:

> Kookaburra sits in the old gum tree,
> Merry merry king of the bush is he;
> Laugh, kookaburra, laugh, kookaburra,
> Gay your life must be.

In a more literary vein, Henry Wadsworth Longfellow based his epic verse about a semi-legendary sixteenth-century Mohawk leader, *The Song of Hiawatha* (1855), on the drum-like THUMP-thump beat of trochaic tetrameter, a hard-handed rhythmic pattern that became the butt of satirists. In a salute to native lore, Longfellow writes:

> Nor forgotten was the Love-song,
> The most subtle of all medicines,
> The most potent spell of magic,
> Dangerous more than war or hunting;
> Thus the Love-song was recorded,
> Symbol and interpretation.

trope [trohp]   any fanciful or non-literal language or figure of speech; also, the musical dialogues of Christian church liturgy, such as the *Quem Quaeritis* [Whom Do You Seek], a medieval Easter piece that is a forerunner of English drama.

troubadour [TROO•buh•dohr] a vagabond, singing *trouvère*, or poet of the Middle Ages who wandered Southern

France composing verse *fabliaux*, canticles, serenades, *aubades* or sunrise songs, *canzonettas, chansons de geste* or heroic verse and lyric tributes to chivalry and courtly love, the forerunner of the sonnet.

A notable work from the thirteenth century is the catalog of Beuern Poems or *Carmina Burana*, a cycle of minstrelsy composed by European students, priests, and jongleurs in a melange of Latin and modern European languages. The text allies pastoral nature worship with litanies, love plaints, courtship songs, antiecclesiastical satire and parody, odes, paeans, and doggerel, for example, the sexual innuendo of this couplet:

> All that Venus bids me do,
> Do I with erection.

tz'u [tsuh]   a lyric metrical pattern taken from musical rhythms and supplied with lyrics according to a predetermined rhyme scheme. Tz'u was the verse form of "Peonies," by Chinese poet Li Ch'ing-chao (twelfth century A.D.)

U

understatement   a deliberate lessening of description, either as a result of great restraint or of irony. The opposite of hyperbole or overstatement, understatement, also called litotes, is the method of Julius Caesar's simplistic announcement of military victory in "Veni, vidi, vici," [I came, I saw, I conquered], and of René Descartes's terse summation of human uniqueness in "Cogito ergo sum" [I think, therefore I am]. Colette creates humor in brevity in *Gigi* (1945): "The three great stumbling blocks in a girl's education ... *homard a l'americaine* [lobster served in the American style, with a tomato and shallot sauce], a boiled egg, and asparagus."
See also litotes.

understudy   a stand-in or substitute for an actor. The understudy memorizes lines and cues, then waits backstage in case the primary actor is unable to perform. The best known understudy in American theater is Shirley MacLaine, who stepped in for ailing Joan McCrackin to perform Bob Fosse's tricky choreography in "Steam Heat," a production number in Richard Adler and Jerry Ross's *The Pajama Game* (1954).

unities   among seventeenth- and eighteenth-century classicists, a dramatic convention of time, place, and action that requires drama to structure its plot in one setting in a 24-hour period. One of the objects of nineteenth-century romanticism was to replace this rigidity with less restriction on creativity. Still viable in modern times, a tight observance of the three unities controls Marsha Norman's taut suicide play, *'night Mother* (1982).

universality [yu•nih•vuhr•SA•lih•tee]   a quality, topic, or theme that applies to all people at all times. The cyclical humanistic motifs of growing up, getting an education, selecting a mate, and creating a new family all precede the greater theme, which is the anticipation or dread of old age and death, a pervasive topic in Japanese haiku.

The universality of George's grief for his wife Emily in Thornton Wilder's *Our Town* (1938) is less significant than the fact that George, too, will join the spirits in the Grover's Corners cemetery and will separate himself from the goals and longings of earthly life. For this reason, the theme of recurrent human situations transcends the town in New Hampshire and extends to all human families that have ever lived or will live on earth.

utopia   fiction, nonfiction, and scripture that is set in an inviting haven, a perfect world that frees residents from perennial wrangles and debates over equality, family life, government, religion, strife, and money, as in the South Sea respite in Herman Melville's *Typee* (1846), feminist stronghold in Charlotte Perkins Gilman's *Herland* (1915), and robot-driven island in Karel Capek's play *R. U. R.* (1921).

Utopian settings are frequently temporary escapes, retreats, or unattainable goals, as found in the garden home of Eden in the book of Genesis (ca. 950 B.C.), the island in William Shakespeare's *The Tempest* (ca. 1610–1611), the New World in Alexis de Tocqueville's *Democracy in America* (1835), the dreamscape of Lewis Carroll's *Alice in Wonderland* (1865), Ayn Rand's forest cabin in *Anthem* (1937), the woods in Henry David Thoreau's *Walden* (1854), the jungle in W. H. Hudson's *Green Mansions* (1904), the refuge in William Golding's *Lord of the Flies* (1954), the religious respite envisioned in Alex Haley's *The Autobiography of Malcolm X* (1965), and the futuristic evolution in Arthur C. Clarke's *Childhood's End* (1953).

See also dystopia.

Veda [VAY•duh]   a compendium of four canonical books—the *Rigveda*, *Atharvaveda*, *Samaveda*, and *Yajurveda* (1000 B.C.), written by Aryans from north central Asia who settled the Indian subcontinent. These intellectual works, the earliest Hindu scripture and sacred lore, are comprised of metrical hymns and chants, prayers, sacrificial rites, liturgical formulas, magic spells, and incantations composed in early Sanskrit.

Venn diagram   a method of character or theme study that groups com-

mon elements in the shared oval of two overlapping circles, for example, aspects of immaturity in the title characters of William Shakespeare's *Romeo and Juliet* (ca. 1593–1595), or noble and altruistic character traits in the protagonists of the novels by Barbara Kingsolver or Pat Conroy. A literary extension of set theory, the Venn diagram derives from the work of English logician John Venn in the 1920s.

victorianism   the rigidly moral, priggish aspect of literature written during the reign of England's Queen Victoria, who ruled the expanding British Empire from 1837 to 1901. Victoria modeled for her subjects the religiosity and prim, family-centered lifestyle that became an international standard of probity and decency. Biographer Lytton Strachey composed studies of Victoriana in *Eminent Victorians* (1918), which includes portraits of Florence Nightingale, Cardinal Manning, and other dignitaries of the era, and in *Queen Victoria* (1921).

Charlotte Brontë's *Jane Eyre* (1847) displays the era's high moral tone, earnest outlook, and expectation of justice through her protagonist, who maintains both virginity and honor by refusing an offer of an illicit relationship with her employer, Edward Rochester. Jane's triumph over injustice derives from unswerving values, sexual propriety, and the upright behavior becoming a woman of her station and middle-class upbringing. Another aspect of victorianism—a belief in education and enterprise—applies to Jane's fictional career, which departs from dependence on relatives after she is educated at Lowood and introduced to the teaching profession.

vignette [vih•NYEHT]   a brief, vivid scene that elucidates a theme, character, or topic in a literary work. The precision of vignette is an element of Jean Toomer's *Cane* (1923), Spaniard Juan

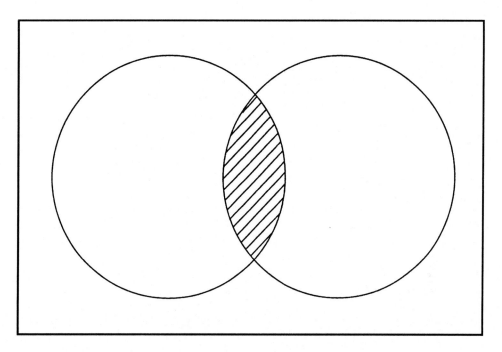

Venn Diagram. (Raymond M. Barrett, Jr.)

Ramón Jiménez's "I Shall Not Return" (1953), and Fernán Silva Valdés's "The Gaucho Troubadour" (1963), a poem from Uruguayan cowboy tradition.

Significant vignettes from American literature include Anne Newport Royall's *Sketches of History Life and Manners in the United States* (1826), Augustus Baldwin Longstreet's humorous *Georgia Scenes* (1834), George Washington Cable's regional vignettes in *Strange True Stories of Louisiana* (1889), and the evocative lyricism of Mary Hunter Austin's Southwestern essays in *The Land of Little Rain* (1903), which examines interrelated forms of life in the Mojave Desert. Sandra Cisneros constructs her young adult novel *The House on Mango Street* (1989) from loosely connected vignettes and episodes that exemplify the rhythms of life in a Hispanic neighborhood.

vision   a   literary   device   that

allows characters to move beyond reality to a dreamscape, mental retreat, afterlife, or meeting with supernatural beings, for example, a glimpse of the gods in John G. Neihardt's *Black Elk Speaks* (1932), in which vengeful deities would

> come in a whirlwind out of the west and would crush out everything on this world, which was old and dying. In that other world there was plenty of meat, just like old times; and in that world all the dead Indians were alive, and all the bison that had ever been killed were roaming around again.

Significant literary visions occur in other religious texts—the book of Genesis, the final books of the New Testament (A.D. 90–95) and the Koran (610), Joseph Smith's *The Book of Mormon* (1830)—as well as in Samuel Taylor Coleridge's poem "Kubla Khan" (1798), a fictional bout of amnesia in Mark Twain's historical novel *A Connecticut Yankee in King Arthur's Court*

(1886), Edward Bellamy's utopian retreat to the past in *Looking Backward* (1887), William Morris's futurism in *News from Nowhere* (1890), and Richard Adams's escapist beast fable *Watership Down* (1972).

W

    waka [WAH•kah] an early 31-syllable, five-line verse form related to the *tanka*, for example, Yosano Akiko's feminist reflection on love, *Tangled Hair* (1907), a sensuous verse collection in the style of the Greek Sappho or the French essayist Colette. Fujiwara no Teika's nocturnal image exemplifies the tight subtle allusiveness of *waka*:

> The floating bridge of
> The dream of a brief spring night
> Breaks off and in
> The sky ribbons of trailing
> Cloud drift away from the peak.

    Nearly 2,000 of these deeply individualistic poems were collected in thirteenth-century Japan in the *Shinkokinshu*, a carefully arranged, 20-book anthology sponsored by the Emperor Gotoba, who was an amateur composer of *waka*.

    The *waka*, which was popular in the Japanese court in the mid-eighth century and remains influential to current times, contains complex emotions and poetic techniques that capture such austere aesthetic ideals as beauty, solitude, and mystery.

    whimsy a blend of bizarre, capricious, or fantastic elements and surprise events or outcomes in an imaginative literary work, as found in the bird denizens of the quirky, grandiose Cloudcuckooland in Aristophanes's comedy *The Birds* (414 B.C.) and the tricky characters of William Shakespeare's *A Midsummer Night's Dream*

(ca. 1593–1595), in which the mischievous Puck transforms the actor Bottom with an ass's head.

    Without warning, whimsy often makes a mental leap from reality to free association or flights of fantasy, producing unforeseen connections or unexpected meetings of characters, for example, Alice's conversation with a caterpillar in Lewis Carroll's *Alice in Wonderland* (1865), eccentric characters in Edward Lear's limericks in *The Book of Nonsense* (1846), silly escapes in Joel Chandler Harris's *Uncle Remus: His Songs and His Sayings* (1880), the creation of a robot factory in Karel Capek's dystopic play *R. U. R.* (1921), unusual companions in L. Frank Baum's *The Wizard of Oz* (1900), surprise developments in Mary Chase's sentimental comedy of manners, *Harvey* (1944), unusual images in Robert Frost's poem "The Telephone" (1916), and peculiar animals and fantastic beings in Norton Juster's children's fantasy, *The Phantom Tollbooth* (1960) and Richard Adams's mythic beast fable, *Watership Down* (1972).

    A favorite twentieth-century model of whimsy is Bilbo Baggins, the unlikely burglar in J. R. R. Tolkien's *The Hobbit* (1937). Bilbo is the unwilling hero who faces poisonous spiders, elves, dwarves, and trolls before retiring to the serenity and security of his underground home. Less capricious are the nostalgic individualists in Truman Capote's *The Grass Harp* (1951) and the romantic escapist who dominates *Breakfast at Tiffany's* (1958).

    Incidental whimsy dots numerous works, for instance, Edmond Rostand's *Cyrano de Bergerac* (1897), Maya Angelou's *I Know Why the Caged Bird Sings* (1970), Ray Bradbury's *Dandelion Wine* (1957), and Gabriel García Márquez's saga *One Hundred Years of Solitude* (1967), in which the daunted suitor, inventor Pietro Crespi, languishes from unrequited love. In his room, he kills himself behind locked doors after setting clockworks to chime a bizarre death notice to the outside world.

wisdom literature   prose and verse that showcases ethical truth, experience, and moral guidance above considerations of plot, setting, and character, for example, the pithy humanism found in homily, fable, parable, and aphorism. Wisdom is the focus of the biblical book of Proverbs and other scriptural works, the Indian *Bhagavad-Gita* (500 B.C.), Marcus Aurelius's *Meditations* (ca. 180 A.D.), Sadi's *Gulistan* (13th century), John G. Neihardt's visionary *Black Elk Speaks* (1932), and the speeches of Gandhi.

Contemporary wisdom literature ranges over a wide spectrum: the writings of poet-philosopher Kahlil Gibran, educator Marian Wright Edelman, humanist Elie Wiesel, and Abenaki storyteller and savant Joseph Bruchac.

wit   an intellectual form of humor arising from incongruity or fancy, often demonstrated through sharp, artful, or sophisticated arrangement of words or insightful images, for example, Saki's observations, "No more privacy than a goldfish" and his dogs howling constantly "like the cherubim which rest not day or night." Oscar Wilde produced a large body of entertaining aphorisms, such as "I can resist everything except temptation." Mark Twain was an American genius at wit, as demonstrated by his comic aphorisms. He was skilled at the balanced statement, as in "When angry, count four; when very angry, swear," and periodic sentence, as in "Nothing so needs reforming as other people's habits."

See also aphorism, incongruity.

yarn   a bold lie or highly embroidered personal experience told by a first-person narrator who performed an exploit or observed a phenomenon. A variety of tall tale, the yarn is a constant in oral tradition, for example, the Appalachian Jack tales of storyteller Ray Hicks and "The Mule Egg" and "The Snake-Bit Hoe Handle" (1988), reminiscences told as a part of Doc McConnell's Old Medicine Show, a stage presentation in the Appalachian tradition that celebrates humor and humanity.

Appendix A:
Literary Prize Winners

Poet Laureate Consultant in Poetry to the Library of Congress

1937–1941	Joseph Auslander	1971–1973	Josephine Jacobsen
1943–1944	Allen Tate	1973–1974	Daniel Hoffman
1944–1945	Robert Penn Warren	1974–1976	Stanley Kunitz
1945–1946	Louise Bogan	1976–1978	Robert Hayden
1946–1947	Karl Shapiro	1978–1980	William Meredith
1947–1948	Robert Lowell	1981–1982	Maxine Kumin
1948–1949	Leonie Adams	1982–1984	Anthony Hecht
1949–1950	Elizabeth Bishop	1984–1985	Robert Fitzgerald
1950–1952	Conrad Aiken		(in absentia)
1952	William Carlos Williams	1984–1985	Reed Whittemore
1956–1958	Randall Jarrell	1985–1986	Gwendolyn Brooks
1958–1959	Robert Frost	1986–1987	Robert Penn Warren
1959–1961	Richard Eberhart	1987–1988	Richard Wilbur
1961–1963	Louis Untermeyer	1988–1990	Howard Nemerov
1963–1964	Howard Nemerov	1990–1991	Mark Strand
1964–1965	Reed Whittemore	1991–1992	Joseph Brodsky
1965–1966	Stephen Spender	1992–1993	Mona Van Duyn
1966–1968	James Dickey	1993–1995	Rita Dove
1968–1970	William Jay Smith	1995–1997	Robert Hass
1970–1971	William Stafford	1997–	Robert Pinsky

Nobel Prize for Literature

1901   René Sully-Prudhomme (French)
1902   Theodor Mommsen (German)
1903   Bjørnstjerne Martinus Bjørnson (Norwegian)
1904   José Echegaray y Eizaguirre (Spanish) and Frédéric Mistral (French)
1905   Henryk Sienkiewicz (Polish)
1906   Giosuè Carducci (Italian)
1907   Rudyard Kipling (British, born in India)
1908   Rudolf Christoph Eucken (German)
1909   Selma Ottilia Lovisa Lagerlöf (Swedish)
1910   Paul Johann Ludwig von Heyse (German)
1911   Maurice Maeterlinck (Belgian)
1912   Gerhart Hauptmann (German)

1913	Rabindranath Tagore (Indian)
1914	No award given
1915	Romain Rolland (French)
1916	Carl Verner von Heidenstam (Swedish)
1917	Karl A. Gjellerup (Danish) and Henrik Pontoppidan (Danish)
1918	No award given
1919	Carl Friedrich Georg Spitteler (Swiss)
1920	Knut Pedersen Hamsun (Norwegian)
1921	Anatole France (French)
1922	Jacinto Benavente y Martínez (Spanish)
1923	William Butler Yeats (Irish)
1924	Wladyslaw Stanislaw Reymont (Polish)
1925	George Bernard Shaw (British, born in Ireland)
1926	Grazia Deledda (Italian)
1927	Henri Bergson (French)
1928	Sigrid Undset (Norwegian, born in Denmark)
1929	Thomas Mann (German)
1930	Sinclair Lewis (American)
1931	Erik Axel Karlfeldt (Swedish)
1932	John Galsworthy (English)
1933	Ivan Alekseyevich Bunin (French, born in Russia)
1934	Luigi Pirandello (Italian)
1935	No award given
1936	Eugene O'Neill (American)
1937	Roger Martin du Gard (French)
1938	Pearl S. Buck (American)
1939	Frans Emil Sillanpää (Finnish)
1940	No award given
1941	No award given
1942	No award given
1943	No award given
1944	Johannes Vilhelm Jensen (Danish)
1945	Gabriela Mistral (Chilean)
1946	Hermann Hesse (Swiss, born in Germany)
1947	André Paul Guillaume Gide (French)
1948	Thomas Stearns Eliot (British, born in the United States)
1949	William Faulkner (American)
1950	Bertrand Arthur William Russell (British)
1951	Pär Fabian Lagerkvist (Swedish)
1952	François Mauriac (French)
1953	Sir Winston Leonard Spencer Churchill (British)
1954	Ernest Miller Hemingway (American)
1955	Halldór Kiljan Laxness (Icelandic)
1956	Juan Ramón Jiménez (Spanish)
1957	Albert Camus (French)
1958	Boris Leonidovich Pasternak (Russian)
1959	Salvatore Quasimodo (Italian)
1960	St. John Perse (French)
1961	Ivo Andrić (Yugoslavian)
1962	John Steinbeck (American)
1963	George Seferis (Greek)
1964	Jean-Paul Sartre (French)—declined
1965	Mikhail Aleksandrovich Sholokhov (Russian)
1966	Nelly Sachs (Swedish, born in Germany) and Shmuel Yosef Agnon (Israeli, born in Poland)

1967	Miguel Angel Asturias (Guatemalan)
1968	Yasunari Kawabata (Japanese)
1969	Samuel Beckett (Anglo-French, born in Ireland)
1970	Alexander Isaevich Solzhenitsyn (Russian)
1971	Pablo Neruda (Chilean)
1972	Heinrich Böll (German)
1973	Patrick White (Australian)
1974	Eyvind Johnson (Swedish) and Harry Edmund Martinson (Swedish)
1975	Eugenio Montale (Italian)
1976	Saul Bellow (American)
1977	Vicente Aleixandre (Spanish)
1978	Isaac Bashevis Singer (American, born in Poland)
1979	Odysseus Elytis (Greek)
1980	Czeslaw Milosz (Polish-American)
1981	Elias Canetti (Bulgarian)
1982	Gabriel García Márquez (Colombian)
1983	Sir William Golding (British)
1984	Jaroslav Seifert (Czechoslovakian)
1985	Claude Simon (French)
1986	Wole Soyinka (Nigerian)
1987	Joseph Brodsky (Russian-American)
1988	Naguib Mahfouz (Egyptian)
1989	Camilo José Cela (Spanish)
1990	Octavio Paz (Mexican)
1991	Nadine Gordimer (South African)
1992	Derek Walcott (West Indian)
1993	Toni Morrison (American)
1994	Kenzaburo Oe (Japanese)
1995	Seamus Heaney (Irish)
1996	Weslawa Szymborska (Polish)
1997	Dario Fo (Italian)

Pulitzer Prize for Drama, Fiction, and Poetry

	Drama	*Fiction*	*Poetry*
1917	No award given	No award given	No award given
1918	Jesse Williams	Ernest Poole	Sara Teasdale
1919	No award given	Booth Tarkington	Carl Sandburg
			Margaret Widdemer
1920	Eugene O'Neill	No award given	No award given
1921	Zona Gale	Edith Wharton	No award given
1922	Eugene O'Neill	Booth Tarkington	Edwin A. Robinson
1923	Owen Davis	Willa Cather	Edna St. Vincent Millay
1924	Hatcher Hughes	Margaret Wilson	Robert Frost
1925	Sidney Howard	Edna Ferber	Edwin A. Robinson
1926	George Kelly	Sinclair Lewis	Amy Lowell
1927	Paul Green	Louis Bromfield	Leonora Speyer
1928	Eugene O'Neill	Thornton Wilder	Edwin A. Robinson
1929	Elmer Rice	Julia Peterkin	Stephen Vincent Benét
1930	Marc Connelly	Oliver LaFarge	Conrad Aiken
1931	Susan Glaspell	Margaret Ayer Barnes	Robert Frost
1932	George S. Kaufman	Pearl Buck	George Dillon
	Morrie Ryskind		
	Ira Gershwin		

	Drama	Fiction	Poetry
1933	Maxwell Anderson	T. S. Stribling	Archibald MacLeish
1934	Sidney Kingsley	Caroline Miller	Robert Hillyer
1935	Zoë Akins	Josephine Johnson	Audrey Wurdemann
1936	Robert Sherwood	Harold Davis	Robert Coffin
1937	Moss Hart George S. Kaufman	Margaret Mitchell	Robert Frost
1938	Thornton Wilder	John Marquand	Marya Zaturenska
1939	Robert Sherwood	Marjorie Kinnan Rawlings	John Gould Fletcher
1940	William Saroyan	John Steinbeck	Mark Van Doren
1941	Robert Sherwood	No award given	Leonard Bacon
1942	No award given	Ellen Glasgow	William Rose Benét
1943	Thornton Wilder	Upton Sinclair	Robert Frost
1944	No award given	Martin Flavin	Stephen Vincent Benét
1945	Mary Chase	John Hersey	Karl Shapiro
1946	Russel Crouse Howard Lindsay	No award given	No award given
1947	No award given	Robert Penn Warren	Robert Lowell
1948	Tennessee Williams	James Michener	W. H. Auden
1949	Arthur Miller	James Cozzens	Peter Viereck
1950	Richard Rodgers Oscar Hammerstein II Joshua Logan	A. B. Guthrie, Jr.	Gwendolyn Brooks
1951	No award given	Conrad Richter	Carl Sandburg
1952	Joseph Kramm	Herman Wouk	Marianne Moore
1953	William Inge	Ernest Hemingway	Archibald MacLeish
1954	John Patrick	No award given	Theodore Roethke
1955	Tennessee Williams	William Faulkner	Wallace Stevens
1956	Albert Hackett Frances Goodrich	MacKinlay Kantor	Elizabeth Bishop
1957	Eugene O'Neill	No award given	Richard Wilbur
1958	Ketti Frings	James Agee	Robert Penn Warren
1959	Archibald MacLeish	Robert Taylor	Stanley Kunitz
1960	Jerome Weidman George Abbott Sheldon Harnick Jerry Bock	Allen Drury	W. D. Snodgrass
1961	Tad Mosel	Harper Lee	Phyllis McGinley
1962	Frank Loesser Abe Burrows	Edwin O'Connor	Alan Dugan
1963	No award given	William Faulkner	William Carlos Williams
1964	No award given	No award given	Louis Simpson
1965	Frank Gilroy	Shirley Ann Grau	John Berryman
1966	No award given	Katherine Anne Porter	Richard Eberhart
1967	Edward Albee	Bernard Malamud	Anne Sexton
1968	No award given	William Styron	Anthony Hecht
1969	Howard Sackler	N. Scott Momaday	George Oppen
1970	Charles Gordone	Jean Stafford	Richard Howard
1971	Paul Zindel	No award given	W. S. Merwin
1972	No award given	Wallace Stegner	James Wright
1973	Jason Miller	Eudora Welty	Maxine W. Kumin
1974	No award given	No award given	Robert Lowell
1975	Edward Albee	Michael Shaara	Gary Snyder
1976	Michael Bennett	Saul Bellow	John Ashbery

	Drama	*Fiction*	*Poetry*
1976	James Kirkwood		
	Nicholas Dante		
	Edward Kleban		
1977	Michael Cristofer	No award given	James Merrill
1978	Donald Coburn	James McPherson	Howard Nemerov
1979	Sam Shepard	John Cheever	Robert Penn Warren
1980	Lanford Wilson	Norman Mailer	Donald Justice
1981	Beth Henley	John Kennedy Toole	James Schuyler
1982	Charles Fuller	John Updike	Sylvia Plath
1983	Marsha Norman	Alice Walker	Galway Kinnell
1984	David Mamet	William Kennedy	Mary Oliver
1985	Stephen Sondheim	Alison Lurie	Carolyn Kizer
	James Lapine		
1986	No award given	Larry McMurtry	Henry Taylor
1987	August Wilson	Peter Taylor	Rita Dove
1988	Alfred Uhry	Toni Morrison	William Meredith
1989	Wendy Wasserstein	Anne Tyler	Richard Wilbur
1990	August Wilson	Oscar Hijuelos	Charles Simic
1991	Neil Simon	John Updike	Mona Van Duyn
1992	Robert Schenkkan	Jane Smiley	James Tate
1993	Tony Kushner	Robert Butler	Louise Glück
1994	Edward Albee	E. Annie Proulx	Yusef Komunyakaa
1995	Horton Foote	Carol Shields	Philip Levine
1996	Jonathan Larson	Richard Ford	Jorie Graham
1997	No award given	Martin Dressler	Lisel Mueller

Booker McConnell Prize

Administered by the National Book League in the United Kingdom, the Booker McConnell literary prize of £20,000 is open to full-length novels written in English by authors from the United Kingdom, Commonwealth, Eire, Pakistan, and South Africa.

1969	P. H. Newby	1983	J. M. Coetzee
1970	Bernice Rubens	1984	Anita Brookner
1971	V. S. Naipauul	1985	Keri Hulme
1972	John Berger	1986	Kingsley Amis
1973	J. G. Farrell	1987	Penelope Lively
1974	Nadine Gordimer and	1988	Peter Carey
	Stanley Middleton	1989	Kazuo Ishiguro
	(co-winners)	1990	A. S. Byatt
1975	Ruth Prawer Jhabvala	1991	Ben Okri
1976	David Storey	1992	Michael Ondaatje and
1977	Paul Scott		Barry Unsworth
1978	Iris Murdoch		(co-winners)
1979	Penelope Fitzgerald	1993	Roddy Doyle
1980	William Golding	1994	James Kelman
1981	Salmon Rushdie	1995	Pat Barker
1982	Thomas Kineally	1996	Graham Swift

Appendix B: Time Line
of World Literature

The following are innovations, works, and collections derived from the text and comprise some of the landmarks in world literature.

1350 B.C.	Akhenaten, "Hymn to the Sun"
1200 B.C.	*Gilgamesh*
1100 B.C.	*Kalevala*
1000 B.C.	*Rigveda*
9th century B.C.	*I Ching*
ca. 850 B.C.	Homer, *Iliad* and *Odyssey*
8th century B.C.	Hesiod, *Works and Days*
7th century B.C.	*Gathas*
6th century B.C.	Confucius, *Analects; Shih Ching* or *The Book of Songs*
600 B.C.	Aesop's Fables; *Exodus*
545 B.C.	Imr-ul-kais, *Moallakat*
500 B.C.	*Bhagavad-Gita*
5th century B.C.	Pindar's odes
475 B.C.	*Shijung*
441 B.C.	Sophocles, *Antigone*
438 B.C.	Euripides, *Cyclops*
416 B.C.	Plato, *Symposium*
411 B.C.	Aristophanes, *Lysistrata*
409 B.C.	Sophocles, *Oedipus Rex*
4th century B.C.	Aristotle, *The Poetics;* Plato, *The Republic; Zuo Zhuan*
300 B.C.	*Ramayana;* Lao-tzu, *Tao Te Ching*
3rd century B.C.	*Mahabharata; Dhammapada; Vedantasutras*
235 B.C.	Apollonius, *Argonautica*
186 B.C.	Plautus, *Menaechmi*
1st century B.C.	Buddhist *Dhammapada*
90 B.C.	Sima Qian, *Shiji*
58–52 B.C.	Julius Caesar, *Gallic Commentaries*
55 B.C.	Catullus's love poems
45 B.C.	Cicero, *De Oratione*
37 B.C.	Phaedrus, Aesopic Fables; Virgil, *Eclogues*
30 B.C.	Horace, Odes
19 B.C.	Virgil, *Aeneid*
8 B.C.	*Zhanguoce*
1 B.C.	Ovid, *Art of Love*
1st century A.D.	Longinus, *On the Sublime;* Vyasa, *Puranas*
14	Livy, *Histories*

60	Petronius, *Satyricon*
65	Lucan, *Pharsalia*
90-95	New Testament
2nd century	*Buddha-carita*
114	Pliny the Younger, "The Eruption of Vesuvius"
115	Plutarch, *Parallel Lives*
121	Suetonius, *Lives of the Caesars*
160	Apuleius, *The Golden Ass*
180	Marcus Aurelius, *Meditations*
222	*Li-chi*
4th century	Patanjali, *Yoga Sutra*
300	Ossian, *Fingal*
425	T'ao Ch'ien, "Returning to Live in the Country"
450	*Widsith*
460	Kalidasa, *Shakuntala*
530	*Wen xuan*
7th century	al-Khansa, "On Her Brother"; *Manyoshu* or *Book of Ten Thousand Leaves*
600	*Beowulf*
613	"Al-fatih," the essence of the Koran
650	*Mu'allaqat* or *The Seven Golden Odes*
8th century	Han-Shan, *Cold Mountain*; Lady Otomo, "Love's Complaint"; Li Po's lyric poetry; Tu Fu's anti-war verse
720	*Nihonshoki*
9th Century	al-Jahiz, *The Book of Animals*
800	Bidpai's version of the *Panchatantra*
810	Li Ho, "Joys of the Honorable Princess"
820	Han Yu's essays
845	Po Chu-Yi, "Song of Everlasting Regret"
870	*Lay of the Host of Igor*
10th century	Badi al-Zaman, *Maqamat*; classic Arabic ghazal; *Ise monogatari*; *Kokinshu*; *Exeter Book*
925	Ki no Tsurayuki, *Tosa Diary*
970	Michitsuma's mother, *Kagero Diary*
1000	Murasaki Shikibu, *Genji*; Firdausi, *Shahnamah*
1005	Abu al-Fadl Ahmad, *Maqamat Al-Hamadhani*
1030	Abu Muhammad 'Ali ibn Ahmad ibn Hazm, *The Ring of the Dove*
1050	*Sarashina Diary*; Sei Shonagon, *The Pillow Book*; Ma'arri, *Meditations*
1070	Ouyang Hsiu's political essays
1080	*Chanson de Roland*
12th century	Jayadeva, *Gita Govinda*; Li Ch'ing-chao's poetry
1100	"The Destruction of Dá Derga's Hostel"; Su Shi's poetry
1120	Abu Muhammad al-Qasim, *Maqamat al-Hariri*
1130	Omar Khayyám, *The Rubá'iyát*
1135	Geoffrey of Monmouth, *History of the Kings of Britain*
1140	*El Cid*
1150-1250	*Edda*
1160	*Ysengrimus*
1175	Marie de France, *Fables*
1177	Farid ud-Din 'Attar, *The Conference of the Birds* 1190; Lady Dabu, *The Poetic Memoirs*
13th Century	Ibn'l Farid's poetry; Rumi, *Mathnawi* and *Divani Shamsi Tabriz*; St. Francis of Assisi, "All Creatures of Our God and King"; *Sundiata*
1200	*Niebelungelied*; Elyas ebn Yusuf Nezami, *Quintet*; *Sumiyoshi Monogatari*
1205	Layamon, *Brut*
1212	Kamo no Chomei, "Account of a Ten-Foot Square Hut"

1225   *The Tale of Heike*
1230   *Carmina Burana*
1250   *Roman de Renart; Saga of Gunnlaug Serpent-Tongue*
1270   *Berta of Hungary*
1275   Guan Hanqing, *Injustice to Don E* (ca. 1275)
14th century   Hafiz, *Divan; Koryo Songs; Shuihu Zhuan*
1321   Dante, *The Divine Comedy*
1350   Yoshida Kenko's *Essays in Idleness; Sir Gawain and the Green Knight*
1353   Giovanni Boccaccio, *Decameron*
1375   John Barbour, *Bruce; Sanguo zhi yanyi*
1377   Ibn Khaldun, *Muqaddimah*
1385   Geoffrey Chaucer, *The Canterbury Tales*
15th century   *Everyman;* Seami Motokiyo, *Atsumori*
1447   *Songs of Flying Dragons*
1450   Thomas Malory, *Le Morte D'Arthur*
1462   François Villon, *Le Grand Testament*
1490   Nur al-Din 'Abd al-Rahman Jami, *The Seven Thrones*
16th century   Lope de Rueda, *The Olives*
1515   *Till Eulenspiegel*
1516   Ariosto, *Orlando Furioso*
1517   Nicolo Machiavelli, *The Prince*
1520   John Skelton, *Colin Clout*
1550   Angelo Beolco begins the *commedia dell'arte*
1564   François Rabelais, *Gargantua and Pantagruel*
1570   Wu Chengen, *Journey to the West*
1572   Luis Vaz de Camoëns, *Os Lusiadas [The Luciad]*
1575   Torquato Tasso, *Jerusalem Delivered*
1578   John Lyly, *Euphues: The Anatomy of Wit*
1585   Ho Nansorhon, "A Woman's Sorrow"
1587   Raphael Holinshed, *Chronicles of England, Scotland and Ireland*
1593   Christopher Marlowe's *Dr. Faustus*
1593-1595   William Shakespeare, *A Midsummer Night's Dream* and *Romeo and Juliet*
1595-1596   William Shakespeare, *Richard II*
1596   Edmund Spenser, *The Faerie Queene*
1599   William Shakespeare, *Julius Caesar*
1599-1600   William Shakespeare, *Hamlet*
17th century   Chikamatsu Monzaemon, kabuki drama
1603-1606   William Shakespeare, *Macbeth*
1609   Powhatan, "Algonquian Confederacy Speech"
1610-1611   William Shakespeare, *The Tempest*
1615   Miguel de Cervantes, *Don Quixote*
1616   Pierre Abélard, "Letters of Héloise and Abélard"
1620   Tulsidas, *Ramcaritmanas*
1632   Bernal Díaz del Castillo, "The True History of the Conquest of New Spain"
1637   John Milton, *Lycidas*
1642   Richard Lovelace, "To Althea"
1648   Robert Herrick, "To the Virgins, to Make Much of Time"
1650   Anne Bradstreet, "The Prologue"
1651   John Milton, "On His Blindness"; Yun Sondo, *The Angler's Calendar*
1657   Blaise Pascal, *Pensées*
1659   Molière, *Les Précieuses ridicules*
1664   Molière, *Tartuffe*
1665   François La Rochefoucauld, *Maximes*
1667   John Milton, *Paradise Lost;* Aphra Behn, *The Rover*
1675   Pu Songling, *Liaozhai Zhi*

1678 John Bunyan, *The Pilgrim's Progress*
1686 Nagai Saikaku, *The Life of an Amorous Woman*
1688 Aphra Behn, *Oroonoko*
1690 Kim Man-jung, *The Cloud Dream of the Nine*
1694 Jean de La Fontaine, Reynard the Fox fables
1697 Charles Perrault, *Mother Goose Stories*
18th century *Hyaku Monogatari; Shaka*
1700 William Congreve, *The Way of the World*
1711 Alexander Pope, *An Essay on Criticism*
1719 Daniel Defoe, *Robinson Crusoe*
1722 Daniel Defoe, *Moll Flanders*
1726 Jonathan Swift, *Gulliver's Travels*
1728 John Gay, *The Beggar's Opera*
1729 Jonathan Swift, "A Modest Proposal"
1733–1758 Benjamin Franklin, *Poor Richard's Almanack*
1740 Samuel Richardson, *Pamela*
1741 Jonathan Edwards, "Sinners in the Hands of an Angry God"
1743 Alexander Pope, *The Dunciad*
1748 Takedo Izumo, *The Treasury of Loyal Retainers*
1751 Thomas Gray, "Elegy Written in a Country Churchyard"
1754 *The Song of a Faithful Wife*
1755 Samuel Johnson, *Dictionary of the English Language*
1759 Voltaire, *Candide*
1766 Samuel Goldsmith, *The Vicar of Wakefield*
1775 Richard Sheridan, *The Rivals;* Thomas Jefferson, *Declaration of Causes and Necessity of Taking of Arms*
1776 Phillis Wheatley, "To His Excellency, George Washington"
1778 Fanny Burney, *Evelina*
1779 John Newton, *Olney Hymns*
1780 Pak Chiwon, *Yorha ilgi*
1782 Choderlos de Laclos, *Dangerous Liaisons*
1791 Tsao Hsueh-chin, *The Dream of the Red Chamber*
1792 Mary Wollstonecraft, *A Vindication of the Rights of Woman*
1794 Anne Radcliffe, *Mysteries of Udolpho*
1796 Robert Burns, "O, My Luve's Like a Red, Red Rose"
1798 Samuel Taylor Coleridge, "Kubla Khan" and *The Rime of the Ancient Mariner;* Thomas Malthus, *An Essay on the Principle of Population as It Affects the Future of Society*
1804 William Wordsworth, "Intimations of Immortality"
1805 Sir Walter Scott, *The Lay of the Last Minstrel*
1806 Lady Hong of Hyegyong Palace, *A Record of Sorrowful Days*
1813 Jane Austen, *Pride and Prejudice*
1816 Lord Byron, *The Prison of Chillon;* Herman Melville, "Bartleby, the Scrivener"
1818 Mary Shelley, *Frankenstein*
1819 John Keats, "Ode on a Grecian Urn"; Washington Irving, "Rip Van Winkle"
1820 John Keats, "The Eve of St. Agnes"; Raja Rammohum Roy, *The Precepts of Jesus, a Guide to Peace and Happiness*
1820 Percy Bysshe Shelley, "Ode to the West Wind"; *Walum Olum*
1822 Jacob and Wilhelm Grimm, *Kinder-and Hausmärchen;* Washington Irving, "The Legend of Sleepy Hollow"
1823 Clement Moore, "A Visit from St. Nicholas"
1824 Lord Byron, *Don Juan*
1826 James Fenimore Cooper, *The Last of the Mohicans*
1827 Heinrich Heine, "The Lorelei"

1830   Adam Kidd, *The Huron Chief;* Joseph Smith, *Book of Mormon*
1832   William Gilmore Simms, "The Swamp Fox"
1833   Antoine LeClaire, *The Autobiography of Black Hawk*
1835   Alexis de Tocqueville, *Democracy in America;* Hans Christian Andersen,
          Tales; William Gilmore Simms, *The Yemassee*
1835–1838   Davy Crockett, *Crockett Almanacks*
1836   Angelina Grimké, *Appeal to the Christian Women of the South*
1839   Charles Darwin, *Voyage of the Beagle;* Charles Dickens, *Oliver Twist*
1841   Edgar Allan Poe, "The Murders in the Rue Morgue"; George Catlin, *Letters
          and Notes on the Manners, Customs and Condition of the North American
          Indians During Eight Years' Travel Amongst the Wildest Tribes of Indians of
          North America;* Henry Wadsworth Longfellow, *Ballads and Other Poems*
1842   Robert Browning, "My Last Duchess" and "Soliloquy of the Spanish Clois-
          ter"; Thomas Babington Macaulay, *Lays of Ancient Rome*
1843   Charles Dickens, *A Christmas Carol;* Edgar Allan Poe, "The Gold Bug";
          Søren Kierkegaard, *Fear and Trembling*
1844   Elizabeth Barrett Browning, "The Cry of the Children"
1845   Alexandre Dumas Père, *The Count of Monte Cristo;* Frederick Douglass,
          Narrative of the Life of Frederick Douglass
1846   Edward Lear, *The Book of Nonsense;* Francis Parkman, *The Oregon Trail*
1847   Charlotte Brontë, *Jane Eyre;* Emily Brontë, *Wuthering Heights*
1848   William Makepeace Thackeray, *Vanity Fair*
1849   Edgar Allan Poe, "Annabel Lee"
1850   Alfred Tennyson, *In Memoriam;* Charles Dickens, *David Copperfield;* Edgar
          Allan Poe, *The Poetic Principle;* Nathaniel Hawthorne, *The Scarlet Letter*
1851   Herman Melville, *Moby-Dick;* Sojourner Truth, "Ain't I a Woman?"
1852   Harriet Beecher Stowe, *Uncle Tom's Cabin*
1853   Matthew Arnold, "Sohrab and Rustum"
1855   Henry Wadsworth Longfellow, *The Song of Hiawatha;* Walt Whitman, *Song
          of Myself*
1857   Charles Baudelaire, *Les Fleurs du Mal;* Elizabeth Gaskell, *Life of Charlotte
          Brontë;* Gustave Flaubert, *Madame Bovary;* Henry Wadsworth Longfel-
          low, *Evangeline;* Hiawatha's speech in Henry Rowe Schoolcraft's *Historical
          and Statistical Information Respecting the History, Condition and Prospects of
          the Indian Tribes of the United States*
1859   Charles Dickens, *A Tale of Two Cities;* R. B. Stratton, *Captivity of the Oat-
          man Girls: Being an Interesting Narrative of Life Among the Apache and
          Mohave Indians*
1860   George Eliot, *The Mill on the Floss;* "The Corrido of Kansas"
1861   Charles Dickens, *Great Expectations;* George Eliot, *Silas Marner;* Harriet
          Ann Brent Jacobs, *Incidents in the Life of a Slave Girl, Written by Herself*
1863   Henry Wadsworth Longfellow, *Tales of the Wayside Inn*
1864   Frederick Douglass, "What the Black Man Wants"
1865   Lewis Carroll, *Alice in Wonderland;* Victor Hugo, *Les Misérables*
1866   Caroline Augusta Ball, "The Jacket of Gray"; Fyodor Dostoevsky, *Crime
          and Punishment;* Walt Whitman, "When Lilacs Last in the Dooryard
          Bloom'd"
1867   Benjamin Franklin, *Autobiography*
1869   Frances Ellen Watkins Harper, *Moses: A Story of the Nile;* Louisa May
          Alcott, *Little Women;* Nikolai Tolstoy, *War and Peace;* Pole Sienkiewicz,
          Quo Vadis
1870   Asadullah Khan Ghalib's ghazals
1872   Lewis Carroll, "Jabberwocky"; Samuel Butler, *Erewhon*
1875   George Washington Cable, "Jean-ah Poquelin"
1876   Leo Tolstoy, *Anna Karenina;* Mark Twain, *The Adventures of Tom Sawyer*

1877   Chief Joseph, "I Will Fight No More Forever"; Sidney Lanier, "Song of the Chattahoochee"
1878   Thomas Hardy, *The Return of the Native*
1879   George Washington Cable, *Old Creole Days;* Henrik Ibsen, *A Doll's House;* Joel Chandler Harris, "Negro Folklore: The Story of Mr. Rabbit and Mr. Fox, as Told by Uncle Remus"
1880   George Washington Cable, *The Grandissimes*
1882   Bankim Chandra Chatterjee, *Anandamath*
1883   Joel Chandler Harris, *Nights with Uncle Remus;* Robert Louis Stevenson, *Treasure Island;* Sarah Winnemucca, *Life Among the Piutes, Their Wrongs and Claims*
1884   Mark Twain, *The Adventures of Huckleberry Finn*
1885   Alfred, Lord Tennyson, *Idylls of the King*
1886   Henry James, *The Bostonians;* Mark Twain, *A Connecticut Yankee in King Arthur's Court;* Robert Louis Stevenson, *Dr. Jekyll and Mr. Hyde* and *Kidnapped;* Thomas Hardy, *The Mayor of Casterbridge*
1887   Edward Bellamy, *Looking Backward*
1888   Crocker Howard, *Shenandoah;* King David Kalakaua, *The Legends and Myths of Hawaii;* Oscar Wilde, *The Happy Prince and Other Tales*
1889   Gerard Manley Hopkins, "Inversnaid"
1890   Rudyard Kipling, *Barrack Room Ballads;* William Morris, *News from Nowhere*
1891   Emily Dickinson, "I'm Nobody"; Hamlin Garland, *Main-Travelled Roads;* Oscar Wilde, *The Picture of Dorian Gray*
1892   George Bird Grinnell, *Blackfoot Lodge Tales*
1893   Stephen Crane, *Maggie, a Girl of the Streets*
1894   John Muir, *The Mountains of California;* Kate Chopin, *Bayou Folk*
1895   H. G. Wells, *The Time Machine;* Stephen Crane, *The Red Badge of Courage;* Thomas Hardy, *Jude the Obscure;* A. B. Paterson, "Waltzing Matilda"
1896   A. E. Housman, "The Loveliest of Trees"
1897   Edmond Rostand, *Cyrano de Bergerac;* Lewis Osborn Innis, *Carmelita, the Belle of San Jose*
1898   Oscar Wilde, *The Ballad of Reading Gaol*
1899   Frank Norris, *McTeague;* Kate Chopin, *The Awakening*
1900   Elizabeth Cady Stanton and Susan B. Anthony, *A History of Women's Suffrage;* Jack London, "To Build a Fire"; James Weldon Johnson and John Rosamund Johnson, "Lift Ev'ry Voice and Sing"; L. Frank Baum, *The Wonderful Wizard of Oz*
1901   Booker T. Washington, *Up from Slavery;* Yosano Akiko, *Tangled Hair*
1902   August Strindberg, *Dream Play;* Charles Eastman, *Indian Boyhood;* Jack London, *The Call of the Wild;* Joseph Conrad, *Heart of Darkness;* Owen Wister, *The Virginian*
1903   Mary Hunter Austin, *The Land of Little Rain*
1904   Geronimo's speech in *The Life of Tom Horn;* J. M. Barrie, *Peter Pan;* John Millington Synge, *Riders to the Sea*
1905   O. Henry, "The Gift of the Magi"; *Original Journals of the Lewis and Clark Expedition*
1906   Afifa Karam, *Badiyah and Fuad;* Upton Sinclair, *The Jungle*
1907   O. Henry, *Heart of the West;* Natsume Soseki, *Theory of Literature*
1909   Mori Ogai, *Vita Sexualis*
1910   John Lomax, *Cowboy Songs and Other Frontier Ballads;* Juan Ramón Jiménez, *Elegías lamentables;* O. Henry, "The Ransom of Red Chief"; *The Zen Substitute*
1911   Edith Wharton, *Ethan Frome*
1912   Joseph Conrad, *The Secret Sharer;* Rudyard Kipling, *Just-So Stories;* Zane Grey, *Riders of the Purple Sage*

1913   George Bernard Shaw, *Pygmalion;* Willa Cather, *O Pioneers!*

1914   John Reed, *Insurgent Mexico;* Robert Frost, "Mending Wall" and "The Death of the Hired Man"; Rupert Brooke, *The War Sonnets*

1915   Charlotte Perkins Gilman, *Herland;* Edgar Lee Masters, *Spoon River Anthology;* Akutagawa Ryunosuke, "The Rasho Gate"; Franz Kafka, "The Metamorphosis"; James G. Frazer, *The Golden Bough;* Somerset Maugham, *Of Human Bondage*

1916   Amy Lowell, "Patterns"; Ezra Pound, "In a Station of the Metro"; James Joyce, *Portrait of the Artist As a Young Man;* John Muir, *A Thousand Mile Walk to the Gulf;* Rabindranath Tagore, *The Hungry Stones;* Robert Frost, "Birches"

1918   Lytton Strachey, *Eminent Victorians;* Muhammad Iqbal, *Mysteries of Selflessness;* Mary Hunter Austin, *The Trail Book*

1920   Carl Jung, *Modern Man in Search of a Soul;* Wilfred Owen, "The Parable of the Old Man and the Young"

1921   Karel Capek, *R. U. R.;* Lytton Strachey, *Queen Victoria;* Yevgeny Zamyatin, *We*

1922   Allen Tate, "Ode to the Confederate Dead"; Hermann Hesse, *Siddhartha;* Katherine Anne Porter, "María Concepción" and "The Garden Party"; Rainer Maria Rilke, *Duino Elegies;* T. S. Eliot, "The Wasteland"

1923   D. H. Lawrence, *Studies in Classic American Literature;* e. e. cummings, "in Just—"; Lu Hsun, *Call to Arms;* Edna St. Vincent Millay, *Sonnets from an Ungrafted Tree;* Jean Toomer, *Cane;* Robert Frost, "Stopping by Woods on a Snowy Evening"

1924   Johan Bojer, *The Emigrants;* John Crowe Ransom, "Bells for John Whiteside's Daughter"; Sherwood Anderson, "I'm a Fool"; St. John Perse, *Anabasis;* Thomas Mann, *The Magic Mountain*

1925   Countee Cullen, "Heritage"; Theodore Dreiser, *An American Tragedy*

1926   Willa Cather, *My Antonia;* Han Yong-un, *Your Silence*

1927   James Weldon Johnson, "The Creation"; O. E. Rölvaag, *Giants in the Earth;* Paul Green, *In Abraham's Bosom;* Thornton Wilder, *The Bridge of San Luis Rey;* Virginia Woolf, *To the Lighthouse*

1928   Julia Mood Peterkin, *Scarlet Sister Mary;* Margaret Mead, *Coming of Age in Samoa;* Mary Hunter Austin, *Children Sing in the Far West;* Stephen Vincent Benét, *John Brown's Body;* Virginia Woolf, *Orlando*

1929   Erich Maria Remarque, *All Quiet on the Western Front;* Jun'ichiro, Tanizaki, *Some Prefer Nettles;* Ernest Hemingway, *A Farewell to Arms;* Thomas Wolfe, *Look Homeward, Angel;* William Faulkner, *The Sound and the Fury*

1930   Fugitive Agrarians, *I'll Take My Stand;* Jaishankar Prasad, *Kamayani;* Noel Coward, *Private Lives;* William Faulkner, *As I Lay Dying*

1931   Eugene O'Neill, *Mourning Becomes Electra;* Pearl Buck, *The Good Earth*

1932   Aldous Huxley, *Brave New World;* Frank B. Linderman, *Pretty Shield, Medicine Woman of the Crows;* John G. Neihardt, *Black Elk Speaks;* W. B. Yeats, *Crazy Jane*

1933   Sholem Asch, *Three Cities;* Lao She, "The Grand Opening"; William Butler Yeats, "The Second Coming"

1934   James Hilton, *Good-bye Mr. Chips;* James T. Farrell, *Studs Lonigan;* John and Alan Lomax, *American Ballads and Folk Songs;* Lillian Hellman, *The Children's Hour;* Monteiro Lobato, "The Farm Magnate"; Robert Graves, *I, Claudius;* William Carlos Williams, "The Red Wheelbarrow"; Wovoka's speech, *The Story of the American Indian*

1935   DuBose Heyward and George Gershwin, *Porgy and Bess;* Hsiao Hung, *Market Street;* Laura Ingalls Wilder, *Little House on the Prairie;* Richard Wright, "Between the World and Me"; Zora Neale Hurston, *Mules and Men* (1935)

1936 Claire Booth, *The Women;* Margaret Mitchell, *Gone with the Wind;* Moss Hart and George S. Kaufman, *You Can't Take It with You*

1937 Alfonsina Storni, "She Who Understands"; Ayn Rand, *Anthem;* Isak Dinesen, *Out of Africa;* J. R. R. Tolkien, *The Hobbit;* John Steinbeck, *Of Mice and Men;* Paul Green, *The Lost Colony;* Nagai Kafu, *A Strange Tale from East of the River;* Shiga Naoya, *A Dark Night's Passing;* Stephen Vincent Benét, "The Devil and Daniel Webster"; Richard Wright, *Black Boy;* Zora Neale Hurston, *Their Eyes Were Watching God*

1938 John Dos Passos, *U. S. A.;* Ibuse Masuji, *Waves: A War Diary;* Marjorie Kinnan Rawlings, *The Yearling;* Thornton Wilder, *Our Town*

1939 Antonio Machado, "The Crime Was in Granada"; Dalton Trumbo, *Johnny Got His Gun;* Jean-Paul Sartre, "The Wall"; John Steinbeck, *The Grapes of Wrath;* Lillian Hellman, *The Little Foxes*

1940 Anton Chekhov, *The Cherry Orchard;* Carson McCullers, *The Heart Is a Lonely Hunter;* Hilda Doolittle, "The Pear Tree"; Richard Wright, *Native Son* and "How 'Bigger' Was Born"; Walter Van Tilburg Clark, *The Ox-Bow Incident*

1941 Edna Ferber, *Giant;* W. J. Cash, *The Mind of the South*

1942 Albert Camus, *The Myth of Sisyphus;* Mari Sandoz, *Crazy Horse: The Strange Man of the Oglalas;* William Faulkner, "The Bear"; Zora Neale Hurston, *Dust Tracks on a Road*

1943 Ayn Rand, *The Fountainhead;* Czeslaw Milosz, "Song of a Citizen"

1944 Jean Anouilh, *Antigone;* Mary Chase, *Harvey;* Muriel Rukeyser, "Who in One Lifetime"

1945 Caroline Gordon, "The Captive"; George Orwell, *Animal Farm;* Tennessee Williams, *The Glass Menagerie*

1946 Albert Camus, *The Stranger;* Carson McCullers, *The Member of the Wedding;* Dylan Thomas, "Do Not Go Gentle into That Good Night"; Nikos Kazantzakis, *Zorba, the Greek;* Robert Penn Warren, *All the King's Men*

1947 Marjory Stoneman Douglass, *The Everglades: River of Grass;* Ralph Ellison, *Invisible Man*

1948 Alan Paton, *Cry, the Beloved Country;* Kawabata Yasunari, *Snow Country;* Bertolt Brecht, *The Caucasian Chalk Circle* (1948); Thomas Heggen and Joshua Logan, *Mr. Roberts*

1949 Arthur Miller, *Death of a Salesman;* George Orwell, *1984;* Jack Schaefer, *Shane;* Joseph Campbell, *The Hero with a Thousand Faces*

1950 Kermit Hunter, *Unto These Hills;* Ray Bradbury, "There Will Come Soft Rains"; William Faulkner, Nobel Prize acceptance speech; Américo Paredes, "El Corrido de Gregorio Cortéz"

1951 Hermann Hesse, *Siddhartha;* J. D. Salinger, *The Catcher in the Rye;* Julio Cortázar, *Bestiary;* Richard Rodgers and Oscar Hammerstein, *The King and I*

1952 Anne Frank, *Diary of a Young Girl;* Ernest Hemingway, *The Old Man and the Sea;* Flannery O'Connor, *Wise Blood;* Samuel Beckett, *Waiting for Godot*

1953 Arthur Miller, *The Crucible;* Conrad Richter, *The Light in the Forest* (1953); Isak Dinesen, "Babette's Feast"; Joseph Epes Brown, *The Sacred Pipe;* Juan Ramón Jiménez, "I Shall Not Return"; Nguyen Thi Vinh, "Thoughts of Hanoi"; Ray Bradbury, *Fahrenheit 451;* Yukio Mishima, *The Damask Drum*

1954 William Golding, *Lord of the Flies*

1955 Flannery O'Connor, "A Good Man Is Hard to Find"; J. R. R. Tolkien, Ring Trilogy; Jerome Lawrence and Robert E. Lee, *Inherit the Wind;* Randall Jarrell, "The Death of the Ball Turret Gunner"; Tennessee Williams, *Cat on a Hot Tin Roof*

1956 Camara Laye, *The Radiance of the King;* Friedrich Dürrenmatt, *The Visit;*

James Agee, *A Death in the Family*; John Ashbery, *Some Trees*; Manuel Rojas, "The Glass of Milk"; Naguib Mahfuz, *Bayn al Qasrayn*

1957   Boris Pasternak, *Dr. Zhivago*; Isaac Bashevis Singer, *Gimpel the Fool*; Jerome Lawrence and Robert Edwin Lee, *Auntie Mame*; Northrop Frye, *Anatomy of Criticism*; Ray Bradbury, *Dandelion Wine*; V. S. Naipaul, *The Mystic Masseur*

1958   Harry Golden, *Only in America*; Enchi Fumiko, *Masks*; Sandra Cisneros, *The House on Mango Street*; T. H. White, *The Once and Future King*

1959   Chinua Achebe, *Things Fall Apart*; Ariyoshi Sawako, *The River Ki*; Günter Grass, *The Tin Drum*; James Michener, *Hawaii*; James Vance Marshall, *Walkabout*; Lorraine Hansberry, *A Raisin in the Sun*; Robert A. Heinlein, *Starship Troopers*; William Gibson, *The Miracle Worker*

1960   Elie Wiesel, *Night*; Pinter, *The Caretaker*; Harper Lee, *To Kill a Mockingbird*; Randall Jarrell, "The Woman at the Washington Zoo"; Robert Bolt, *A Man for All Seasons*

1961   Allen Ginsberg, "Kaddish"; Joseph Heller, *Catch-22*; Pablo Antonio Cuadra, "The Jaguar Myth"; Rachel Carson, *Silent Spring*

1962   Anthony Burgess, *A Clockwork Orange*; Flannery O'Connor, *The Violent Bear It Away*; Manuelo Azuelo, *The Underdogs*

1963   Alexander Solzhenitsyn, *One Day in the Life of Ivan Denisovich*; Fernán Silva Valdés, "The Gaucho Troubadour"; Heinrich Böll, *The Clown*; John Le Carré, *The Spy Who Came in from the Cold*; Julio Cortázar, *Hopscotch*; Mark Twain, *Letters from the Earth*; Martin Luther King, Jr., "Letter from a Birmingham Jail"; Sylvia Plath, *The Bell Jar*; Tawfiq al-Hakim, *The River of Madness*

1964   Saul Bellow, *Herzog*; Theodora Kroeber, *Ishi*

1965   Alex Haley, *The Autobiography of Malcolm X*; Katherine Anne Porter, "The Jilting of Granny Weatherall"; Neil Simon, *The Odd Couple*; Thomas Berger, *Little Big Man*

1966   Jean Rhys, *Wide Sargasso Sea*; Tawfiq al-Hakim, *The Fate of a Cockroach*; Kurt Vonnegut, *Slaughterhouse-Five*; Susan Sontag, "Notes on Camp"; Ghassan Kanafani, *The Literature of Resistance in Occupied Palestine . 1948–1966*; Truman Capote, *In Cold Blood*

1967   Chaim Potok, *The Chosen*; Daniel Keyes, *Flowers for Algernon*; Gabriel García Márquez, *One Hundred Years of Solitude*; Joyce Carol Oates, *A Garden of Earthly Delights*; William Styron, *The Confessions of Nat Turner*

1968   Arthur C. Clarke, *2001: A Space Odyssey*; Eldridge Cleaver, *Soul on Ice*; James Goldman, *The Lion in Winter*; Joan Didion, *Slouching Toward Bethlehem*; Ka-Tzetnik, *The Clock Overhead*; May Swenson, "Women"; N. Scott Momaday, *House Made of Dawn*; Octavio Paz, *Cuento de los Jardines*

1969   Eliot Wigginton, *The Foxfire Book*; Ezra Pound, *Cantos*; John Fowles, *The French Lieutenant's Woman*; Ursula K. Le Guin, *The Left Hand of Darkness*

1970   Dee Brown, *Bury My Heart at Wounded Knee*; James Dickey, "Angina"; Maya Angelou, *I Know Why the Caged Bird Sings*; Toni Cade Bambara, *The Salt Eaters*

1971   Ernest Gaines, *The Autobiography of Miss Jane Pittman*; John Gardner, *Grendel*

1972   David Caudeiron and Alwin Bully, *Speak Brother Speak*; Harriette Arnow, *The Dollmaker*; Pat Conroy, *The Water Is Wide*; Richard Erdoes, *Lame Deer: Seeker of Visions*; Ursula Le Guin, Earthsea Trilogy

1973   Alice Childress, *A Hero Ain't Nothin' but a Sandwich*; Freddie Rhone, *Calabash Alley*; Hugh Leonard, *Da*; John Hersey, *Hiroshima*; Rudolfo Anaya, *Bless Me, Ultima*

1974   James Michener, *Centennial*; Stanislaw Lem, "The First Sally (A) OR Trurl's Electronic Bard"

1975   Adrienne Rich, *Charleston in the 1860s: Derived from the Diaries of Mary Boykin Chesnut;* Bruce St. John, "Bajan Litany"; Maxine Hong Kingston, *The Woman Warrior;* Ruth Prawer Jhabvala, *Heat and Dust*

1976   Alex Haley, *Roots: The Saga of an American Family;* Barbara Jordan, "Who Then Will Speak for the Common Good?"; James Dickey, "May Day Sermon"; Marge Piercy, *Woman on the Edge of Time;* Ntozake Shange, *for colored girls who have considered suicide/when the rainbow is enuf*

1977   Allen Tate, "Ode to the Confederate Dead"; Anita Desai, *Fire on the Mountain;* Colleen McCullough, *The Thorn Birds;* Kamala Markandaya, *The Honeycomb*

1978   Adrienne Rich, *Twenty-one Love Poems*

1979   Beth Henley, *Crimes of the Heart;* Harvey Fierstein, *Torch Song Trilogy*

1980   Umberto Eco, *The Name of the Rose*

1981   Leslie Marmon Silko, "Lullaby"

1982   Alice Walker, *The Color Purple;* Gary Soto, "Like Mexicans"; Isabel Allende, *House of the Spirits;* Marsha Norman, *'night Mother;* T. Coraghessan Boyle, *Water Music;* Thomas Keneally, *Schindler's List*

1983   Diane Wolkstein and Samuel Noah Kramer, *Inanna: Queen of Heaven and Earth, Her Stories and Hymns from Sumer;* Paula Gunn Allen, *The Woman Who Owned the Shadows*

1984   Allan Gurganus, *Oldest Living Confederate Widow Tells All;* Wole Soyinka, *A Play of Giants*

1985   Carlos Fuentes, *Old Gringo;* Margaret Atwood, *The Handmaid's Tale;* Rigoberto Menchu, *I, Rigoberto*

1986   Alfred Uhry, *Driving Miss Daisy;* August Wilson, *Fences;* E. R. Braithwaite, *To Sir with Love;* Elie Wiesel, Nobel Prize acceptance speech; Larry McMurtry, *Lonesome Dove;* Mark Mathabane, *Kaffir Boy;* Rita Dove, *Thomas and Beulah*

1987   Kaye Gibbons, *Ellen Foster;* Toni Morrison, *Beloved*

1988   Barbara Kingsolver, *The Bean Trees;* John Ehle, *The Trail of Tears: The Rise and Fall of the Cherokee Nation;* Paul Monette, *Borrowed Time;* Robert Harling, *Steel Magnolias;* Paulo Coelho, *The Alchemist*

1989   May Swenson, "How Everything Happens"; *The Songs of Henry Lawson*

1990   Barbara Kingsolver, *Animal Dreams;* Derek Walcott, *Omeros;* Kazuo Ishiguro, *Remains of the Day;* Michael Crichton, *Jurassic Park*

1991   Victor Villaseñor, *Rain of Gold*

1992   Amy Tan, *The Kitchen God's Wife;* Laura Esquivel, *Like Water for Chocolate;* Michael Ondaatje, *The English Patient;* Paul Keens-Douglas, "Tanti at the Oval"; Sylvia López-Medina, *Cantora*

1993   Ernest Gaines, *A Lesson Before Dying;* Leslie Marmon Silko, "Yellow Woman"; Lois Lowry, *The Giver;* Maya Angelou, "On the Pulse of the Morning"

1994   Nikki Giovanni, *Racism 101*

1995   Ellen Gilchrist, "Rhoda"; Nelson Mandela, *The Long Walk to Freedom*

1996   *Winter Quarters, The 1846–1848 Life Writings of Mary Haskin Parker Richards;* Margaret Walker, *Jubilee*

1997   Charles Frazier, *Cold Mountain;* Colleen McCullough, *Caesar;* Sonia Sanchez, *Does Your House Have Lions?*

1998   Barbara Kingsolver, *The Poisonwood Bible*

Bibliography

Abrams, M. H. *A Glossary of Literary Terms.* Toronto: Holt, Rinehart and Winston, 1971.

Baldick, Chris. *The Concise Oxford Dictionary of Literary Terms.* Oxford: Oxford University Press, 1990.

Banerji, Sures Chanra, and Chhanda Chakraborty. *Folklore in Ancient and Medieval India.* Calcutta: Punthi Pustak, 1991.

Barnet, Sylvan, Morton Berman, and William Burton. *A Dictionary of Literary Terms.* New York: Little, Brown, 1960.

Beckson, Karl, and Arthur Ganz. *Literary Terms: A Dictionary.* Noonday, 1989.

Bhullar, Harsangeet Kaur. "The Ghazal—Then and Now," http://home1. pacific.net.sg/~loudon/ghazal.htm.

Brogan, T. V. F., ed. *The New Princeton Handbook of Poetic Terms.* Princeton: Princeton University Press, 1994.

Brown, Lesley. *The New Shorter Oxford English Dictionary.* Kinsington: Clarendon Press, 1993.

Cavendish, Marshall. *Man, Myth and Magic.* New York: Marshall Cavendish, 1970.

Cordozo-Freeman, Inez. "José Ines Chavez García: Hero or Villain of the Mexican Revolution?" *Bilingual Review,* Jan.-Apr. 1993, 3-14.

Cuddon, J. A. *A Dictionary of Literary Terms and Literary Theory.* Oxford: Blackwell Reference, 1991.

"Darpana Academy of Performing Arts," http://www.darpana.com/drama.htm.

Feldman, Susan, ed. *The Storytelling Stone.* Troubridge: Laurel Books, 1965.

Fifer, Elizabeth. *Maxine Hong Kingston, Narrative Technique and Female Identity.* Lexington: University Press of Kentucky, 1985.

Gassner, John, and Edward Quinn, eds. *The Reader's Encyclopedia of World Drama.* New York: Thomas Y. Crowell, 1969.

Gibb, H. A. R. *Arabic Literature: An Introduction.* Oxford: Oxford University Press, 1963.

"Giovannni in London, or The Libertine Reclaimed," http://artsci.washington.edu/drama-phd/tugio.html.

"A Glimpse of Turkish Theatre," http://www.mfa.gov.tr/GRUPD/theatre2.htm.

"The Green Man," http://www.inanna.com/ygdrasil/greenman.html.

"The Green Man," http://www.mhd.dk/greenman/greenman.htm.

"Haiku," http://asnic.utexas.ed/asnic/countries/japan/haiku.html.

Henry, Laurie. *The Fiction Dictionary.* Chicago Story Press, 1995.

Hunt, Nancy L. "Mexico's Many Musics," *Studies in Latin American Popular Culture,* 1992, 239-248.

Jones, Alison. *Dictionary of World Folklore.* New York: Larousse, 1995.

Kamat, Dr. Jyotsna. "Bangà-Ranga: Bengali Theater," http://www.karmat.com/kalranga/wb/vangrang.htm

Kato, Shuichi. *A History of Japanese Literature.* Kyoto: Kodansha International, 1979.

Leiter, Samuel L. *Kabuki Encyclopedia: An English-Language Adaptation of Kabuki Jiten.* London: Greenwood, 1979.

MacDonald, Richard. "What Is a Tanka?," http://home1.pacific.net.sg /~loudon/rick.htm.

Maggio, Rosalie. *The New Beacon Book of Quotations by Women.* Boston: Beacon Press, 1996.

A Manual of Style: A Guide to the Basics of Good Writing. Wings Books, 1986.

Merriam-Webster's Collegiate Dictionary. Springfield, MA: Merriam-Webster, Inc., 1993.

Merriam-Webster's Reader's Handbook. Springfield, MA: Merriam-Webster, Inc., 1997.

Miller, James E., Robert O'Neal, and Helen M. McDonnell, eds. *Italian Literature in Translation.* Reading, MA: Scott, Foresman & Co., 1970.

Moke, Susan. "The Literary Legacy of Classical Arabic Poetry," http://www.indiana.edu/~rugs/rca/v17n3/p7.html.

Nair, Maya. "Mohiniyattam—Origin, Growth and Content," http://www.kerala.org/culture/mohiniattam-maya.html.

Packard, William. *The Poet's Dictionary: A Handbook of Prosody and Poetic Devices.* New York: HarperPerennial, 1989.

Powell, Michelle. "Opposites Do Not Attract: Punch and Judy for New Times," http://www.fas.harvard.edu/~art/opposites.html.

"Punch and Judy History," http://www.primenet.com/~freshdlc/PJ hist.html.

Reichhold, Jane. "Japanese Poetry Terms," http://xxx.faximum.com/aha.d/ japgloss.htm.

Rosenberg, Donna. *Folklore, Myths, and Legends.* Lincolnwood, Ill.: NTC Publishing, 1997.

Snodgrass, Mary Ellen. *The Encyclopedia of Fable.* Santa Barbara, Calif.: ABC-Clio, 1998.

_____. *The Encyclopedia of Frontier Literature.* Santa Barbara, Calif.: ABC-Clio, 1997.

_____. *The Encyclopedia of Satirical Literature.* Santa Barbara, Calif.: ABC-Clio, 1997.

_____. *The Encyclopedia of Southern Literature.* Santa Barbara, Calif.: ABC-Clio, 1997.

_____. *The Encyclopedia of Utopian Literature.* Santa Barbara, Calif.: ABC-Clio, 1996.

Werner, Louis. "Singing the Border News," *Americas*, Nov./Dec. 1994, 48-50.

"What Is Bugaku?" http://nimbus.ocis.temple.edu/~kotsuki/bugaku.html.

Yu, Ning. "A Strategy Against Marginalization: The High and Low Cultures in Kingston's China Men," *College Literature*, Oct. 1996, 73-88.

Index

Numbers in **boldface** refer to pages with illustrations.